The Athlete as National Symbol

The Athlete as National Symbol

*Critical Essays on Sports
in the International Arena*

Edited by
NICHOLAS VILLANUEVA, JR.

McFarland & Company, Inc., Publishers
Jefferson, North Carolina

This book has undergone peer review.

ISBN 978-1-4766-7117-8 (print)
ISBN 978-1-4766-3835-5 (ebook)

LIBRARY OF CONGRESS AND BRITISH LIBRARY
CATALOGUING DATA ARE AVAILABLE

Library of Congress Control Number 2020000469

© 2020 Nicholas Villanueva, Jr.. All rights reserved

No part of this book may be reproduced or transmitted in any form or by any means, electronic or mechanical, including photocopying or recording, or by any information storage and retrieval system, without permission in writing from the publisher.

Front cover: Team USA marches into Fisht Olympic Stadium during the opening ceremony of the 2014 Olympic Winter Games on February 7 in Sochi, Russia (IMCOM Public Affairs)

Printed in the United States of America

McFarland & Company, Inc., Publishers
  Box 611, Jefferson, North Carolina 28640
    www.mcfarlandpub.com

For Ryan Dale Villanueva

Acknowledgments

This book would not have been possible without the financial support of the University of Colorado, Boulder. The following support enabled me to explore research opportunities and seek out the brilliant scholars who contributed to this edited collection: Department of Ethnic Studies research support, and the College of Arts and Sciences Fund for Excellence. Additionally, I wish to extend my thanks to my colleagues who encourage my research and provide me with a department full of intellectual stimulation: Arturo Aldama, Joanne Belknap, Clint Carroll, Angelica Lawson, Daryl Maeda, Jessica (Yesika) Ordaz, Hillary Potter, Reiland Rabaka, Enrique Sepúlveda, and Seema Sohi. I would also like to thank the peer reviewers for their careful attention and effective feedback.

I am grateful for the friends in my life who provide social and intellectual support: Kathy Thoen, Chris Brandt, Thomas Hodde, Steve Harrison, and Erin Stone. I am indebted to my Broomfield, Colorado, friends who provide me a place to write, and their friendships that are important to my success: Heather Crandall, Colin Cleary, Josh Swetsky, Kirby Spinney, and Troy Scoggins. Samantha (Sam) Ward—you are loved and missed by so many friends. I would like to thank my family, including my sister, who is the greatest and most vocal supporter of my career; my father for teaching me how to work hard and never settle for less than my best effort; and my late mother Patricia (Patsy) Villanueva, who inspired me to be proud of the person I am. Most importantly, I wish to thank my best friend and partner, Ryan, for his encouragement, support, and ability to make me laugh through some of the more stressful moments.

Table of Contents

Acknowledgments	vi
Introduction	1

Part One: Race, Gender and Social Justice

Land of the Free? Sporting Nationalism and White Privilege in the United States NICHOLAS VILLANUEVA, JR.	9
Diversity and Organizational Productivity: Examining the Role of Race and Gender in U.S. Olympic Team Success at the 2012 London Games JOMILLS H. BRADDOCK II, CHRISTINA SANCHEZ VOLATIER, ADRIENNE MILNER, ASHLEY B. MIKULYUK *and* MARVIN P. DAWKINS	24

Part Two: Sport and National Identity

"Damn!—welly good white man's game": Race, Golf and the Struggle for Social Justice in South Africa, c. 1890–1991 HENDRIK SNYDERS	47
National Heroes or Disgusting Nazis? Soccer Patriotism, German National Identity and the "Gaucho Gate" Incident After the FIFA World Cup 2014 YANNICK KLUCH	71
National Identities and International Sport: What About the Women? ALI BOWES	88

Part Three: Athletes and the Global Spectacle

A Fatwa for German Soccer
    BRUCE S. BURNSIDE   113

A Cause Without a Rebel: In Search of a Palestinian Sporting Hero
    JON DART   138

Part Four: Media Re-Presentation of Nationhood and Sport

Team Orders: Mass Media Complicity with State Nationalisms Expressed Through Motorsport
    ZACHARY T. ANDROUS   167

Taking Our Ball and Staying Home: Nationalistic Exceptionalism and Cultural Imperialism in U.S. Sports Coverage and Leagues
    JARED BAHIR BROWSH   190

About the Contributors   217

Index   219

Introduction

NICHOLAS VILLANUEVA, JR.

Scholars have been intrigued by the formation of nation-states and the phenomenon of nationalism for decades. From Benedict Anderson's *Imagine Community* to the most recent publication by Gary Gerstle, *Liberty and Coercion: The Paradox of American Government*, literature on the nation-state has examined regionalism and nationalism among the people. The essays in this collection explore nationalism through the microcosm of sport, identifying historical moments when athletes became national symbols through their actions on and off of the playing field. Divided into four parts—Race, Gender and Social Justice; Sport and National Identity; Athletes and the Global Sport Spectacle; and Media Re-Presentation of Nationhood and Sport—this volume hopes to provoke critical thinking about sport and its place in society.

Many people believe the myth that sport builds character, keeps our youth out of trouble, and promotes healthy bodies and minds. Anyone involved with sport, the idea goes, will be a better person for it, because sport is "essentially good, and ... its purity and goodness is transferred to all who participate in it."[1] Acceptance of this myth is believed to lead to emotional unity within a sporting social world. But it can also lead to detachment from non-sporting groups, elitism in sport, success at any cost, and ambivalence toward social responsibility.

Acceptance of the great sports myth contributes to many of the social problems in sport. In the United States, this myth can be traced back to the early 20th century. Historians of the ancient world might date the origins of the myth to Greece and the Olympic Games. For the purposes of this volume, it is assumed that the modern, international sport myth emerged in the 1890s, with the rebirth of the Olympic Games. Pierre de Coubertin, considered the father of the modern Olympic Games, worked tirelessly to bring back the games in an effort to keep men strong, and credited sport with having the power to build men's character. Supporting this belief in the power of sport were leaders like Theodore Roosevelt. As president of the United States, Roosevelt believed that football was an example of hyper-masculinity, a necessary characteristic of U.S. identity.

Roosevelt believed in the ideals of hard work and "manly strife."[2] As police commissioner of New York City, Roosevelt appointed recruits, and based his importance on physical exams and physical qualifications rather than playing politics. Roosevelt received a commission in a volunteer unit for the Spanish-Cuban-American War of 1898—First Volunteer Cavalry. Of the 1,000 available positions, Roosevelt "filled a majority of places with cowboys, hunters, and prospectors of the West and Southwest, men who bore the closest resemblance to his fabled backwoodsman."[3] He described these men as a "splendid set ... with weather-beaten faces, and eyes that looked a man straight in the face without flinching ... there could be no better material for soldiers than that afforded by these grim hunters of the mountains, these wild rough riders of the planes."[4] In 1899, Roosevelt gave a speech in Chicago titled *A Strenuous Life*, summing up what he believed should be the moral character of American citizens. In his speech he argued against men living a complacent life and that women need not fear childbirth.

In sport, by 1907, critics of American football believed the sport to be too dangerous. In the first years of the 20th century, deaths of teenagers and adults from injuries sustained in football were commonplace. Historians credit Roosevelt with saving the sport of football. He was critical of those attempting to ban the sport saying, "The sports especially dear to a vigorous and manly nation are always those in which there is a certain slight element of risk.... It is mere unmanly folly to try to do away with the sport because the risk exists."[5] Yet, he did understand the importance of altering the rules for player safety. In 1906, with the implementation of the forward pass, only eleven deaths occurred on the field of play, which was a significant improvement from the previous year.[6] Roosevelt and other proponents of football are credited with saving the game, and the changes made it more "American" than the previous version that developed out of European rugby.

Football became an important part of masculine identity. In the early 20th century, a gender ideology developed in sport that marginalized women and anyone who was a critic of its significance in U.S. society. Football was so revered that it was used as a recruiting tool during World War I. In the spring of 1917, the United States ended its isolationist approach and entered the war. By fall, the United States Navy created the Navy Special Services football team, with former college players who had enlisted in the war effort. Paddy Driscoll of Northwestern University, Charlie Bachman and Hugh Blacklock of the University of Michigan, and Jimmy Conzelman of Washington University were sent to the Great Lakes Naval Training Center (GLNTC) near Lake Bluff, Illinois. It was at the GLNTC where they learned their initial role in the war effort was to drum up military support through football. Historian Rich Cohen examined this team and remarked, "If you look at the first busts in the NFL Hall of Fame, you'll be looking at much of the navy's World War I team."[7] He remarked that the team defeated just about every football powerhouse in the country. The games "were meant to boost morale and serve as a recruiting tool."[8] Conflating the United States military with football allowed spectators of the sport to see it as truly "American" and, when the soldiers returned victorious, so too was the connection between service and support of the "combat" on the field of play. Thus, the great sports myth became embedded in the nationalist milieu of sport in the United States and abroad.

Building on the great sport myth is the sense of bonding and emotional unity that is created within a sporting social world. This unity appears on the surface level as supporting and protective. However, it can become enforcing rather than supporting and insulating rather than protecting. The Larry Nassar scandal of sexual abuse with USA Gymnastics, and as a team physician at Michigan State University, exposed that the social world of elite gymnastics, and the problems within the organization, were insulated from external interference for over two decades. The support seemed non-existent when athletes complained about abuse. Instead, the hierarchy of power within the organization followed the chain of command, leaving the survivors of sexual abuse without the support network they needed. A social world in sport that becomes so insulated has the potential to have a culture of abuse become part of everyday life. Rather than accept social problems in the sporting world as outliers, the scholars in this book ask the more difficult question, "What is wrong with sport that allows racist, sexist, and xenophobic acts to occur?" This is the challenge with questioning the great sport myth—recognizing and accepting that sport does not always lead to positive character development. For some, understanding the sport does not improve the lives of all who participated is a major paradigm shift, almost what it was like when people learned the earth wasn't flat.

The essays in Part One, "Race, Gender and Social Justice," examine national identity within two high-profile sporting institutions: the NFL and the Olympic Games. In the collection's opening essay, Nicholas Villanueva, Jr., examines the critical backlash against NFL quarterback Colin Kaepernick and other protesting black athletes via social media. Kaepernick's protest revealed the structural racism that exists in sport in the United States. This essay argues that a cumulative array of societal factors, including a pro-military ideology in the post–9/11 world, a history of racial oppression in the United States, and the interaction of the NFL with spectators that systemically privilege white athletes over non-white athletes, has led to the exclusion of black athletes from the "imagined community" of the NFL fan base, because of their perceived unpatriotic actions.

Coauthors Jomills H. Braddock II, Christina Sanchez Volatier, Adrienne Milner, Ashley B. Mikulyuk and Marvin P. Dawkins continue the discussion of social justice in sport with an examination of diversity on the United States Olympic team. The authors argue that increasingly diverse national sporting teams are directly linked to productivity. Although researchers have found that both gender and racial diversity are positively associated with productivity and effectiveness across a broad range of organizational contexts in the U.S., this relationship remains relatively unexplored in sport organizations. Because sport organizations both reflect and reproduce racism and sexism in the larger social structure, the U.S. Olympic Team, or TEAM USA, serves as a symbol of social justice in terms of nationalism and inclusion. Their findings reveal a clear, but often unacknowledged benefit of racial diversity for American Olympic success.

Part Two explores "Sport and National Identity." In the opening essay, Hendrik Snyders attempts to map the contours of the history of black golf in South Africa, especially its players, clubs, competitions and administrators, as well as their difficulties and successes. As such, it further attempts to assist with the burial of some of the prevailing myths that continue to ascribe certain sports inequalities (especially with regard to race) to natural evolution, individual disinterest or psychological, emotional and physical unsuitability.

In "National Heroes or Disgusting Nazis? Soccer Patriotism, German National Identity and the 'Gaucho Gate' Incident After the FIFA World Cup 2014," Yannick Kluch delves into the topic of German identity in soccer, looking in particular at the 'Gaucho Gate' controversy, which ignited after players of the German national soccer team, celebrating their 2014 FIFA World Cup victory, performed a dance that overtly mocked their Argentinian opponents. The controversial nature of the dance created major uproar in both national and international media landscapes, with Uruguayan journalist Victor Hugo Morales describing the German national team soccer players as "disgusting Nazis."

Ali Bowes examines the relationship between women, the construction of nations, and the reproduction of national identities, a topic that remains under-researched, particularly in the realm of sport. In "National Identities and International Sport: What About the Women?," Bowes argues that women have been regularly excluded in literature on sporting nationalisms, and because women have been written out of the nation, and subsequently out of analyses on sport and the nation, their experiences have been ignored. This essay demonstrates the need to ask those athletes who actually act as representatives of the nation about their identities and sense of belonging, and begins to address the relative absence of research on women, sport and national identity.

Part Three takes a provocative look at "Athletes and the Global Spectacle." In the opening essay, Bruce S. Burnside draws on legal anthropological theory and German and religious studies to track the various actors that helped enact what became a national drama in the media around the issue of fatwa and sport, including the Council, the League, the player's union, the team, and Al-Azhar University in Cairo. Burnside argues that the Central Council for Muslims in Germany used, what he calls, a relatively benign religious issue (fasting) intersecting with a professional sport with strong links to ongoing identity formation in Germany, to position Islam as compatible with professional German sports and thus with German identity writ large. He maps the deeply intertwined history of German nationalism and sport as well as the more recent policy changes that have opened up citizenship paths (since 2000) of those with Muslim backgrounds and what role Islam should play in German social and legal life.

In "A Cause Without a Rebel: In Search of a Palestinian Sporting Hero," Jon Dart assesses the likelihood of Palestinian athletes emerging whose visibility might advance their call for human rights. Attention is given to Mahmoud Sarsak who, as a young Palestinian footballer, was arrested when he tried to travel from Gaza to the West Bank to sign a professional contract. Accused of involvement in violent anti–Israeli actions, he was held for three years before being released without charge. Dart discusses how calls for social justice for the Palestinians have come primarily from non–Palestinian sports men and women, such as footballers Eric Cantona, Cristiano Ronaldo and Joey Barton, and English cricketer Moeen Ali, who was reprimanded for wearing wristbands embossed with the phrases "Save Gaza" and "Free Palestine" during a match.

Part Four, "Media Re-Presentation of Nationhood and Sport," analyzes mass media representation, or re-presentation, of national identity and sport. In this section's first essay, Zachary T. Androus analyzes mass media presentations of riders competing in the International Motorcycling Federation Road Racing World Championship (currently trademarked as MotoGP by rights holder Dorna Sports), to show how they discursively enact and reify state claims to national legitimacy by representing the riders as paragons of their state nationalities.

Finally, in the collection's final essay, Jared Bahir Browsh brings this international examination of athletes as national figures back to the United States. Browsh examines media coverage and professional league marketing to show the evolution of this nationalistic attitude toward sports in the United States. Browsh studies the dearth of media attention toward sports that lack American involvement and dominance, to the constant attempts to expand the footprint of domestic professional sports leagues in the United States around the world through expansion and player recruitment.

This collection explores the restrictive ideology of nationalism in international sport. To understand the dominant narrative of nationalism, it is important not to conflate patriotism with nationalism. As historian Maurizio Viroli stated, "The language of patriotism invites individuals to remain culturally defined, interested, and passionate, and tries to instill in them a culture of liberty, and interest in the Republic, a love of the common good; it does not aim to dictate what rational moral individuals ought to do, but to make those who love liberty stronger than the champions of oppression and discrimination."[9] Nationalism might be quite the opposite. It is a restrictive ideology with a set of rules placed upon a society by the dominant group who controls most institutions. In sport, that dominant group is largely white, male, heterosexual, and Christian. Benedict Anderson argued that nationalism is an "imagined community" built upon cultural artifacts. The authors of the following essays interrogate our great sports myth through the perspective of athletics to learn how, and at what intersectional moments, sporting identities can challenge dominant ideologies about sport and understand the realities of athletes as national symbols.

NOTES

1. Jay Coakley, *Sport and Society: Issues and Controversies* (New York: McGraw-Hill, 2017), p. 11.
2. Theodore Roosevelt, *The Strenuous Life: Essays and Addresses* (Mineola, NY: Dover, 2012).
3. Gary Gerstle, *American Crucible: Race and Nation in the Twentieth Century* (Princeton, NJ: Princeton University Press, 2001), 27.
4. Ibid.
5. John J. Miller, *The Big Scrum: How Teddy Roosevelt Saved Football* (New York: Harper Perennial, 2011), 132–133.
6. Ibid., 212.
7. Rich Cohen, *Monsters: The 1985 Chicago Bears and the Wild Heart of Football* (New York: Farrar, Straus and Giroux, 2013), 35–36.
8. Ibid.
9. Maurizio Viroli, *For Love of Country: An Essay on Patriotism and Nationalism* (New York: Oxford University Press, 1997), 16.

PART ONE
Race, Gender and Social Justice

Land of the Free?

Sporting Nationalism and White Privilege in the United States

NICHOLAS VILLANUEVA, JR.

"The language of patriotism invites individuals to remain culturally defined, interested, and passionate, and tries to instill in them a culture of liberty, and interest in the republic, a love of the common good; it does not aim to dictate what rational moral individuals ought to do, but to make those who love liberty stronger than the champions of oppression and discrimination."[1]

Abstract

This study of Colin Kaepernick's protest examines the current topic of racial injustice in the United States, politics and sport, and the critical backlash against Kaepernick and other black athletes via social media. His protest revealed the structural racism that exists in sport in the United States. This essay argues that a cumulative array of societal factors, including a pro-military ideology in the post–9/11 world, a history of racial oppression in the United States, and the interaction of the NFL with spectators that systemically privilege white athletes over non-white athletes, has led to the exclusion of black athletes from the "imagined community" of the NFL fan base, because their perceived unpatriotic actions. This essay argues that the timing of Kaepernick's protest, in a U.S. political climate more polarizing than any other, during an Olympiad year that intensified a nationalistic milieu, and at a sporting venue that lionizes military service persons, his protest of the U.S. national anthem led to a "perfect storm" of racists reactions and hateful comments about an athlete and his protest over racial injustice in the United States.

"O'er the land of the free and the home of the brave!" The final words of the U.S. national anthem are immediately followed by boisterous cheers and applauds at sporting events. These symbols of nationhood, nationalism, and pride—the American flag and anthem—are used in the ceremony and tradition that is part of American sporting nationalism. At baseball games from coast to coast and encompassing professional, amateur, and club teams, this ceremony evolved after September 11, 2001, to include, and almost replace, "Take me out to the ballgame" with "God Bless America." In the 21st-century world, sport and nationalism combine to exemplify a desire for homogeneity that includes members of a social world that are patriotic to the state and excludes any outlier that appears to disrespect the militant ceremony that exists during a sporting event. Sporting nationalism and society have clashed in the 21st century. Football and baseball are no longer simply a game, but a space where national identity is defined and contested. During the summer and fall of 2016, athletes used this space to contest national identity and bring awareness to the social inequality that exists in U.S society. It is this playing field that has become a contested space for something much more than a game. In this land of the free, these brave athletes and fans are standing up to racial injustice. In doing so, some have opposed the ceremonial playing of the national anthem with a peaceful protest of kneeling. For the dominant group of white males in sport and society, this was seen as unpatriotic. Dominant narratives revealed there is a privilege in sport that precludes athletes of color from making any statement that is not in line with dominant white society.

On Friday, August 26, 2016, Colin Kaepernick drew the attention of multiple media outlets when he refused to stand with his hand over his heart during the playing of the national anthem before the start of a preseason game against the Green Bay Packers. He refused to stand for the anthem before the previous game one week earlier, but this time he attracted the attention of the sports media. Kaepernick stated, "I am not going to stand up to show pride in a flag for a country that oppresses black people and people of color.... To me, this is bigger than football and it would be selfish on my part to look the other way. There are bodies in the street and people getting paid leave and getting away with murder."[2] Kaepernick's demonstration continued what other protests started, such as the black lives matter protests, to push for a national conversation about racism and discrimination in this country. This site of protest, however, entered living rooms across the country, while football fans were preparing to watch the beginning of another season. This location, on the football field, and the protest of the national anthem, received mixed responses. According to a Yahoo Sports survey by Jay Busbee, sportswriter, and author of *Earnhardt Nation*, 47 percent of the respondents opposed the Kaepernick protest, 32 percent supported it, and 21 percent were either neutral or did not know how they felt about his actions.[3] Busbee concludes that "at least 44 percent of Americans want their football to be about football ... or, if it gets political, only about the kind of protests with which they agree."[4]

Football has not been solely about football for years. In the 21st-century world, football has been infused with nationalism and has symbolized American pride in our nation's military. Football ideology is one predicated on militaristic terminology. As Dave Zirin examined in his documentary, *Not Just a Game*, players often parallel their games with that of combat, arguing that they are "going to battle," and, "It's war!" Zirin explained that the military presence is embedded in football games. Military appreciation can be found throughout stadiums, armed forces recruiting stations are set up in or around the facility. Even uniforms were redesigned for military appreciation day to have team colors displayed in a camouflage print.[5] This is not by chance, the Department of Defense spent over $53 million on patriotic displays at sporting events, according to a report by Senators John McCain and Jeff Flake of Arizona. NFL franchises are not the only recipients of "paid patriotism," the National Guard spent $88 million over three years sponsoring Dale Earnhardt, Jr.'s Sprint Cup car. The dominant narrative in sport, and especially true for football, is that politics favorable to the dominant fan group, or sporting world, is acceptable. Patriotism and pride in symbols like the flag and songs like the national anthem and "God Bless America," are expected by the masses of spectators actively participating in the ceremonial playing of the national anthem. It is at that moment where interpretations of American identity and American nationalism are learned and understood. According to Dave Zirin, "It's here [sport] where societal and cultural meaning play out, our very notions about who we are and how we see each other, not only as Americans, but as individuals.... And as we will see, sports culture produces stories that become the dominant narratives that makes certain ways of seeing the world normal, conventional, just the way it is. While at the same time, actively trying to silence anything or anybody who doesn't fit in this accepted frame."[6] It is this dominant narrative about patriotism and nationalism that Colin Kaepernick challenged with his peaceful protest against racial injustice in America, a protest that has angered millions of Americans more than the subject of his protest.

To understand the dominant narrative of patriotism and nationalism, a definition is required for both. When polling a college class on Critical Sports Studies at the University of Colorado, Boulder, the meaning of patriotism was largely understood by a majority of respondents. Moreover, they argued that patriotism involved some action and was a conscious decision to act.

They believed that anyone could be a patriot as long as they love their country and perform some action acknowledging their adoration. However, when asked about nationalism fewer students responded, and most of the students argued that nationalism appeared to have rules for inclusion. Patriotism is an emotional attachment that an individual has to a nation. This attachment, or a love for country, transcends static nationalistic ideals of homogeneity and exclusion of the non-statesman, and is inclusive of cultural diversity. A heterogeneous State can share this love of country and ceremoniously come together and actively demonstrate this through patriotism. As historian Maurizio Viroli stated, "the language of patriotism invites individuals to remain culturally defined, interested, and passionate, and tries to instill in them a culture of liberty, and interest in the Republic, a love of the common good; it does not aim to dictate what rational moral individuals ought to do, but to make those who love liberty stronger than the champions of oppression and discrimination."[7] These attachments can be for cultural reasons, ethnic reasons, or, in the case of the United States, historical reasons. Nationalism is much different. It, as Benedict Anderson argued, is an "imagined community" that is built upon cultural artifacts. These cultural artifacts, or characteristics, are historical, and their meanings can change over time. The dominant group in U.S. society is made up of white, heterosexual men. As dominant members, historically, this group defined U.S. national identity and, thus, U.S. citizenship. Since sport is a microcosm of our larger society, it is no surprise that white, heterosexual men define the ideology of sport and embrace a nationalistic identity that celebrates hyper-masculinity, heteronormativity, and whiteness—with players and fans unnoticing that sport is an arena of white privilege. This "imagined community" of sport, exemplified in the sporting world of football, is imagined because players and fans from small towns to urban cities may never meet each other, but they unknowingly come together in front of their televisions each week, waiting patiently for their sporting heroes to lead their team to victory. Or, as Anderson wrote: "because the members of even the smallest nation will never know most of their fellow-members, meet them, or even hear of them, yet in the minds of each lives the image of their communion."[8] Colin Kaepernick's actions, while some can argue are exercising his patriotic duty to protest injustice, were largely seen by members of the dominant sporting world as disrespectful, unpatriotic, and not part of their "imagined community."

This study of the Kaepernick protest examines the current topic of racial injustice in the United States, politics and sport, and the critical backlash against Kaepernick and other black athletes via social media. His protest revealed structural racism that exists in sport in the United States. This essay argues that a cumulative array of societal factors that include a pro-military ideology in the post–9/11 world, history of racial oppression in the

United States, and the interaction of the NFL with spectators that systemically privilege white athletes over non-white athletes, led to the exclusion of black athletes from the "imagined community" of sport. A superficial counter argument claims that there is a large number of black athletes in sport today, thus, denying that white privilege exists in sport. However, having the power to determine what the sporting nationalism script allows, is at the core of white privilege in sport, and dominant white males make those decisions. The Kaepernick protest occurred as Americans entered the final months of a presidential race that exposed racism and xenophobia, and allowed voters to support a candidate that made racist and sexist comments. Yet, the national uproar making media headlines was black athletes and their peaceful protest against racial inequality. This essay argues that the timing of Kaepernick's protest, in a U.S. political climate more polarizing than any other, during an Olympiad year that intensified a nationalistic milieu, and at a sporting venue that lionizes military veterans, led to a "perfect storm" of racists reactions and hateful comments about athletes of color and their protest over racial injustice in the United States, that exposed white privilege in sport.

During the month of August 2016, when Colin Kaepernick began his protest, the sporting milieu was at its patriotic peak of a four-year cycle—the Olympiad. Only five days after the closing ceremonies of the Rio 2016 Olympic Games, Kaepernick began his demonstration. For two weeks the sporting world focused on the Latin American country of Brazil, and fans cheered on their nation's athletes with nationalistic rhetoric and patriotic displays of support. Politics and sport have had an uneasy relationship during the Olympiad. Host nations use the games for international prestige and national pride, yet social issues and political unrest have historically been at the forefront of the games. In 1936 Berlin, Germany, patriotism and nationalism were propagated throughout the country in movie theaters that broadcasted recorded events with German athletes victorious. The games are remembered for African American Jesse Owens' gold medal triumph in a track and field stadium that included Adolf Hitler. This is the dominant sport narrative that has survived: a hatred for Hitler brought Owens into the dominant sport narrative. Excluded from our historical memory is the segregated society of the United States that Owens returned to after traveling throughout Europe as a free man. In the London press, the *Spectator* referred to Owens as "the hero of these Games," yet even the *Atlanta Constitution*, considered "the most liberal of Southern newspapers, did not publish photographs of any black U.S. Olympians."[9] Upon returning to the U.S., President Franklin D. Roosevelt failed to congratulate the Olympic champion. However, the dominant group in U.S. society has preserved the story of Owens' triumph through generations as a story of breaking down the color line, leaving out the embarrassing truth that Owens experienced freedom on the track & field in Nazi Germany.

From the Berlin games that exposed race and nationhood to the 2014 Sochi Olympic games that identified human rights violations against the LGBTQ community in Russia, politics have played an important role in the international event. Human rights groups called for a boycott of the 2014 Sochi Olympic games because of the passage of "Anti-Gay propaganda laws." Russian Parliament members argued that the laws were aimed at "protecting children." However, these laws conflated homosexuality with pedophilia, a belief propagated in the United States as well through Christian religious extremists. Even with a call for action against Russia, the games continued without a boycott. It is not surprising that heteronormativity in the sporting world prevailed.[10]

Political statements were made in Rio 2016 as well. During the opening ceremonies, ten athletes marched into the stadium from Democratic Republic of the Congo, Ethiopia, South Sudan, and Syria, with one unifying flag—the flag of the Olympic Games. These athletes arrived in Rio de Janeiro as expatriates, refugees who fled social and political upheaval in their home country. This political statement, during a global refugee crisis that has hundreds of thousands displaced, and risking their lives seeking refuge, presented these men and women as heroes who persevered through monumental challenges. Refugees from nations, when seen as young, struggling displaced athletes, find their way into the dominated sport narrative, even when only months earlier, xenophobic political leaders such as Governor Mike Pence of Indiana called for the refusal of Syrian refugees in his state.[11] Refugee athletes at the 2016 Games did not win any medals, but their journey to the games symbolized their commitment to sport even without the flag of their home country. The heroism of these athletes, their stories of sacrifice and loss, provided the world an image of refugees that found a place in the hearts of many in the audience of the opening ceremony.

Three nights after the opening ceremony, one of the premiere events of the games awarded gold, silver, and bronze medals—the women's gymnastics team final. The team for the United States won the gold medal, and Gabby Douglas, an African American female team member, inadvertently disrupted this nationalistic discourse. Douglas, a 2012 Olympic gold medalist, helped the team to a second consecutive team gold medal. During the medal ceremony, Douglas stood with her teammates, sang along to the national anthem, but with her hands at her side. Immediately, social media posts ignited a firestorm of criticism that the athlete was dishonoring the Stars and Stripes. August 9, 2016, was the second anniversary of the death of Michael Brown, shot and killed by a Ferguson, Missouri, police officer. Brown's death and multiple other deaths of unarmed black men by white police officers were the impetus behind the Black Lives Matter movement. As Douglas stood on the podium of the medal ceremony social media bullies began to speculate her motivation behind not placing her hand on her heart. Anonymous strangers like @ReallyRick of Cookeville, Tennessee, posted, "Just because you didn't make the all-around finals doesn't mean you have to be a disrespectful bitch Gabby Douglas!"[12] Numerous posts criticized the twenty-year-old African American athlete criticizing her attitude, her lack of excitement while watching teammates perform, and her hair. Was all of this stemming from not placing her hand over her heart? Not exactly. One week later U.S. track and field shot putters Ryan Crouser and Joe Kovacs won gold and silver medals, respectively. During their medal ceremony, neither athlete placed their hand over their hearts. Social media lacked any condemnation of these two athletes and their "refusal" to honor the national anthem. Their privilege as white males protected them from ridicule, leaving the dominant white audience to believe there must have been some acceptable reason for their inaction. For Douglas, systemic racism that exists in social institutions led to her condemnation through cyberbullying and exposed a privilege that exists for white, male athletes.

Cyberbullying of black athletes is the 21st-century version of lynching in the United States. Lynching in the U.S. has a long history, mostly targeting people of color—African Americans for racialized justifications and Hispanics, primarily of Mexican descent, for nationalistic reasons.[13] According to the NAACP, lynching is defined by four categories for their historical record keeping. First, a murder must have occurred; second, there must be three or more perpetrators involved; third, it must occur extra-legally, public condemnation rather than official means of law and order; and fourth, the purpose was an act of vengeance or tradition. While cyberbullying attacks are not always lethal, they are a form of collective violence.

The practice of lynching in the United States has its origin early in the 1760s among South Carolinians, known as "regulators," who used extra-legal measures to punish outlaws. The term "lynching" may have originated from Charles Lynch of Bedford County, Virginia, "when he and his friends informally tied and whipped pro–British sympathizers during the American Revolution," and first appeared in print in 1817 as "Lynch's Law."[14] Initially, a lynching referred to a group of men who whipped or beat an outlier to society. By the third and fourth decades of the 19th century, white southerners were using such assaults, now usually ending in death, to pursue rebellious slaves. Lynching then moved west with the gold rush, and westerners defended the practice as necessary to bring order to the frontier. Following reconstruction, southern whites used lynching to intimidate black southerners and establish a social order of segregation. The decade of the 1890s accounts for more lynching of African Americans than any other decade. After the turn of the century, the Ku Klux Klan reemerged in 1916 and their campaign of 100 percent Americanism targeted not only African Americans, but ethnic Mexicans,

Jews, Catholics, and Eastern European immigrants. There were more known lynchings of ethnic Mexicans between 1910 and 1920 than any other 20th-century decade. As the century progressed, civil rights activists, white and non-white, became targets of lynching mobs. Following this evolution of "judge lynch," 21st-century cyberbullying of black athletes can be seen as part of the tradition of lynching as public shaming in the social world of sport.

Cyberlynching is in accord with the definition of lynching if there is community shaming, public versus law enforcement response to the perceived social violation, three or more perpetrators, and as a response that is justified as tradition or revenge. For Gabby Douglas, there were thousands of comments about her actions on the medal podium, definitely more than three perpetrators, and these cyberbullies justified their actions as revenge for insulting the U.S. flag during the playing of the national anthem. Douglas was expected to follow a script that required her hand over her heart or a salute to the flag. The perpetrators immediately launched their cyberattack, and the mob grew in numbers. Social media platforms such as Twitter and Facebook allowed people to post their comments and attacks, often lambasting the young woman in terms of how she should act as a national figure. These attacks were not carried out on U.S. Track and Field shot putters Ryan Crouser and Joe Kovacs. These white men received no criticism for not following the same patriotic script. Either a racial ideology or gender ideology, or possibly both, privileged them to be free to enjoy their gold-medal moment the way they desired.

Similar to lynching of the 20th century, cyber lynching is racialized. Newspapers and African American institutions led the way in collecting data on lynching cases, with the *Chicago Tribune* publishing cumulative annual totals beginning in 1883. In 1912, the Tuskegee Institute began publishing the *Negro Yearbook: An Encyclopedia of the Negro*, which included the annual lynching records collected by the Institute since 1892. According to Tuskegee Institute records, 3,445 of the 4,742 known lynchings that occurred between 1882 and 1964 targeted African Americans. The remaining 1,297 victims are listed as "white."[15] Violations of a racial hierarchy by African Americans led to most of these extra-legal executions. White mobs targeted black men for speaking to white women, suspected sexual relations with white women, and for not addressing a white woman respectfully. However, the lynching of black men occurred too for nationalistic reasons when black men were found wearing a U.S. Army uniform. In 1919, William Little of Blakely, Georgia, was lynched for wearing his World War I uniform, this continued following World War II when 56 black veterans were beaten or lynched for the same reason. White men formed mobs when their racial hierarchy appeared to be violated. A hierarchy that credited military service and success in the World Wars with white superiority.

Cyberbullying of Gabby Douglas began long before the 2016 Olympic games. Douglas became the first African American woman to win the Olympic All-Around gold medal at the 2012 London Olympic games. She bested U.S. athlete Jordyn Wieber, the 2011 World All-Around Champion during the preliminary competition, qualifying her for the event final, where she won the gold medal ahead of two Russian athletes. But Douglas did not fit the image of an Olympic gold medalist for a segment of the fan base of the sport. Following her victory, Douglas was criticized for her appearance and most notably for her hair. Even Douglas was surprised, "Really? I won two gold medals and made history and my hair is trending?"[16] Trending, but not with positive comments.

The sixteen-year-old Olympic gold medalist received thousands of insulting and racists comments following her successful Olympic journey to London. Upon returning to the U.S., Douglas made media appearances that included an interview with Oprah Winfrey. During that interview, Douglas revealed that she was bullied at her gym in Virginia, Excalibur Gymnastics. Douglas felt isolated, was concerned about over performing and standing out. She remembered going home and crying. She recalled an athlete preparing to mount the uneven bars, and when requesting that someone "scrape the bar," a technique necessary for prepping the apparatus, the girl questioned, "Why doesn't Gabby do it, she's our slave?"[17] In 2010, Douglas left Excalibur for West Des Moines, Iowa, to train with elite coach Liang Chow, of Chow's Gymnastics & Dance—U.S. National Team Training Center. Over one thousand miles from her family, Douglas moved to work with the best coaches. Chow, at that time, was best known for grooming U.S. gymnast Shawn Johnson to become an Olympian. Four years earlier Johnson won the silver medal in the all-around competition at the Beijing Olympic Games. In 2012, Douglas became Chow's greatest success story by topping Johnson's achievement winning the all-around gold medal. However, to the dissatisfaction of cyberbullies on social media, Douglas was not their picturesque gymnast, and the cyber lynching began. The criticism continued to 2016, following her appearance on the medal podium during the ceremony where she did not hold her hand over her heart. Douglas was the first African American woman to win the most coveted title in gymnastics, the Olympic all-around gold medal, but continues to be remembered for her hair and as an unpatriotic athlete. Moreover, Chow's gym's website does not have Douglas prominently positioned on the home page for future young girls to aspire to be; Chow is pictured instead with silver medalist Shawn Johnson, a white woman.

Following the conclusion of the Olympic games in August 2016, sports fans turned their attention to the National Football League. Awaiting them was Colin Kaepernick who had decided that racial injustice in the U.S. needed more attention. In a symbolic move, Kaepernick refused to stand up for the national anthem. His purpose was to bring attention to the racial injustice that befell African Americans, specifically for police disproportionately targeting African Americans, a racial profiling that has led to the death of these victims. Kaepernick became a pariah for his refusal to "show pride in a flag for a country that oppresses black people and people of color."[18] Karl Taro Greenfield of the *Los Angeles Times* opined, "the interconnected worlds of social and sports media threw a patriotic fit."[19] The masses of sports fans took to social media to attack Kaepernick for dishonoring the flag during the patriotic tradition of standing on the sideline, holding a hand over their heart during the singing of the Star Spangled Banner. However, this "tradition" only began in 2009. Following the Kaepernick backlash, NFL spokesman Brian McCarthy confirmed that this is a relatively new practice. Before 2009, NFL players remained in their locker room until after the fans participated in their patriotic script. The decision to include the players was an attempt to strengthen the ties between the U.S. military and the NFL.

Football has a long history with the military. Early 20th-century political figures like Theodore Roosevelt revered football for the toughness of this uniquely "American" sport. Although football evolved from rugby, a sport that originated in Warwickshire, England, American exceptionalism in sport claimed it as its own. Not surprisingly since the same has happened in the past with baseball, that evolved from traditionally British "ball and bat" games, and basketball, which was invented by a Canadian. Roosevelt was a man known for his belief that citizens of the Republic should live a "strenuous life" not a life of "ignoble ease."[20] To Roosevelt, men needed to instill these qualities in their sons and that we needed to "admire the man who embodies victorious effort."[21] As for women, Roosevelt believed in a gender ideology that privileged men. Roosevelt scorned women who feared motherhood and childbirth, he argued, "when women fear motherhood, they tremble on the brink of doom; and well it is they should vanish from the earth, where they are fit subjects for the scorn of all men."[22] Roosevelt's love of football, a game he is credited with saving from near extinction because of the dangers associated with the sport, was not as strong as his love for U.S. military servicemen.

Young men who sacrificed for the good of the nation he held in his highest regard. Moreover, during World War I, years after he held the office of the presidency, Roosevelt lauded young boys who were too young to serve for doing their part for the country. "Boy Power," as it was referred to by the Department of Labor, was a patriotic war initiative, encouraging young men to enroll with the understanding that they were doing their part. Representatives from the Department of Agriculture met in St. Louis during the week of November 5 to 10, to evaluate the success of "Boy Power" from the previous summer. The representative members opined, "that schoolboys rightly trained would make capable farm helpers and would be a potent factor in winning the war against Germany."[23] William E. Hall, the national director of the Boys' Working Reserve, received a letter from former President Theodore Roosevelt expressing his support for the loyalty to the nation the program championed:

> One of the great benefits you confer is that of making a boy realize that he is part of Uncle Sam's team; that he is doing his share in the great war, that he holds his services in trust for the Nation, and that although it is proper to consider the question of material gain and the question of his own desires, yet that what he must most strongly consider at this time is where his services will do most good to our people as a whole. I earnestly wish you every success in your wise and patriotic effort.
>
> Faithfully yours, Theodore Roosevelt[24]

It was at this moment, during the recruitment of men to enlist in the U.S. Army for World War I, that the intersection of football and military emerged in 20th-century popular culture. The team from West Point dominated college football, and during the 1917 season, traveled through Midwestern factory towns recruiting young men for military service.[25]

Today, spectators who criticize Kaepernick for his political protest before an NFL game, fail to notice just how political their game has become. Military flyovers are commonplace at football games, and honoring local military personnel for their service at halftime events is an ordinary practice. Even the singing of the national anthem became politicized in recent years. Not by Colin Kaepernick, but the NFL. In 2009, the NFL made it a requirement for players to exit their locker rooms before the singing of the national anthem. The U.S. military and the NFL came to the agreement that players should, and would, stand for the national anthem over seven years before Kaepernick's protest. Kaepernick didn't politicize football, the U.S. federal government and the NFL already had a well-established ideology in place. An ideology that politicized football as an American tradition that supported the U.S. military in the post–9/11 world. Not doing so was an action that left a player out of this social world of sport. The dominant group constructing these rules turned a blind eye toward disproportionate incarceration rates among African American men, gross violations of the "equal protection" clause of the 14th Amendment of the U.S. Constitution, and the unnecessary murder of young black men during "routine" traffic stops. Moreover, they lambasted the peaceful protest of an athlete taking a knee for 90 seconds before a football game.

Other black athletes followed Kaepernick's lead. Jordan Danberry, Tatiyna Smith, Kiara Williams, Jailyn Mason, Yasmeen Ratliff, and Briunna Freeman, members of the University of Arkansas women's basketball team joined a growing number of black athletes across the country kneeling to protest racial injustice in the United States.[26] In October, two women separately kneeled during their singing performance of the national anthem before a Miami Heat basketball game. Singer Leah Tysse knelt while singing the final lyrics "Land of the free, and home of the brave." Tysse responded to questions via her Facebook page:

> The sad reality is, as a white American, I am bestowed a certain privilege in this nation that is not enjoyed by all people. Black families are having much different conversations with their children about how to interact with the police than white families. Let's be honest. Until we can recognize that white privilege exists we cannot have a dialogue about race.[27]

Later during the month of October, prior to a preseason game between the Miami Heat and the Philadelphia 76ers, Denasia Lawrence, an African American woman who works part-time for the Heat organization, took a knee as she sang the entire national anthem. She stated via Facebook:

> I took the opportunity to sing AND kneel; to show that we belong in this country AND that we have the right to respectfully protest injustices against us. I took the opportunity to sing AND kneel to show that, I, too, am America…[28]

Three University of Nebraska football players protested racial injustice in the United States by kneeling during the anthem prior to a September 24, 2016, football game against Northwestern University in Evanston, Illinois. Senior linebacker Michael Rose-Ivey, DaiShon Neal, and Mohamed Barry peacefully protested anti-black violence by taking a knee. Their actions were followed by a firestorm of racist comments and death threats by University of Nebraska fans and a member of the university board of regents. Rose-Ivey publically addressed the fans on September 26, 2016, with an impassioned statement about his experience following that game:

> Even though I am a college graduate. Even though I am blessed to play college football at the highest level.… Even though I am a healthy being. And even though I am fully conscious, I will still endure racism. I will still be referred to on Facebook as a clueless, confused nigger, by former high school classmates, friends, peers, and even Husker fans. Some people believe DaiShon, Mohamed, and myself should be kicked off the team or suspended. While some say we deserve to be lynched or shot just like the other black people that have died recently.[29]

Rose-Ivey appeared upset, confused, and angry, not just from the previous statement, but from what was to follow: "Another believed that since we didn't stand for the Anthem that we should be hung before the Anthem for the next game. These are actual statements we received from fans."[30] Head coach Mike Riley offered support for his players and stated: "Obviously, this is a choice they have made for personal reasons and that's the beautiful thing about the United States that they can do that."[31] Higher up the university administrative rank, Regent Hal Daub voiced his frustration with the players, fueling the hateful rhetoric of some Husker fans. Daub stated, "It's a free country, they don't have to play football for the university either.... They won't take the risk to exhibit their free speech in a way that places their circumstance in jeopardy, so let them get out of uniform and do their protesting on somebody else's nickel."[32] Rather than address the racist comments made by students and fans, and rather than acknowledge the death threats these young men received, one of the first questions Daub asked was if these were "scholarship" athletes. Thus, believing that he has the power to remove them from the team for not following the dominant sports ideological script associated with the national anthem. When powerful white men in sport or society overlook racism in the name of 100 percent Americanism, they give credibility to hateful speech and help members of this dominant group in society rationalize discrimination.

One hundred percent Americanism was a theme historically popular with the rise of the Second Ku Klux Klan from 1916 through the 1920s. Along with their anti-immigrant, nativists campaigns, the Klan was most popular with Christian conservatives that were anti–Catholic and anti–Semitic. Klan membership peaked in the 1920s with a range between three to six million members.[33] Often thought of as a Southern phenomenon, Klan membership thrived throughout the United States. In 1920, Nebraska reported having 1,296,372 residents, and by 1921, 45,000 of them were official members of the Klan. With a strong history of the KKK in this state, it is easier to understand why the three Nebraska football players lacked the privilege of support from high-ranking state officials. Making the environment even more volatile was the 2016 presidential election race. Nativist political rhetoric today echoes a similar call to arms of one hundred years ago. Nativist views gained increased traction during the 2015–2016 Republican primary race, with plans to exclude Muslim refugees, repatriate non–U.S. citizens, and construct a wall that will prevent Mexican "killers and rapists" from entering the United States.[34] Following the election of Barrack Obama, Republican leaders struggled with how they could galvanize poor white voters. Historian Carol Anderson argued how they strategized to "unelect a black president" in her book, *White Rage: The Unspoken Truth About Our Racial Divide*. Anderson reported that a Republican Senator stated, "We need to get the angry white vote."[35] By 2016, white rage boiled over and hate speech became campaign sound bites. Nativist and anti–Black Lives Matter rhetoric gained increased traction with white supporters of Donald Trump. Even his "hot mic" comments that should have drawn intense criticism were accepted by a faction of the dominant white society, because of his anti-politically correct-message. Alt-right and Anti-PC supporters were more concerned with maintaining white power than social injustice targeting U.S. citizens of color. When told something is not politically correct, this base of Trump followers realize they must follow new social rules that impede their privileged history. By November of 2016, Trump convinced a significant number of citizens that hate speech was acceptable. These voters embraced him as their president and elected a man that insulted women, incited the rhetoric of violence at campaign rallies, and stereotyped Mexicans as murderers and rapists. He became a symbol of 100 percent Americanism in its most blatantly racist origin.

Black athletes in 2016 exposed the racial injustice that exists in U.S. society today. Gabby Douglas became the target of hate speech, not for a protest, but because of a perceived protest, with her hand absent from her heart during the national anthem. One week later, two white men stood stoically during the playing of the U.S. national anthem, their hands absent from their chest, privileged and safe from any major backlash for their lack of action. The only difference is they were white men in the arena of sport. Kaepernick's protest led other young and politically active black men to protest as well, only to receive death threats by white fans. Kaepernick himself may never start or even play professional football again, but he helped reveal the lack of progress our nation has made in the 21st century. What is largely overlooked is the truly patriotic actions he made by protesting oppression, which was a founding principle of our nation. Why should African Americans stand during an anthem that was written in 1812? It was written for white men. The final words "O'er the land of the free, and the home of the brave" were penned while slavery existed and would continue for more than fifty years to follow. Moreover, the second verse of the national anthem, one that is not sung, condemns the actions of slaves who took up arms with the British in the War of 1812, who were fighting for their hope for "independence." I argue that the progress of the civil rights era has come to the point of contestation once again. Society today can no longer look back at the 1950s and 1960s and say, "Look how far we have come!" No, not when the microcosm of sport in 2016 revealed the racism and white privilege that continues to exclude black athletes from sporting nationalism and excludes African Americans in the United States from what Benedict Anderson called an *Imagined Community*.

Notes

1. Maurizio Viroli, *For Love of Country: An Essay on Patriotism and Nationalism* (New York: Oxford University Press, 1997).
2. Steve Wyche, "Colin Kaepernick Explains Why He Sat During National Anthem," August 27, 2016, nfl.com, http://www.nfl.com/news/story/0ap3000000691077/article/colin-kaepernick-explains-why-he-sat-during-national-anthem.
3. Jay Busbee, "Yahoo Poll: Half of Americans Oppose Kaepernick's Protest," Yahoo Sports, September 19, 2016, http://sports.yahoo.com/news/yahoo-poll-half-of-americans-oppose-kaepernicks-protest-154103124.html.
4. Ibid.
5. *Not Just a Game*. Directed by Jeremy Earp (Media Education Foundation, 2010).
6. *Not Just a Game*. Directed by Jeremy Earp (Media Education Foundation, 2010).
7. Maurizio Viroli, *For Love of Country: An Essay on Patriotism and Nationalism* (New York: Oxford University Press, 1997), 16.

8. Benedict Anderson, *Imagined Communities: Reflections on the Origin and Spread of Nationalism* (London: Verso, 1993), 2–6.

9. Allen Guttmann, "Berlin 1936: The Most Controversial Olympics," in Alan Tomlinson and Christopher Young, *National Identity and Global Sports Events: Culture, Politics, and Spectacle in the Olympics and the Football World Cup.* 71–72.

10. Laura Smith-Spark and Phil Black, "Protests, Boycott Calls as Anger Grows Over Russia Anti-gay Propaganda Laws," CNN http://www.cnn.com/2013/08/01/world/europe/russia-gay-rights-controversy/index.html.

11. Stephanie Wang, "Pence Stops Syrian Refugee Resettlement in Indiana," *Indianapolis Star*, November 16, 2015.

12. Emma Gray, "Haters, Leave Olympic Champion Gabby Douglas the F Alone," *Huffington Post*, August 15, 2016.

13. Nicholas Villanueva, Jr., *Lynching of Mexicans in the Texas Borderlands* (Albuquerque: University of New Mexico Press, 2017).

14. Stephen J. Leonard, "Judge Lynch in Colorado, 1859–1919," *Colorado Heritage* (Autumn, 2000), 4.

15. Campbell Robertson, "History of Lynching in the South Documents Nearly 4,000 Names," *New York Times*, February 10, 2015.

16. Julee Wilson, "Gabby Douglas Hair: Olympian's Mom, Natalie Hawkins Responds to Daughter's Hair Critics," *Huffington Post*, August 7, 2012.

17. Gabby Douglas, "Interview with Oprah Winfrey Sparks Firestorm Online," *The Hollywood Reporter*, August 28, 2012.

18. Karl Taro Greenfield, "Colin Kaepernick's Problem: Angry Responses Always Drown Out the Reason for a Protest," *Los Angeles Times*, September 2, 2016.

19. Ibid.

20. Theodore Roosevelt, *The Strenuous Life: Essays and Addresses* (New York: Dover, 2009).

21. Ibid.

22. Ibid.

23. "Boy Power: Official Bulletin of the United States Boys' Working Reserve, Department of Labor," *United States Boy's Working Reserve*, vol. I, no. 2, December 15, 1917, 1.

24. Ibid., 5.

25. Rich Cohen, *Monsters: The 1985 Chicago Bears and the Wild Heart of Football* (New York: Picador, 2014).

26. "Lady Razorbacks Take Knee During National Anthem Before Exhibition Game," THV11 (CBS) Little Rock, Arkansas, November 4, 2016, http://www.thv11.com/sports/lady-razorbacks-take-knee-during-national-anthem-before-exhibition-game/347529511.

27. Jose Martinez, "Women Takes a Knee During National Anthem Performance Prior to Heat-76ers Game," October 22, 2016, http://www.complex.com/sports/2016/10/denasia-lawrence-takes-knee-during-national-anthem-performance.

28. Ibid.

29. Andrew Joseph, "Nebraska Regent Wants Football Players Kicked Off the Team for Anthem Protests," *USA Today*, September 27, 2016.

30. Ibid.

31. Ibid.

32. Tyler Tynes and Richard Johnson, "Emails Show a Nebraska Regent Was 'Embarrassed' by Cornhusker Football Players' Protest," *SB Nation*, October 20, 2016, https://www.sbnation.com/college-football/2016/10/25/13337820/nebraska-cornhusker-football-players-protest-kneel-national-anthem.

33. Rory McVeigh, "Structural Incentives for Conservatives Mobilization: Power Devaluation and the Rise of the Ku Klux Klan, 1915–1925," *Social Forces*, Vol. 77, No. 4 (June 1999), p. 1463.

34. Amber Phillips, "Here Are 12 Other Times Donald Trump Vilified Illegal Immigrants," *The Washington Post*, July 1, 2015.

35. Carol Anderson, *White Rage: The Unspoken Truth of Our Racial Divide* (New York: Bloomsbury, 2017).

Diversity and Organizational Productivity

Examining the Role of Race and Gender in U.S. Olympic Team Success at the 2012 London Games

JOMILLS H. BRADDOCK II,
CHRISTINA SANCHEZ VOLATIER,
ADRIENNE MILNER, ASHLEY B. MIKULYUK
and MARVIN P. DAWKINS

Abstract

Although researchers have found that both gender and racial diversity are positively associated with productivity and effectiveness across a broad range of organizational contexts in the U.S., this relationship remains relatively unexplored in sport organizations. Because sport organizations both reflect and reproduce racism and sexism in the larger social structure, the U.S. Olympic Team, or TEAM USA, serves as a symbol of social justice in terms of nationalism and inclusion. Although a number of economists have examined social and demographic correlates of Olympic success (medal counts) across nations, race and gender typically have not been considered.

This study examines the association between racial/gender diversity and the performance (medals won) of the 2012 U.S. Olympic Team. Athlete data was gathered from the U.S. Olympic Team (TEAM USA) website. Data pertaining to United States' medal counts was collected from the NBC website and from London 2012, the official website of the London Olympic Games. Our descriptive analysis utilizes a parity index to compare the relative success or productivity of different race and gender athletes by employing an odds ratio indicator.

TEAM USA had a substantially higher representation of whites (72 percent), compared to athletes of color (28 percent), however, athletes of color accounted for a disproportionate share of total medals won. The parity index (1.38) indicates that athletes of color earned a 38 percent greater share of total team medals than their white teammates, and this pattern was consistent among both male and female.

These findings reveal a clear, but often unacknowledged benefit of racial diversity for American Olympic success.

> Diversity and inclusion are core values at the USOC because they make us better as an organization.
> —United States Olympic Committee (USOC)
> CEO Scott Blackmun[1]

The United States is becoming increasingly racially diverse, and demographic projections suggest that the nation may become majority minority by mid-century.[2] As a result, understanding the impact of growing racial-ethnic diversity has become a central focus of social, political, and academic debates. At the macro-level, scholars often frame this debate around questions of whether macro-level diversity is beneficial for national growth and productivity, or whether culturally diverse societies are more or less efficient than culturally homogeneous ones.[3] Similar debates also occur with regard to the impact of diversity at the meso- or organizational level examining diversity's impact on productivity or innovation of particular firms and businesses.

Research on the impact of diversity has produced mixed results.[4] Some studies suggest that diversity creates potential benefits for production and innovation[5] while other studies suggest that demographic diversity is associated with potential costs.[6] However, numerous studies have found a positive association between diversity and a wide range of outcomes: increased sales revenue, expanded customer base, greater market shares, and relative profits[7]; higher productivity[8]; job creation and economic growth[9]; and stimulation of innovation, cross-cultural cooperation and production.[10] In essence, organizational diversity, rather than homogeneity, seems to be associated with both cultural vitality and economic success. Indeed, research has shown that diversity has positive effects on creativity, innovation, and performance across different levels of social organization including firms, communities, and nations.

Nevertheless, while researchers have found that diversity can enhance productivity and effectiveness across a range of organizational and institutional contexts in the U.S. and abroad, there are very few studies of this relationship in sport contexts. In this regard, the present study breaks new ground in examining the impact of race-ethnic diversity on the productivity or effectiveness of a meso-level sports organization—the 2012 U.S. Olympic team. This study focuses specifically on Team USA's performance during the 2012 London Games. Because of the widely hailed impact of American women and gender diversity on Team USA's success in the London Games,[11] in this analysis, we seek to expand understanding of diversity effects in sports contexts by examining the relationship between Team USA's race-ethnic diversity and productivity in terms of medals won overall and separately for males and females. We also examine these relationships for Team USA overall, and by type of sport.

Nationalism and International Sport Competition

For the United States, and many other nations, the Olympics represents much more than an international platform to demonstrate athletic prowess. The Olympic Games, like other international sports mega-events (e.g., FIFA World Cup, Rugby World Cup, etc.), provide a global showcase for countries to project an idealized image of their national character.[12] For example, in his weekly address to the nation, President Barack Obama touted the diversity of the 2016 U.S. Olympic Team. He proclaimed that "Team USA reminds the world why America always sets the gold standard: We're a nation of immigrants that finds strength in our diversity and unity in our national pride" and encouraged Americans to "cherish this opportunity to come together around one flag."[13] In many ways, President Obama's remarks should not be surprising. The Olympic Games have long been considered a global stage for projecting *American exceptionalism*—the distinct character of the United States as a free nation rooted in democratic ideals and personal liberty. For example, many Americans pointed to Jesse Owens's four track-and-field medals in the 1936 Berlin games as an example of the virtues of the nation's diversity and democratic values. Celebrating Owens' historic accomplishments served to undermine Adolf Hitler and the Nazis' claim to racial Aryan superiority. Ironically, this took place in an era—nearly two decades prior to the *Brown v. Board of Education* ruling—when racial segregation in the U.S. was not only still widespread, but sanctioned by law in many locations. Following his victorious return to the U.S., Jesse Owens was reduced to racing against horses to survive financially. Similarly, in 1948, with Jim Crow segregation still in place, USOC official Gustavus T. Kirby suggested that U.S. Olympics flag-bearers should be flanked by two figures communicating athletes as national symbols, "one of whom should be a woman and the other a Negro"[14] in order to communicate "that the United States team has been and will be always made up of men and women, those of the white race, and those of other races."[15]

More recently, the American media has used mega sports events to emphasize similar egalitarian virtues in highlighting the growing racial and ethnic diversity of U.S. Winter Olympic teams and the significant progress toward gender parity in the composition of our Summer Olympic teams. Indeed, researchers have demonstrated nationalistic tendencies in the American media's coverage of the U.S. Olympic teams. For example, the success of American athletes are more likely to be attributed to their superior competitive orientation, concentration, composure, and commitment,[16] while the successes of athletes from other nations are more likely to be attributed to superior athletic skills or experience.[17]

Other nations have also sought to use the Olympic platform in similar ways. For example, leading up to the 1936 Olympics, Adolf Hitler viewed the Berlin Games as an opportunity to demonstrate the virtues of Germany's national character and commitment to Aryan superiority.

Additionally, during the Cold War, both the United States and the Soviet Union tried to prove their cultural and national superiority through symbolic victories at the Olympics.

It has also been argued that in some modern societies, the Olympic Games and other international sports mega-events help to maintain national unity.[18] In South Africa, for example, even though rugby was seen as a symbol of Apartheid, both white and black South Africans acknowledged that victory in the 2007 World Rugby Championship as well as hosting the World Football Championship in 2010 represented important symbolic milestones in the erection of a new national unity and racial reconciliation.[19] Similar arguments have been made about the Olympic Games and national pride. M.D.R. Evans and Jonathan Kelly's[20] comparative analysis of 24 countries found that across national boundaries, respondents indicate they gain a sense of national pride from sports performances and smaller countries may gain an even greater return from athletic events.[21] However, demographic differences may exist in this area. For example, Bryan Denham[22] demonstrated that national sporting pride is stronger among men than among women, and among the less educated than among more highly educated individuals.

Olympic success also influences international prestige, and nations continue to invest in this area.[23] Historically, the former Soviet Union, and more recently, China have invested substantial amounts of private and public money to improve their athletic competitiveness in international sports mega events as a way to advertise their political and economic systems.[24] In addition, Eastern European countries have begun to devote attention to improving their Olympic medal index with hopes of enhancing national awareness, pride, and unity through top-level sports.[25]

Race and the Summer Olympic Games[26]

Although many Americans may think of Jessie Owens' success in the 1936 Berlin Games as the beginning of minority involvement, athletes of color have had a long history of participation in the "modern" Olympic Games which began with the Athens Olympics in 1896. Indeed, two African American men earned medals at one of the earliest modern Olympic Games at St. Louis in 1904: Joe Stadler earned silver in the standing high jump and George Poage earned bronze medals in both the 200-meter and 400-meter hurdles. Four years later, John Baxter Taylor, Jr., the son of former slaves, and student-athlete at the University of Pennsylvania, became the first African American to win an Olympic gold medal as a member of the men's medley relay team at the 1908 Summer Olympics in London. African American women's Olympic participation was delayed because of race and gender discrimination, as Louise Stokes and Tidye Pickett qualified in track and field for the 1932 Los Angeles Olympics but were barred from participation because of their race. However, four years later, both Stokes and Pickett became the first African American women to represent United States in the 1936 Berlin Games. Eighteen African Americans earned membership on Team USA in 1936, including Jesse Owens, whose four-gold-medal performance undermined Hitler's claims of Aryan superiority. In 1948, Alice Coachman, a Tuskegee Institute student-athlete, set a high jump record and became the first African American woman to win an Olympic gold medal. Most experts would agree that Wilma Rudolph was perhaps the most dominant early African American female Olympic athletes. She overcame childhood polio to win three gold medals in track events at the 1960 Olympics (the 100-meter dash, 200-meter dash, and 400-meter relay). Rudolph was also the first American woman, of any race, to win three gold medals. These accomplishments led to her becoming the first African American woman to win the James E. Sullivan Award—America's highest honor in amateur athletics as well as the Associated Press' "female athlete of the year" in 1960 and 1961. Her African American teammate, two-time silver medalist Willye White, became the first American woman to compete in five Olympic Games (1956, 1960, 1964, 1968 and 1972). These trailblazing African American women were followed by track and field stars such as Jackie Joyner-Kersee and Florence Griffith-Joyner who dominated the Olympics during the 1980s. Joyner-Kersee competed in the long jump and the heptathlon, winning two gold medals at the 1988 Seoul Olympics. She also won a gold medal in heptathlon champ at the 1992 Barcelona Olympic Games. Griffith-Joyner broke several world records at the 1988 Seoul Olympics, earning the title of "fastest woman in the world." She won gold medals in the 100- and 200-sprints and the 4 × 100-meter relay team. Because of their accomplishments, both Joyner-Kersee and Griffith-

Joyner won Sullivan Awards and recognition as the AP's Female Athlete of the Year. In addition, Cheryl Miller led the U.S. women's basketball team to a gold medal in the 1984 Olympics in Los Angeles.

Mexican American Joe Salas became one of the first U.S. Latino Olympians when he was selected to join the U.S. Olympic team. Salas won a silver medal in the 1924 Olympic Games in Paris. After retiring, Salas served as a coach for the U.S. boxing team at the 1932 Los Angeles Olympic Games. In 1984, Mexican American Tracee Talavera became the first Latina to make the U.S women's gymnastics team which won a silver medal at the Los Angeles Olympics. At the 2008 Beijing Olympics, Cuban American Dara Torres became the oldest swimmer to ever compete. Through her long and successful career, Torres earned 12 medals over five Olympic Games beginning in 1984.

In 1948, Asian Americans Sammy Lee and Victoria Manalo made history at the London Olympic Games. Sammy Lee won a gold medal in 10-meter platform diving and a bronze in 3-meter springboard diving in London and later won a gold medal in platform diving at the 1952 Olympics in Helsinki, Finland. At the 1948 Games, Victoria Manalo also won gold medals in platform and springboard competitions at the London Olympic Games becoming both the first woman to win two diving gold medals in the same Olympics and first Asian American woman to win a medal in the Summer Olympic Games. Other notable Asian Americans have followed in their footsteps: Ford Konno, a swimmer who won gold in 1952; Amy Chow, a member of the first-ever American gymnastics team gold to win gold in 1996; Greg Louganis, the first man in 56 years to win Olympic springboard and platform diving titles at the same Olympics; Tomia "Tommy" T. Kono, a weightlifter and three-time Olympic medalist in weightlifting who was inducted, along with Lee, into the U.S. Olympic Hall of Fame in 1990; and Natalie Coughlin, a five time Olympic medalist in swimming in 2004.

Native American Jim Thorpe who won two Olympic track and field gold medals in the 1912 Stockholm Games—and played professional baseball, football and basketball—was arguably one of the greatest athletes of the 20th century. In the Olympics, he won the pentathlon (long jump, javelin, discus, 200m and 1,500m), and the decathlon (100m, long jump, shot put, high jump, 400m, discus, 110m hurdles, pole vault, javelin and the 1,500m). His performance established a world record of 8,412 points, and beat his nearest challenger by almost 700 points, a record which would stand until 1948.

Perhaps more impressive than the accomplishments of athletes of color during racial climates sometimes characterized by open hostility and antipathy, was the fact that many of these athletes trained under less than ideal conditions with limited access to quality equipment and facilities. For example, many of the African American athletes who became Olympic champions attended historically black colleges and universities which lacked the finances needed to provide the quality of training equipment and facilities present in predominantly white institutions. Yet, when Robert Hayes won his first gold medal in the 100-meters competing in the Summer Olympic Games of 1960, little attention was given to the fact that Hayes had experienced inferior training conditions not only at Florida A&M University, but dating back to high school days in Jacksonville, Florida where the only facility to hold competitions for the poorly funded and racially segregated schools of that city was a worn out track at an under-resourced, segregated public park (Wilder Park).

Research on Diversity and Success in Team Sports

Our review located only a few empirical studies on the topic of racial and ethnic diversity and team success in sports contexts. Jessica Weiss and Paul Sommers examined the association between racial composition and success among professional basketball teams and found that team diversity in the NBA appears to be neither an asset nor a liability to team performance (winning percentage).[27] Craig Bogar examined the association between racial composition and success among Atlantic Coast Conference (ACC) men's and women's college basketball teams and found that (1) coaching diversity was unrelated to winning percentage; (2) among women's teams, diversity was positively, though not significantly related to winning percentage; and, (3) among men's teams, diversity was positively, and significantly related to winning percentage.[28] Jürgen Gerhards and Michael Mutz examined the influence of globalization, market value, and cultural diversity on team success in elite men's professional soccer. They found that teams that are composed of *some* players from different national backgrounds perform better, on average, than nationally more homogeneous teams. However, the direction of the association was reversed for teams which included players from *many* different nationalities.[29] Thomas Timmerman examined the relationships between age diversity, racial diversity, and team performance in basketball and baseball with different interaction requirements. Analyzing archival data from 871 professional basketball teams and 1,082 professional baseball teams from 1950 to 1997, he found that (after controlling for team ability) age diversity and racial diversity were negatively associated with basketball team performance and that diversity on both variables was unrelated to baseball team performance.[30] Neither of these studied examined Olympic sports. Interestingly, however, although a number of studies, largely by economists, have sought to identify social and demographic correlates of Olympic success (medal counts) across nations, racial-ethnic diversity typically has not been among the correlates examined. Sanchez Volatier and colleagues (in press) examined how gender diversity impacted the performance of the U.S. Olympic Team over time.[31] They found that Team USA prospers when female athletes are well represented. They also found that at the 2012 London Games, female athletes accounted for a disproportionate share of total medals (78 percent) won by the U.S. Olympic Team, and that the total medals won by American females was in a broader range of sports (including traditionally male-dominated sports) than their male counterparts.

The present study examines the performance of the 2012 U.S. Olympic Team to determine whether race-ethnic diversity, as reflected by significant participation of Athletes of Color (African American, Hispanic, Asian) impacted Team USA's overall success (medals count) in the London Games.

Methods

Data pertaining to United States athletes' participation rates and demographics for the 2012 London Olympic Games was gathered from the U.S. Olympic Team (Team USA) website.[32] Data pertaining to United States medal counts was gathered from the NBC website covering the London Olympics[33] and from London 2012, the official website of the London Olympic Games.[34] Because our analysis examines participation and success of individual athletes rather than national teams, we count medals awarded to each individual athlete. Thus, our analytic medal counts differ from official team medal counts. For example, both the men's and women's basketball earned gold medals. The official team medal count would be two gold medals—one for Team USA women and one for Team USA men. However, each of the twelve members of the men's and women's teams were awarded gold medals, resulting in an individual count of twenty-four gold medals. The same procedure was followed for other team sports (e.g., soccer, volleyball, doubles tennis) in which individual athletes are awarded medals based on their team's success.

Athlete's race was determined by an examination of online media guide photos and photographs from several official USOC and London Olympics websites. Similar procedures for using photographs in racial identification have been used by other sports researchers.[35] Our classifications were made based on how these athletes' race would be perceived by others in the U.S., and are not necessarily reflective of particular athletes' racial self-identification. For athletes with difficult to determine ethnicities or race by picture, last names were taken into account. For these athletes, their biography page was also checked for information such as "place of birth" and "languages." These additional steps most often applied to Latino athletes, Asian athletes and Hawaiian athletes. Hawaiian athletes were classified as Asian for the purposes of this project. Given the study's focus on comparing the success of white and nonwhite athletes, the present analysis categorizes black, Latino, and Asian athletes as athletes of color (AOC). This strategy minimizes potential racial classification problems that might arise regarding biracial or multiracial identity if the study focus involved comparing specific race-ethnic groups.

We assess race-ethnic parity (equality or similarity) in Olympic participation and success using social indicators.[36] Comparing the success of white athletes to AOC differ significantly when different indices are used to present identical data. Suzanne Donovan and Christopher Cross describe three different indices for measuring parity.[37] A risk index could be calculated by dividing the number of whites participating in the Olympics by the total number of white high school and college athletes in the school population. Thus, the risk index would represent the proportion of white Olympic participants. An odds ratio could be calculated by dividing the risk index for whites by the risk index for AOC and would represent a comparative index of risk. If the risk index for a participation indicator is identical for white Athletes and AOC, the odds ratio will equal unity or 1.0. Odds ratios less than unity indicate that AOC are underrepresented relative to white athletes while odds ratios greater than unity would indicate that AOC are overrepresented. Finally, a composition index would be calculated by dividing the number of AOC participating in Olympic athletics by the total number of athletes participating in the Olympics. This measure would represent the proportion of all Olympians who are AOC. The composition index can produce misleading results because it does not control for baseline representation for race-ethnic subgroups. In this project we calculate a parity index by dividing the proportion of Olympic AOC participants by the proportion of white participants. Parity, or unity, is represented by the value 1.0, such that values below 1.0 reflect underrepresentation and values above represent overrepresentation. Our analysis uses the parity index to assess race-ethnic representation and performance in the 2021 London Olympic Games.

Findings

Descriptive results examining race-ethnicity and Team USA athletes' Olympic success, for the full sample, are presented in Table 1. The data reported here show participation rates and medals earned—overall and by sport discipline—for white athletes and AOC. As indicated in the bottom row of Table 1, Team USA had a significantly higher representation of white athletes (71 percent), compared to AOC (29 percent).

Nevertheless, the results in this row of Table 1 also show that relative to their participation, AOC accounted for a disproportionate share of total

Table 1. Race and Team USA Athletes Participation and Medals by Sport (Percent in Parentheses)

	White Athletes		Athletes of Color		AOC/White	All Athletes	
	Participants	Medals	Participants	Medals	Parity Index*	Participants	Medals
Archery	6 (100)	3 (100)	0	0	—	6	3
Athletics	53 (42)	3 (9)	72 (58)	32 (91)	7.48	125	35
Badminton	0	0	3 (100)	0	—	3	0
Basketball	3 (12)	3 (12)	21 (88)	21 (88)	1.00	24	24
Boxing	0	0	12 (100)	2 (100)	—	12	2
Canoe	7 (100)	0	0	0	—	7	0
Cycling	25 (100)	5 (100)	0	0	—	25	5
Diving	11 (100)	6 (100)	0	0	—	11	6
Equestrian	13 (100)	0	0	0	—	13	0
Fencing	13 (65)	3 (75)	7 (35)	1 (25)	.62	20	4
Field Hockey	14 (87)	0	2 (13)	0	0	16	0
Gymnastics	9 (69)	2 (50)	4 (31)	2 (50)	1.00	13	4
Judo	5 (100)	2 (100)	0	0	—	5	2
Pentathlon	3 (100)	0	0	0	—	3	0
Rowing						44	17
Sailing	16 (100)	0	0	0	—	16	0
Shooting	20 (100)	4 (100)	0	0	—	20	4
Soccer	17 (94)	17 (94)	1 (6)	1 (6)	1.00	18	18
Swimming	46 (94)	33 (94)	3 (6)	2 (6)	1.00	49	35
Sync Swimming	2 (100)	0	0	0	—	2	0
Table Tennis	0	0	3 (100)	0	—	3	0
Taekwondo	0	0	4 (100)	1 (100)	—	4	1
Tennis	8 (67)	3 (60)	4 (33)	2 (40)	1.36	12	5
Triathlon	4 (80)	0	1 (20)	0	0	5	0
Volleyball	26 (81)	10 (63)	6 (19)	6 (37)	2.49	32	16
Water Polo	24 (92)	11 (85)	2 (8)	2 (15)	2.03	26	13
Weightlifting	2 (67)	0	1 (33)	0	0	3	0
Wrestling	10 (59)	2 (67)	7 (41)	1 (33)	.70	17	3
TOTALS	381 (71)	116 (61)	153 (29)	73 (39)	1.56	534	189

*Parity Index can only be computed for sport disciplines in which both white athletes and athletes of color participate and earn medals.

medals won by the U.S. Olympic Team in the 2012 London Games. Specifically, AOC comprised 29 percent of Team USA athletes, but won 40 percent of total team medals earned. The overall parity index (1.56) indicates that AOC were 56 percent more likely than white athletes to earn Olympic medals. This finding suggests a clear benefit of race-ethnic diversity to American success in the London 2012 Olympic Games. It also reinforces the results of a recent study[38] documenting the benefits of gender diversity on Team USA's success in the 2012 London Games.

Not only did Team USA athletes of color win a disproportionate share of total medals earned, they did so despite not participating in a broad range of sport disciplines, including archery, canoeing, cycling, diving, equestrian, judo, pentathlon, sailing, shooting, and synchronized swimming. Overall, AOC earned medals in twelve of the seventeen (70 percent) sport categories—athletics, basketball, boxing, fencing, gymnastics, soccer, swimming, taekwondo, tennis, volleyball, water polo, and wrestling—in which they participated. In contrast Team USA's white athletes earned medals in fifteen of the twenty-four (63 percent) sport categories—archery, athletics, basketball, cycling, diving, fencing, gymnastics, judo, rowing, shooting, soccer, swimming, tennis, volleyball, water polo, and wrestling—in which they participated. Among the specific sport disciplines where both white athletes and AOC earned medals, AOC won a disproportionate share of Team USA medals in four categories—athletics, tennis, volleyball, and water polo. In the athletics category, AOC won thirty-two of the thirty-five medals awarded to Team USA. The athletics parity index (7.48) indicates that AOC were seven and one-half times more likely than white athletes to earn medals in this discipline. In the athletics category, AOC won thirty-two (91 percent) of the thirty-five medals awarded to Team USA. The athletics parity index (7.48) indicates that AOC were seven and one-half times more likely than white athletes to earn medals in this discipline. In tennis, AOC represented one-third of participants but won 40 percent of the medals awarded to Team USA in this sport. The tennis parity index (1.36) indicates that AOC were 36 percent more likely than white athletes to earn medals in this discipline. In volleyball, AOC represented just 19 percent of participants but won 37 percent of the medals awarded to Team USA in this sport. The volleyball parity index (2.49) indicates that AOC were roughly two and a half times more likely than white athletes to earn medals in this discipline. In water polo, AOC represented just 8 percent of participants but won 15 percent of the medals awarded to Team USA. The water polo parity index (2.03) indicates that AOC were roughly twice as likely as white athletes to earn medals in this discipline. The success of AOC in athletics may not be surprising given their extensive and long history of involvement in track and field activities. However, their disproportionate Olympic success in tennis, water polo, and volleyball is striking, given their significant underrepresentation in those sports at both the high school and college levels. Overall, AOC were underrepresented as medalists in two sport disciplines. In fencing, AOC represented 35 percent of participants but won 25 percent of the medals awarded to Team USA in this sport. The fencing parity index (.62) indicates that AOC were 38 percent less likely than white athletes to earn medals in this discipline. In wrestling, AOC represented 41 percent of participants but won 33 percent of the medals awarded to Team USA in this sport. The wrestling parity index (.70) indicates that AOC were 30 percent less likely than white athletes to earn medals in this discipline. Overall, the results in Table 1 show that Team USA AOC won a disproportionate share of Olympic medals, even in sport disciplines where they have been traditionally underrepresented.

We turn next to results examining gender differences in the relationship between race-ethnicity and Team USA athletes' Olympic success. Findings for Team USA male athletes are presented in Table 2. The data reported here show male participation rates and medals earned—overall and by sport discipline. As shown in the bottom row of Table 2, Team USA had a significantly higher representation of white male athletes (70 percent), compared to AOC males (30 percent).

Nevertheless, the results in this row of Table 2 reveal that relative to their participation, male AOC accounted for a disproportionate share of total medals won. Among males, AOC comprised 30 percent of Team USA athletes, but won 47 percent of total team medals earned. The overall parity index (1.75) indicates that male AOC were 75 percent more likely than white male athletes to earn Olympic medals.

Not only did Team USA male AOC win a disproportionate share of total medals earned, they did so despite not participating in a broad range of sport disciplines, including archery, canoeing, cycling, diving, equestrian, judo, pentathlon, sailing, shooting, volleyball and water polo. Overall, male AOC earned medals in five—athletics, basketball, gymnastics, swimming, and wrestling—of the fourteen (36 percent) sport categories in which they participated. In contrast Team USA white male athletes earned medals in eight— archery, athletics, basketball, diving, rowing, shooting, swimming, tennis, and wrestling—of the twenty (40 percent) sport categories in which they participated. Among the specific sport disciplines where both white and AOC males earned medals, AOC won a disproportionate share in two categories— athletics and swimming. In the athletics category, male AOC won fifteen of the seventeen medals (88 percent) awarded to Team USA. The athletics parity index (4.90) indicates that among males, AOC were nearly five times more likely than white athletes to earn medals in this discipline. In swimming, AOC males represented just 4 percent of participants but won 6 percent of the medals awarded to Team USA in this sport. The swimming parity index

Table 2. Race and Team USA Male Athletes Participation and Medals by Sport (Percent in Parentheses)

	White Athletes		Athletes of Color		AOC/White	All Athletes	
	Participants	Medals	Participants	Medals	Parity Index*	Participants	Medals
Archery	3 (100)	3 (100)	0	0	—	3	3
Archery	3 (100)	3 (100)	0	0	—	3	3
Athletics	25 (40)	2 (12)	38 (60)	15 (88)	4.90	63	17
Badminton	0	0	2 (100)	0	—	2	0
Basketball	1 (8)	1 (8)	11 (92)	11 (92)	1.00	12	12
Boxing	0	0	9 (100)	0	—	9	0
Canoe	5 (100)	0	0	0	—	5	0
Cycling	12 (100)	0	0	0	—	12	0
Diving	5 (100)	4 (100)	0	0	—	5	4
Equestrian	7 (100)	0	0	0	—	7	0
Fencing	6 (60)	0	4 (40)	0	0	10	0
Field Hockey	NA[1]	NA[1]	NA[1]	NA[1]	NA[1]	NA[1]	NA[1]
Gymnastics	4 (67)	0	2 (33)	1 (100)	—	6	1
Judo	3 (100)	0	0	0	—	3	0
Pentathlon	1 (100)	0	0	0	—	1	0
Rowing	20 (83)	4 (100)	4 (17)	0	—	24	4
Sailing	9 (100)	0	0	0	—	9	0
Shooting	14 (100)	2 (100)	0	0	—	14	2
Soccer	DNQ[2]	DNQ[2]	DNQ[2]	DNQ[2]	DNQ[2]	DNQ[2]	DNQ[2]
Swimming	23 (96)	17 (94)	1 (4)	1 (6)	1.53	24	18
Sync Swimming	NA[1]	NA[1]	NA[1]	NA[1]	NA[1]	NA[1]	NA[1]
Table Tennis	0	0	1 (100)	0	—	1	0
Taekwondo	0	0	2 (100)	0	—	2	0
Tennis	5 (83)	2 (100)	1 (17)	0	—	6	2
Triathlon	1 (50)	0	1 (50)	0	1.00	2	0
Volleyball	16 (100)	0	0	0	—	16	0
Water Polo	13 (100)	0	0	0	—	13	0
Weightlifting	0	0	1 (100)	0	—	1	0
Wrestling	8 (62)	2 (67)	5 (38)	1 (33)	.81	13	3
TOTALS	185 (70)	33 (53)	78 (30)	29 (47)	1.75	263 (100)	62

(1.53) indicates that male AOC were 53 percent more likely than white athletes to earn medals in this discipline. Male AOC were underrepresented as medalists in one sport discipline: AOC males represented 38 percent of wrestling participants but won 33 percent of the medals awarded to Team USA in this sport. The wrestling parity index (.81) indicates that AOC were 19 percent less likely than white athletes to earn medals in this discipline.

Findings for Team USA female athletes are presented in Table 3. The data reported here show female participation rates and medals earned—overall and by sport discipline. As shown in the bottom row of Table 3, Team USA had a significantly higher representation of white female athletes (720 percent), compared to AOC females (28 percent).

The findings in this row show that relative to their participation, female AOC accounted for a disproportionate share of total medals won. Among females, AOC comprised just 28 percent of Team USA athletes, but won 34 percent of total team medals earned. The overall parity index (1.31) indicates that female AOC were 31 percent more likely than white females to earn Olympic medals.

Team USA female AOC won a disproportionate share of total medals earned despite not participating in a broad range of sport disciplines, including archery, canoeing, cycling, diving, equestrian, judo, pentathlon, rowing, sailing, shooting, synchronized swimming, triathlon and weightlifting. Overall, female AOC earned medals in ten—athletics, basketball, boxing, fencing, gymnastics, soccer, taekwondo, tennis, swimming, and water polo—of the fifteen (67 percent) sport categories in which they participated. In contrast, Team USA's white female athletes earned medals in twelve—athletics, basketball, cycling, diving, gymnastics, judo, rowing, soccer, shooting, swimming, tennis, and water polo—of the twenty-four (50 percent) sport categories in which they participated. Among the specific sport disciplines where both white and AOC females earned medals, AOC won a disproportionate share in two categories—athletics and gymnastics. In the athletics category, female AOC won seventeen of the eighteen medals (94 percent) awarded to Team USA. The athletics parity index (13.15) indicates that among females, AOC were roughly thirteen times more likely than white athletes to earn medals in this discipline. In gymnastics, AOC females represented 28 percent of participants but won 40 percent of the medals awarded to Team USA in this sport. The gymnastics parity index (1.26) indicates that female AOC were 26 percent more likely than white athletes to earn medals in this discipline. Female AOC were underrepresented as medalists in one sport discipline: AOC females represented 8 percent of swimming participants but won 6 percent of the medals awarded to Team USA in this sport. The fencing parity index (.74) indicates that AOC were 26 percent less likely than white athletes to earn medals in this discipline.

Table 3. Race and Team USA Female Athletes Participation and Medals by Sport (Percent in Parentheses)

	White Athletes		Athletes of Color		AOC/White Parity Index*	All Athletes	
	Participants	Medals	Participants	Medals		Participants	Medals
Archery	3 (100)	3 (100)	0	0	—	3	3
Archery	3 (100)	0	0	0	—	3	0
Athletics	28 (45)	1 (6)	34 (55)	17 (94)	13.15	62	18
Badminton	0	0	1 (100)	0	—	1	0
Basketball	2 (17)	2 (17)	10 (83)	10 (83)	1.00	12	12
Boxing	0	0	3 (100)	2 (100)	—	3	2
Canoe	2 (100)	0	0	0	—	2	0
Cycling	13 (100)	5 (100)	0	0	—	13	5
Diving	6 (100)	2 (100)	0	0	—	6	2
Equestrian	6 (100)	0	0	0	—	6	0
Fencing	7 (70)	0	3 (30)	1 (100)	—	10	1
Field Hockey	14 (87)	0	2 (13)	0	0	16	0
Gymnastics	5 (71)	2 (67)	2 (28)	1 (33)	1.26	7	3
Judo	2 (100)	2 (100)	0	0	—	2	2
Pentathlon	2 (100)	0	0	0	—	2	0
Rowing	20 (100)	13 (100)	0	0	—	20	13
Sailing	7 (100)	0	0	0	—	7	0
Shooting	6 (100)	2 (100)	0	0	—	6	2
Soccer	17 (94)	17 (94)	1 (6)	1 (6)	1.00	18	18
Swimming	23 (92)	16 (94)	2 (8)	1 (6)	.74	25	17
Sync Swimming	2 (100)	0	0	0	—	2	0
Table Tennis	0	0	2 (100)	0	—	2	0
Taekwondo	0	0	2 (100)	1 (100)	—	1	0
Tennis	3 (50)	1 (33)	3 (50)	2 (67)	2.03	6	3
Triathlon	3 (100)	0	0	0	—	3	0
Volleyball	10 (62)	0	6 (38)	0	0	16	0
Water Polo	11 (85)	11 (85)	2 (15)	2 (15)	1.00	13	13
Weightlifting	2 (100)	0	0	0	—	2	0
Wrestling	2 (50)	0	2 (50)	0	0	4	0
TOTALS	196 (72)	87 (66)	75 (28)	44 (34)	1.31	271	131

*Parity Index can only be computed for sport disciplines in which both white athletes and athletes of color participate and earn medals

Summary and Discussion

Although determining the costs and benefits of diversity has become an increasingly popular topic in the social science literature, few studies have focused on sport in particular to examine if diversity is beneficial for organizational productivity. Additionally, the few studies[39] which examine the relationship between racial diversity and performance in sport have not examined Olympic sports. The current study seeks to help fill this gap in the research by examining how race-ethnic diversity among athletes impacted Team USA's success at the 2012 London Games. Our results reveal a strong positive association between the number of AOC and medals won. Overall the present results support the notion that race-ethnic diversity is beneficial to organizational productivity, including international mega-sports teams such as Team USA. Specifically, our results show that, relative to their participation, AOC accounted for a disproportionate share of total medals won by the United States at the 2012 Olympic Games. This pattern was observed among both male and female Olympians. Although not reported in the current study, we find similar results with regard to the number of gold medals earned by Team USA.

In recent years the USOC has undertaken a number of initiatives to promote equity and inclusion, broadly defined. These efforts have contributed to more gender balanced Olympic teams and increased involvement of diverse racial and ethnic athletes representing Team USA in both the Summer and Winter Games. For example, at the London Games, two black males, and two Latino males, represented Team USA in rowing. Given that rowing is not a sport known for a tradition of diversity, it seems clear that this progress is likely a result of the development and growth of America Rows and USRowing's diversity and inclusion initiative.[40] Diversity challenges remain, however. Among both males and females, there appears to be some degree of "stacking." Athletes of color are heavily concentrated largely in a handful of sport disciplines (e.g., athletics 58 percent; basketball 88 percent; boxing 100 percent; table tennis 100 percent), while white athletes are heavily concentrated in a much larger cluster of sports (e.g., archery 100 percent; canoe 100 percent; cycling 100 percent; diving 100 percent; equestrian 100 percent; sailing 100 percent; shooting 100 percent; soccer 94 percent; swimming 94 percent; volleyball 81 percent; water polo 92 percent). The stacking of AOC in basketball and track—due in large measure to the limited range of sports offered in high minority high schools—may limit the overall productivity of Team USA. One could reasonably argue that if male and female AOC had more equitable access to a wider range of high school sports (e.g., soccer, volleyball, etc.), they could contribute even more to the nation's Olympic success.

Nevertheless, the USOC's diversity efforts also clearly contributed to the success of Team USA. Recent internal assessments by the USOC found that both Summer and Winter Olympics teams that are more diverse tend to win more medals than teams that are less diverse. The findings of the present study, as well as a recent study[41] provide strong corroborating evidence of the positive connection between diversity (racial and gender) and Olympic success.

One might wonder why the "collective" success of AOC and their contribution to Team USA "winning" the medals race at the London Games seems to have passed without recognition. To be sure, the success of individual athletes of color such as Gabby Douglas were widely recognized, but recognition of the accomplishments of AOC as a social category has not received notable acclaim. Considering that the "collective" success of female athletes at the London Games received considerable public notice, it seems reasonable to think that the "collective" success of AOC might also warrant similar attention. Even though women won a majority of Team USA's medals while AOC only won 39 percent, AOC won a disproportionate share overall, as well as among both male and female athletes. The outstanding accomplishments of Team USA's female athletes led to 2012 being proclaimed as the "year of the woman athlete" while there was radio silence regarding the accomplishments of AOC. Could the different responses to Olympic success be rooted in dominant gender and racial ideologies? Stereotypes associated with dominant gender ideology might lead to perceiving women succeeding on "male turf" in elite sports as surprising, while stereotypes associated with dominant racial ideology might lead to expecting superior athletic performance among AOC. In either instance, gendering female athletic performance and racializing AOC athletic performance is problematic. The racialization of athletic performance of AOC reinforces racial stereotypes as well as diminishes the likelihood that the American public would recognize and value the benefits of racial diversity as they might come to value the benefits of gender diversity. Perhaps what is needed in regard to Team USA and Olympic success, is a comprehensive and inclusive, rather than a narrow (gender or race-focused) media and public framing of the benefits of diversity. Fortunately, the USOC appears to recognize this point. According to Scott Blackmun, CEO of the USOC, "[we] need to improve our cultural competency. We need to harness the idea of a diverse talent pool because it's effective, not just because it's fair.... Diversity and inclusion are core values at the USOC because they make us better as an organization."[42]

As a nation of immigrants, the United States in particular is stronger when it's racial and gender diversity are more equitably represented. To that end, diversity and inclusivity initiatives should be strengthened all levels of sport, including interscholastic and intercollegiate sporting opportunities, for women and people of color. In the past, the Olympic Games has been used as a platform to demonstrate not just athletic prowess, but much more than that—national unity. In an increasingly diverse society, Team USA sports, as a platform for diversity and inclusion, has the potential to contribute once again to enhancing national unity in increasingly polarizing times. It is our view, based on our analyses here, that the USOC is well-positioned to broadcast the value of inclusion not just in sports contexts, but to society writ-large.

NOTES

1. TeamUSA Diversity and Inclusion Vision, USOC, accessed February 23, 2017, http://www.teamusa.org/about-the-USOC/Inside-the-USOC/Programs/Diversity-and-Inclusion/USOC-Diversity-And-Inclusion-Scorecards/diversity-and-inclusion-vision.

2. Karen Humes, Nicholas A. Jones, and Roberto R. Ramirez, "Overview of Race and Hispanic Origin, 2010," U.S. Department of Commerce, Economics and Statistics Administration, U.S. Census Bureau, 2011.

3. Tüzin Baycan-Levent and Peter Nijkamp, "Characteristics of Migrant Entrepreneurship in Europe," *Entrepreneurship and Regional Development* 2009 (21): 375–397.

4. Alberto Alesina, and Eliana La Ferrara, "Ethnic Diversity and Economic Performance," *Journal of Economic Literature* 43, no. 3 (2005): 762–800; Elena Bellini, Gianmarco I.P. Ottaviano, Dino Pinelli, and Giovanni Prarolo, "Cultural Diversity and Economic Performance: Evidence from European Regions," In *Geography, Institutions and Regional Economic Performance* (Berlin: Springer, 2013), pp. 121–141; Paul Collier, "Implications of Ethnic Diversity," *Economic Policy* 16, no. 32 (2001): 128–166; Cedric Herring, "Does Diversity Pay?: Race, Gender, and the Business Case for Diversity," *American Sociological Review* 74, no. 2 (2009): 208–224; Marc Hooghe, Tim Reeskens, Dietlind Stolle, and Ann Trappers, "Ethnic Diversity, Trust and Ethnocentrism and Europe: A Multilevel Analysis of 21 European Countries," In *Unpublished Paper Presented at American Political Science Association Annual Meeting*. 2006; Katherine Y. Williams, and Charles A. O'Reilly III, "A Review of 40 Years of Research," *Res Organ Behav* 20 (1998): 77–140; E. Pluribus Unum, and Robert D. Putnam, "Diversity and Community in the Twenty-First Century," (2006); John M. Quigley, "Urban Diversity and Economic Growth," *The Journal of Economic Perspectives* 12, no. 2 (1998): 127–138; Steven Vertovec, "Super-Diversity and Its Implications," *Ethnic and Racial Studies* 30, no. 6 (2007): 1024–1054.

5. Edward P. Lazear, "Globalisation and the Market for Team-Mates," *The Economic Journal* 109, no. 454 (1999): 15–40; Katherine Y. Williams and Charles A. O'Reilly III, "A Review of 40 Years of Research," *Res Organ Behav* 20 (1998): 77–140;

6. Alberto Abadie and Javier Gardeazabal, "The Economic Costs of Conflict: A Case Study of the Basque Country," *The American Economic Review* 93, no. 1 (2003): 113–132; William Easterly, Alberto F. Alesina, and Reza Baqir, "Public Goods and Ethnic Divisions" (1997); Alberto Alesina, and Eliana La Ferrara, "Ethnic Diversity and Economic Performance," *Journal of Economic Literature* 43, no. 3 (2005): 762–800.

7. Cedric Herring, "Does Diversity Pay?: Race, Gender, and the Business Case for Diversity," *American Sociological Review* 74, no. 2 (2009): 208–224.

8. Elena Bellini, Gianmarco I.P. Ottaviano, Dino Pinelli, and Giovanni Prarolo, "Cultural Diversity and Economic Performance: Evidence from European Regions," in *Geography, Institutions and Regional Economic Performance* (Berlin: Springer 2013), pp. 121–141; Francesco D'Amuri, Gianmarco I.P. Ottaviano, and Giovanni Peri, "The Labor Market Impact of Immigration in Western Germany in the 1990s," *European Economic Review* 54, no. 4 (2010): 550–570.; M.A. Manning Manacorda and J. Wadsworth, *The Impact of Immigration on the Structure of Male Wages: Theory and Evidence from Britain*, Centre for Economic Performance (CEP). No. 754. Discussion Paper, 2006; Gianmarco I.P. Ottaviano, and Giovanni Peri, "The Economic Value of Cultural Diversity: Evidence from U.S. Cities," *Journal of Economic Geography* 6, no. 1 (2006): 9–44.

9. Rebecca Harding, Mark Hart, Dylan Jones-Evans, and Jonathan Levie, "Global Entrepreneurship Monitor," London: London Business School (2002); Francesca Froy, and Sylvain Giguère. *From Immigration to Integration: Local Solutions to a Global Challenge* (OECD, 2006).

10. Richard Florida, "Cities and the Creative Class," *City and Community*, 2 (2003): 3-19.

11. Bill Chappell, "Year of the Woman at the London Games? for Americans, It's True," *NPR*, last modified August 10, 2012. http://www.npr.org/sections/thetorch/2012/08/10/158570021/year-of-the-woman-at-the-london-games-for-americans-its-true.

12. Steven W. Pope, "Rethinking Sport, Empire, and American Exceptionalism," *Sport History Review* 38 (2007): 92–120.

13. Lavendar Paige, "Obama: Team USA 'Sets The Gold Standard' with Its Diversity," *Huffington Post*, Aug, 06, 2016. http://www.huffingtonpost.com/entry/obama-olympics-2016_us_57a5ec7be4b021fd9878c4f8.

14. Mark Dyreson, *Crafting Patriotism for Global Dominance: America at the Olympics* (New York: Routledge, 2013).

15. *Ibid.*

16. Andrew C. Billings, and James R. Angelini, "Packaging the Games for Viewer Consumption: Gender, Ethnicity, and Nationality in NBC's Coverage of the 2004 Summer Olympics," *Communication Quarterly* 55, no. 1 (2007): 95–111.

17. Andrew C. Billings, and Susan Tyler Eastman, "Selective Representation of Gender, Ethnicity, and Nationality in American Television Coverage of the 2000 Summer Olympics," *International Review for the Sociology of Sport* 37, no. 3–4 (2002): 351–370.

18. Alan Bairner, *Sports, Nationalism, and Globalization: European and North American Perspectives* (Stony Brook: State University of New York Press, 2001); Raymond Boyle Neil Blain, and Hugh O'Donnell, *Sport and National Identity in the European Media* (Leicester: Leicester University Press, 1993); Richard Giulianotti and Roland Robertson, "Recovering the Social: Globalization, Football and Transnationalism," *Global Networks* 7 (2007): 166–86; Barrie Houlihan, "Sport, National Identity and Public Policy," *Nations and Nationalism* 3 (1997): 113–37; Joseph Maguire, and Emma K. Poulton, "European Identity Politics in Euro 96: Invented Traditions and National Habitus Codes," *International Review for the Sociology of Sport* 34 (1999): 17–29; Lloyd L. Wong and Richard Trumper, "Global Celebrity Athletes and Nationalism Fútbol, Hockey, and the Representation of Nation," *Journal of Sport & Social Issues* 26 (2002): 168–94.

19. John Nauright, *Long Run to Freedom: Sport, Cultures and Identities in South Africa* (Morgantown, WV: Fitness Information Technology, 2010); Saskia Irene Welschen, "Making Sense of Being South African: The Analysis of National Identity Construction in Talk" (paper presented at the ISA World Congress of Sociology, Gothenburg, Sweden, July 11–17, 2010).

20. M.D.R. Evans and Jonathan Kelly, "National Pride in the Developed World: Survey Data from 24 Nations, *International Journal of Public Opinion Research* 14 (2002): 303–338.

21. *Ibid.*; Agnes Elling, Ivo Van Hilvoorde, and Remko Van Den Dool, "Creating or Awakening National Pride Through Sporting Success: A Longitudinal Study on Macro Effects in the Netherlands," *International Review for the Sociology of Sport* 49 (2014): 129–151.

22. Bryan E. Denham, "Correlates of Pride in the Performance Success of United States Athletes Competing on an International Stage," *International Review for the Sociology of Sport* 45 (2010): 457–473.

23. Lincoln Allison and Terry Monnington, "Sport, Prestige and International Relations," *Government and Opposition* 37 (2002): 106–34.

24. Pravin K. Trivedi and David M. Zimmer, "Success at the Summer Olympics: How Much Do Economic Factors Explain?" *Econometrics* 2 (2014): 169–202.

25. Mojca Doupona Topič and Jay Coakley, "Complicating the Relationship Between Sport and National Identity: The Case of Post-Socialist Slovenia," *Sociology of Sport Journal* 27 (2010): 371–389; Welschen, "Making Sense."

26. "Asian American Athletes Represent U.S. at 2012 Olympics," *News America Media*, accessed March 1, 2017, http://newamericamedia.org/2012/07/asian-american-athletes-represent-us-at-2012-olympics.php; Julie Rodriguez, "Honoring Latino Olympians and Par-

alympians at the White House," *The White House*, last modified September 28, 2012, https://www.whitehouse.gov/blog/2012/09/28/honoring-latino-olympians-and-paralympians-white-house; http://www.topendsports.com/events/summer/firsts.htm; Robert Repino, "African Americans at the Olympic Games," *Oxford University Press Blog*, last modified, August 11, 2012, https://blog.oup.com/2012/08/african-americans-at-the-olympic-games/; Robert D. McFadden, "Sammy Lee, First Asian-American Man to Earn Olympic Gold, Dies at 96," *New York Times*, last modified December 3, 2016, https://www.nytimes.com/2016/12/03/sports/sammy-lee-dies-asian-american-olympic-gold.html?_r=0; Melody Merin, "Asian Americans First Won Olympic Gold 60 Years Ago," *IIP Digital*, last modified May 30, 2008, http://iipdigital.usembassy.gov/st/english/article/2008/05/20080530165620xlrennef0.5189478.html#axzz4YFNSV02e; "Notable Asian, Pacific American Athletes and Achievements," *ESPN*, last modified May 20, 2015, http://www.espn.com/blog/statsinfo/post/_/id/105788/notable-asian-pacific-american-athletes-and-achievements; Carolina Moreno, "11 of the Greatest Latino Athletes in Olympic History," *The Huffington Post*, last modified August 12, 2016, http://www.huffingtonpost.com/entry/11-of-the-greatest-latino-athletes-in-olympic-history_us_579fba8be4b08a8e8b5f161e; "Jim Thorpe," *Olympic.org*, accessed March 1, 2017, https://www.olympic.org/jim-thorpe; John X. Miller, "HBCU Olympians from the Past," last modified August 5, 2016, https://theundefeated.com/features/hbcu-olympians-from-the-past/; Dave Zirin, " on the Passing of HBCU and Olympic Coaching Legend Ed Temple," *The Nation*, last modified, September 28, 2016, https://www.thenation.com/article/on-the-passing-of-hbcu-and-olympic-coaching-legend-ed-temple/; Ronda Racha Penrice, "The Black Olympians: Class of 1936," *Ebony*, August 18, 2016, http://www.ebony.com/black-history/black-olympians-1936-games#axzz4YPjPOaCs.

27. Jessica B. Weiss and Paul M. Sommers, "Does Team Racial Composition Affect Team Performance in the NBA?" *Atlantic Economic Journal* 37 (2009): 119–120.

28. Craig T. Bogar, "The Relationship Between Racial Diversity and Winning Percentage: A Study of Men's and Women's Basketball Teams and Coaching Staffs in the Atlantic Coast Conference from 2005–2009," *The Sport Journal* 17 (2014).

29. Jürgen Gerhards and Michael, "Who Wins the Championship? Market Value and Team Composition as Predictors of Success in the Top European Football Leagues," *European Societies* (2016): 1–20.

30. Thomas A. Timmerman, "Racial Diversity, Age Diversity, Interdependence, and Team Performance," *Small Group Research* 31 (2000): 592–606.

31. Christina Sanchez Volatier, Jomills Henry Braddock II, Adrienne N. Milner, Ashley Mikulyuk, and Marvin Dawkins, "Gender Diversity and U.S. Olympic Team Success at the 2012 London Games," in Adrienne Milner and Jomills Henry Braddock, II (eds.), *Women in Sports: Breaking Barriers, Facing Obstacles, Volume One: Sportswomen and Teams* (Santa Barbara, CA: Praeger, Forthcoming).

32. "Team USA: Athletes," *2012 United States Olympic Committee* (2012), retrieved August–December 2012, http://www.teamusa.org/Athletes.aspx.

33. "NBC Olympics: Athletes," *NBC Universal* (2012), retrieved August–December 2012, http://www.nbcolympics.com/athletes/index.html.

34. London 2012 Olympics, "London 2012 Olympics: Athletes," *The Official Website of London 2012 Olympics and Paralympic 2012 Games*, retrieved August–December 2012, http://www.london2012.com/athletes/.

35. Norman R. and Yetman Forrest J. Berghorn, "Racial Participation and Integration in Men's and Women's Intercollegiate Basketball: A Longitudinal Perspective," *Sociology of Sport Journal* 10 (1993): 301–314; Örn B. Bodvarsson and King Banaian, "The Value of Arbitration Rights in Major League Baseball: Implications for Salaries and Discrimination," *Quarterly Journal of Business and Economics* 37 (1998): 65–79; Timmerman, "Racial Diversity"; Weiss and Sommers, "Team Racial Composition."

36. U.S. Commission on Civil Rights, *Social Indicators of Equality for Minorities and Women* (Washington, D.C.: U.S. Government Printing Office, 1978).

37. Suzanne M. Donovan and Christopher T. Cross, *Minority Students in Special and Gifted Education* (Washington, D.C.: National Academy Press, 2002).

38. Christina Sanchez Volatier, Jomills Henry Braddock II, Adrienne N. Milner, Ashley

Mikulyuk, and Marvin Dawkins, "Gender Diversity and U.S. Olympic Team Success at the 2012 London Games," in Adrienne Milner and Jomills Henry Braddock, II (eds.), *Women in Sports: Breaking Barriers, Facing Obstacles, Volume One: Sportswomen and Teams* (Santa Barbara, CA: Praeger, Forthcoming).

39. Craig T. Bogar, "The Relationship Between Racial Diversity and Winning Percentage: A Study of Men's and Women's Basketball Teams and Coaching Staffs in the Atlantic Coast Conference from 2005," *The Sports Journal* 17 (2014); Weiss and Sommers 2009, "Team Racial Composition."

40. "America Rows," U.S. Rowing, Accessed February 23, 2017, http://www.usrowing.org/america-rows/.

41. Sanchez Volatier et al., "Gender Diversity."

42. TeamUSA Diversity and Inclusion Vision.

PART TWO

Sport and National Identity

"Damn!—welly good white man's game"
Race, Golf and the Struggle for Social Justice in South Africa, c. 1890–1991

HENDRIK SNYDERS

Abstract

Bobby Locke, Gary Player, Ernie Els and other famous white South African golfers are internationally known and feted as among the most iconic figures in the history of the game. Their black counterparts such as Papwa Sewgolum (Dutch Open Champion) and Vincent Tshabalala (French Open Champion), the products of a strong golfing tradition among the country's formerly oppressed communities, less so. In comparison to the advances made in the existing scholarship about the struggle of African American golfers for universal recognition and its interconnectedness with the struggle for social justice, the century-long battle of their South African counterparts under the influence of first racial segregation and later institutionalized racism (apartheid), is a largely neglected and forgotten aspect of both South African and international golfing history. This essay attempts to rectify this omission and to map the contours of the history of black golf in South Africa, especially its players, clubs, competitions and administrators, as well as their difficulties and successes. As such, it further attempts to assist with the burial of some of the prevailing myths that continue to ascribe certain sports inequalities (especially with regard to race) to natural evolution, individual disinterest or psychological, emotional and physical unsuitability.

The challenge, implored noted British historian, Wray Vamplew, is to bring the "tough social issues of class, age, gender, and ethnicity into the public history domain of sport."

Roughs, Bunkers and the Silence of the Greens

While South African white golf history for both men and women have been well documented, black Africans are still excluded from the narrative. Typical of this style is Robert Fall's *Golfing in Southern Africa* where no black golf club, association, event or person is featured in his list of the "Who is Who in Southern African golf."[1] Similarly, the *Illustrated African Golfer*, published for a short period before World War II, omitted any reference to this group of South Africans.[2] The only publication with a focus on black golfers remains the pocket-sized booklet published in 1947 by Simon Malaza, secretary of the Transvaal Bantu Golf Union. This booklet, however, is limited in scope and focused strictly on the activities of those that were classified as black African or "Bantu" in terms of the official racial and ethnic terminology of the time.[3] Four recent publications suffered from the same deficiencies. Despite paying attention to the apartheid-era and the few golfers of color such as Papwa Sewgolum and Vincent Tshabalala that made a mark on the international circuit, the general history of black golf, their clubs and associations are skimmed over and as a result remains obscured.[4] Chris Nicholson's biography of Durban Indian golfer Papwa Sewgolum, although significantly better contextualized, still failed to account for the collective golfing legacy of all black golfers. Beyond using, the larger anti-apartheid sport struggle to foreground the achievements of his subject, Nicholson's account also omitted the specific nation-wide golf struggles and its associated nuances.[5] This stands in stark contrast to the healthy growth in the research output dealing with the struggle of African American golfers in the United States of America for recognition.[6] The century-long battle of black South Africans under the influence of racial segregation and later institutionalized racism (apartheid) in comparison, is still a largely neglected and forgotten aspect of both South African and international golfing history.

This essay attempts to rectify this omission and map the contours of black South African golf history, especially its players, clubs, competitions and administrators, as well as their difficulties and successes against the background of the larger struggle against apartheid.

Toward a Black Golfing Tradition, c. 1900–1939

Sources in the Western Cape Archives and Records Services in Cape Town indicated that golf ("Kolf" in Dutch) was played in Cape Town as early as 1843. At stake was the Silver Kolf or Silver Golf awarded to the colony's white resident golfers.[7] Played for on an individual basis, it took another 40 years before the first official golf club in South Africa, the Cape Golf Club, was established in November 1885. The Waterloo Green, a piece of land in front of the military camp in Wynberg, served as a rudimentary golf course for the Royal Scottish Regiment based there. All equipment inclusive of balls, clubs and hole-cutters had to be imported from Scotland.[8] From this humble beginning, the game spread over South Africa by the end of the 19th century. Membership of the newly established clubs extended across the class divide with a growing membership among individuals in both the working class and colonial high society.[9]

The first national open golf championship for white golfers took place in Kimberley from September 26 to October 1, 1892, and laid the foundation for a range of others including the S.A. Amateur Championship that followed a year later and the Johannesburg Christmas Tournament that was hosted in 1895. By 1895, because of the increased popularity of the game, club representatives of the Cape Colony and Orange Free State felt it necessary to further codify their game by defining both the terms "amateur" and "recognized golf club." In the case of the latter, a recognized golf club was defined "as one which keeps up its own links has elected officers, and whose members pay a subscription."[10] Any club or association that lacked own facilities was therefore automatically disqualified from obtaining membership of what later became the SA Golf Union in 1910. With this measure, golf administrators formally aligned themselves with their peers in a range of other sports organizations that used sport to "reinforce white power and difference."[11]

The black colonial elite (both players and sport administrators) were supporters of the idea that "good sport, manliness and love of 'fair play' should be promoted amongst all classes of society."[12] Administrators in particular attempted to use sport, the demonstration of prowess as well as the values of fair play and sportsmanship as indicators of their "fitness to be accepted as full citizens in Cape society."[13] In some instances, attempts were made to convince the colonial authorities to pass legislation to ban tribal amusements and to promote the wider use and appreciation of English and its associated literature.[14] Social segregation that was the prevailing social custom, however, blocked their advancement. *Cape Argus*, one of the Cape Town's oldest newspapers indeed acted as a propagandist of the notion that "the races are best socially apart, each good in their own way, but a terribly bad mixture."[15] As a result, social advancement through the demonstration of prowess in "culturally civilized" sport was curtailed. This, however, did not stop the development of a significant black sporting tradition in sports such as in rugby and cricket during the 19th century. Golf, notwithstanding its perceived reputation as a "source of healthy recreation to which there was no dark side at all," was not among these legacies.[16] As such, it failed to play a role in the building of character and the establishment of civilized credentials as envisaged.[17]

An exhaustive search through the sports columns of the early newspapers, failed to unearth any references to organized golfing activity within the black community during the late 19th and early 20th centuries. There are, however, anecdotal references in various contemporary newspapers about individual attempts by indigenous South Africans in Natal to get to grips with the game.[18] The accuracy of these reports, however, remains in doubt. What is beyond doubt is the fact that the rooting of the game among the local white population, created employment for caddies and other maintenance personnel.[19] Caddy Masters, both black and white, acted as powerful socializing agents and as guardians of the social and racial status quo. They constantly reminded their charges to be well-behaved, obedient, stay within the law and not to harbor or express any political opinions. The general rule was simply to "keep out of politics, play your golf, you'll be fine that way."[20] Non-politic and subservient behavior, however, did not spare them from insults and accusations of being lazy, stupid and ignorant from the white golfing fraternity.[21] This notwithstanding and due to their proximity to the game, a number of caddies acquired a high level of proficiency in playing it, albeit with repaired and discarded golf clubs. With the encouragement and aid of their Caddie Masters, they also participated in informal competitions. This practice continued well into the early 20th century.[22]

From World War I to Apartheid, 1918–1948

The Great War disrupted golf globally and generally retarded the further growth of the South African game. The worldwide effects of the "Great Depression" (1929–39) further delayed its revival. Ironically, the first black golfer of any note emerged during this period. According to contemporary media reports, Ramnath "Bambata" Boodhan, a Durban-based caddie and repairer of clubs under the apprenticeship of white Durban Golf Club professional, George Fotheringham, challenged for higher honors after displaying an aptitude for the game during informal games and victories over some well-known names in white Natal golfing circles. Boodhan, thanks to the assistance of some beneficiaries, entered the British Open in 1929 and became the first black South African golfer to compete internationally.[23] This came at a time that most white golfers erroneously regarded black interest in the game as limited to betting on games and the collection of lost golf balls for decorative or resale purposes.[24] His participation in three further tournaments and intention to qualify as an assistant professional created a new awareness of the existence of black golf prowess in South Africa.

Despite Boodhan's lack of success on the European circuit, his endeavors inspired others and evidently played a role in the formation of a number of golf clubs in Natal, Transvaal and the Cape Province. Among the pioneer clubs that led the process toward the establishment of a distinctive black golfing tradition were the Durban Indian Golf Club (DIGC) (est. 1929), Payneville (1930) and the Wynberg (1931) golf clubs in Johannesburg and Sunningdale Park in Cape Town shortly thereafter. The first regional representative associations, the Transvaal Bantu Golf Union (1936) and the Western Province Colored Golf Union (1937) which endeavored to place black golf on a solid organized footing, only followed five years later. In line with the general practice at the time, both organizations added a racial reference to their respective names to distinguish themselves from their white counterparts.

Following the founding of the first clubs, the game among blacks saw spectacular growth, especially in Transvaal. Within two years after the formation of the TBGU, eight clubs namely the Bobby Jones G.C., Pimville; St Andrews G.C. and Wynberg G.C within Johannesburg as well as clubs in Benoni, Stirtonville; Germiston; Randfontein and Pretoria affiliated.[25] Judging by their names, these clubs and its membership had high aspirations. While St. Andrews in Scotland is globally acknowledged as the spiritual home of golf and therefore the ultimate course for any player to appear on, Wynberg in Cape Town can be regarded as the spiritual home of South African golf. The club name Bobby Jones referred to one of golf's small group of global stars at the time. The act of naming, according to Nauright, extends beyond mere social and "cultural mimicking." It indeed, forms part of a complex and "elaborate process of proving respectability" and the pursuit of social advancement.[26] These developments took place against the backdrop of the first British amateur golf tour to South Africa which was followed by a visit of a British Ladies team in 1933 and two reciprocal tours of South African teams to the United Kingdom in 1937.

From the outset, the new bodies organized their own competitions in the form of small "money-events." This, according to the Transvaal administrators, was not the ideal situation. Furthermore, the quality of organization of these events also left much to be desired. As an ambitious organization, the TBGU's stated objective was to establish a proper "South African Bantu Golf Tournament" played along "amateur sporting rules until times allow for professional contests."[27] This objective was achieved within two years after its founding when the TBGU hosted the first South African Open Championship for blacks on the Wynberg Course in Johannesburg in 1938. This achievement comprehensively rejected the claims of certain white missionaries that the indigenous population lacked the ability and aptitude forms of sports and that "the introduction of organized games amongst raw Natives, I fear, would meet with very little success."[28]

World War II (1939–45), beyond causing a shortage of golf balls ("golf ball famine"), also interrupted the growth path of black golf in South Africa. Due to a lack of proper golf balls, even white golfers had to use any available ball, including wooden ones.[29] Black golfers furthermore joined the war effort and raised funds for the Governor-General's National War Fund through the hosting of a dedicated golf day. This act of patriotism won them the goodwill of the white community and stood them in good stead in the post-war period and with regard to their relationship with individuals and organized bodies such as the Transvaal Professional Golfers Association (TPGA). A representative of the TPGA at the time also assessed the state of the black game as "more physic than scientific."[30]

Apartheid, Course Access and Fraternal Patronage

Three years after the conclusion of World War II, the National Party that strongly opposed South Africa's participation in the conflict, won the South African general election on a political platform that promised white voters the institutionalization of segregation between the races. This event coincided with an unprecedented growth in the popularity of golf among non-whites all over the country. In April 1948, the *SA Golf* magazine noted significant increases in both club membership and competitions from the Cape Karoo to Port Elizabeth, Durban and the Witwatersrand.[31] The Western Province Colored Golfers Association based in Cape Town for example boasted a membership of more than 200 members. By November of the same year, the four provincial associations convened a meeting in Bloemfontein with a view to establish a South African Golf Association for Non-Europeans. On this occasion, the founding members committed to work toward fostering interest in golf among blacks or non–Europeans; improving the standard of play; inculcating the spirit of sportsmanship and encouraging inter-provincial competition.[32] The assembled further resolved to host an annual South African championship tournament concomitantly with its annual general meeting over the Easter period. This was a practice adopted from their white counterparts. The inaugural SA Non-European Open Championships tournament was therefore scheduled to take place in Kimberley the next year against the backdrop of a rapidly changing South Africa.

With their hands on the levers of power, the National Party through the promulgation of a number of key pieces of legislation, started to reconfigure South African society. Among the legislation passed to institutionalize segregation up to 1955, were the Population Registration Act (Act 30 of 1950), the Prohibition of Mix Marriages Act (Act 55 of 1949), the Group Areas Act

(Act 41 of 1951), and the Reservation of Separate Amenities Act (Act 49 of 1953). Although no specific legislation was passed to formalize segregated sport, the legislation around separate amenities left black sportspeople in general and golfers in particular with the poorest facilities. In some areas, provisions of golf courses were the last thing on the agenda. To crown it all, the right to represent South Africa internationally in particular was reserved for white athletes.

As previously alluded to, access to good golf courses for both practice and competition purposes posed a perennial problem for black golfers. As a result, they became almost wholly dependent on the maintenance of strong fraternal relations and the goodwill of their white counterparts for playing purposes. Black golfers also had to engage in constant lobbying of the public authorities inclusive of municipalities, provincial councils and state departments on and off the field. This left very little room for mistakes and from early on the maintenance of a sound administration and cooperation with the authorities instead of confrontation became a key concern for the administrators. In this regard, the *SA Golf* magazine noted:

> There has not been a dissenting voice: and the affairs of the Non-European body, and the manner in which they conduct their affairs, have been examined with intense closeness. There was nothing to which any exception could be taken. Many good people have given money to help the Non-European golfers along the way. That money has been used with discretion, and the officials can produce balance sheets that would satisfy the most painstaking auditor, were he even armed with a microscope.[33]

In the same vein Jock Brews a high profile white administrator and golfing personality, advised the Transvaal Bantu Golf Union that a written constitution and a sound administration is "the only way in which you can command or retain the respect and help of your well-wishers—European or Bantu."[34]

Applications for the development of new facilities by the organized black golfing fraternity, posed its own challenges. Such applications were frequently declined based on the principle that such amenities could only be provided when the "provisions of the Group Areas Act had been applied."[35] When the East London chapter of the international service and philanthropic organizations, Rotary, in 1961 offered to build a golf course for black golfers in the area, Bantu Affairs Department officials responsible for the policing of residential segregation between Colored's, Africans and Indians insisted that the proposed facility should be for the exclusive use of those classified as "Bantu" (African). As a result, the project never materialized.[36] This way of reasoning lay behind the late or general non-delivery of golf courses for black communities. The first dedicated golf course for Africans in the Durban district on the banks of the Umgeni River as a result, was only opened in April 1959 as part of the Umgeni Bantu Sports Ground. This practice of combining different sporting codes in one facility, however, brought its own set of problems. When the Durban Indian Sports Grounds Association during the same year attempted to persuade the Durban City Council to establish a nine-hole golf course on the Springfield Sports Ground, cricketers who shared the same facilities objected. Opening and maintenance of a golf course on a multi-sport facility would not only have interfered with their sport but would have unfairly denied other codes sufficient access to practice their activities.[37] The situation in the Cape Province was no better and up to the mid-1960s, there were no golf courses for black residents in the main concentration areas of Cape Town, Paarl and Worcester.[38]

To circumvent the many constraints faced by them, black golf administrators were forced to become creative. Clubs as a matter of strategy often elected reputable white individuals as patrons in the hope of using them as goodwill ambassadors in their negotiations for access to playing facilities. Patrons were often the main source and facilitators of donations of trophies, medals and the modest prize-money that was at stake and that served as an incentive to the participants.[39] The effectiveness of patrons always depended on their status and stature within white society and therefore accounted for the varying nature of the level of funding for competitions observed between the provinces, regions and cities. White golfers in turn, often extended fraternal courtesies such as donations and support in rule interpretation to their black counterparts.[40] The nature of this relationship, however, had its own drawbacks. The patron like the caddie master, contributed significantly toward the pacification and general docility of both golfers and their administrators and their steering away from anti-apartheid organization that were propagating for political and social change.

Resistance, Reaction and International Isolation, 1950–1970

Following the introduction of apartheid, the black community in 1952 embarked on a civil disobedience campaign in an attempt to change the situation. The response of the apartheid state was harsh and brutal and saw large numbers of anti-apartheid activists assaulted, arrested, jailed and banned from political activity. This temporarily disrupted the activities of various anti-apartheid organizations and activists. Unperturbed by the state response, various sporting bodies established the Coordinating Committee for International Recognition (CCIR) in 1955. This decision was motivated by the realization that the strategy of seeking international recognition through uncoordinated and individual efforts was inadequate and lacked coherence. Neither the SA Non-European Golf Association nor any of its affiliates, however, participated in this process. It is safe to assume that given their struggles for facilities and sponsorship, that the black golfing fraternity were intent on protecting rather than to jeopardies their network of patrons and their limited but continued access to white golf courses. This stance effectively relegated them to the status of passive observers rather than active agents for change.

The CCIR from the onset lobbied a range of international sports federation and campaigned for the exclusion of all race-based South African teams. By 1957, the organization tasted the first fruits from its efforts when it succeeded in effecting the expulsion of the white table tennis body from the International Table Tennis Federation. The black and non-racial South African Table Tennis Board (SATTB) was admitted in their stead. The apartheid government, however, refused travel documents to the SATTB and extended this ban to all others opposed to the political system. It also decreed that black international participation would only be allowed in cases where the participants were affiliated and recognized members of the relevant white sports body.[41] This was a deliberate, cynical and calculated attack on the anti-apartheid sports struggle since the Native Laws Amendment Act promulgated in 1952, explicitly prohibited racial mixing or membership of civic organizations such as sport clubs, churches and schools. Furthermore, the Separate Amenities Act prohibited the full use of racially designated facilities.

Following a deliberate intimidation and bullying campaign by the apartheid state, the CCIR succumbed to fear and timidity and disappeared from the sports-political front.[42] The South African Sports Association (SASA) took its place in 1958 and campaigned for the inclusion of all athletes irrespective of race, into representative South African teams. It also condemned the Springbok, the national sports emblem, as a symbol of racism. Claiming to represent an estimated 70,000 athletes, except for golfers who once again remained distant from the new body, SASA attempted to negotiate with their white counterparts in to hope of effecting change. Negotiation, however, failed which forced the organization to change tactics. It yet again embarked on direct lobbying of international control bodies in the hope of forcing a change of the status quo.[43] Concomitantly, the organization tried to convince local sponsors of key white sports events to make rejection of racial segregation a precondition for their financial support.[44] SASA also operated as a vigilance organization and campaigned against the continuation of racially exclusive contests. In this regard, it opposed a proposed government-sanctioned and racial tour of West Indian cricketers captained by Frank Worrell in 1959. In the face of growing public opposition, the proposed tour was cancelled. In retaliation, the apartheid government extended the refusal of travel documents to SASA representatives. Like in the case of the CCIR, SASA likewise became the target of systematic repression, intimidation and persecution at a time that the white South African amateur golf team entered the Eisenhower Trophy golf competition in Scotland.[45]

The travel ban, initially did not directly affect apolitical individuals such as champion Durban Indian golfer, Sewsunker Papwa Sewgolum who dominated black competitions and who thanks to the sponsorship of his employer was afforded an opportunity to travel overseas in May 1959 to participate in the British and Dutch Golf Open.[46] Ironically, Sewgolum competed with his white compatriot, Gary Player in the former tournament; an act that at home would have been a contravention of South African law. Sewgolum's subsequent victory in the Dutch Open to match that of fellow compatriots Syd Brews (1934 and 1935) and Bobby Locke (1939) formally announced the international arrival of black South African golf.

The year 1960 was declared the "Year of the Pass" by the African National Congress (ANC) and the start of a campaign aimed at forcing the government to abolish the pass laws. This legislation was also the target of a similar campaign by the Pan Africanist Congress (PAC), the ideological and political opponents of the former organization. These two bodies were the most prominent anti-apartheid bodies on the political front at the time given their status as the representatives of the majority black African population. The campaign, conceived as a non-violent civil disobedience campaign and scheduled to start on March 21, however, took a turn for the worse. During the protest, the police at Sharpeville on the Witwatersrand killed 69 unarmed demonstrators. This set in motion an orgy of violence and counter violence followed by the banning of black political organizations including the African National Congress (ANC) and Pan Africanist Congress (PAC) under the Unlawful Organizations Act (Act 34 of 1960). Furthermore, a State of Emergency was declared which was followed by harsh repression of the opponents by the apartheid state.[47] A large number of political leaders and sports administrators including Dennis Brutus, the leader of the SASA were arrested. A significant number were either forced into exile or placed under house arrest. This came about, merely three months after Sewgolum's victory in the South African Non-European Open Championship (SANEOC) at Milnerton. On the occasion, the SA Non-European Golf Association (SANEGA) also held its annual general meeting and contrary to the stipulations of the Native Laws Amendment Act, elected an inclusive leadership representative of both Colored and "Bantu" or African members in the persons of Alfred Maqubela (president—Transvaal), Peter Louw (vice-president—Western Province) and D. Phala (secretary—Orange Free State).[48] This small act of defiance, however, failed to attract any notice or adverse consequences, probably because of the standing of the existing body in the eyes of its white patrons.

In the wake of the Sharpeville shootings, exiled anti-apartheid activists together with anti-apartheid solidarity organizations in the United Kingdom that over time evolved into the Anti-Apartheid Movement (AAM) initiated a boycott campaign against segregated sport. South Africa, however, continued to participate in international competitions as a member of the International Olympic Committee and other international sports federations. Furthermore, the South African Olympic Committee (SAOC), the country's official Olympic body, consistently denied involvement or the presence of any form of racial discrimination within its operations.[49] Black golf, however, continued on its set path and stayed clear from resistance politics. This did not help Sewgolum who, despite winning two successive Dutch Open tournaments in 1961 and 1963, in the words of Gary Player, upon his return "had to revert to a sporting life of second-class status in which he needed official permission to compete each week against white golfers, for whom he was more than a playing match."[50]

Against the background of the international anti-apartheid campaign, the South African government on March 29, 1961, reaffirmed its commitment to apartheid sport and its opposition to integrated national teams and incoming tours by mixed-race international teams. Concomitantly, government institutions received strict orders to enforce the applicable legislation without fear or favor and to prevent any undermining of the system.[51] As a result, a number of tours were canceled. Ironically, it equally deprived white sports men and women of foreign competition.

With the promulgation of the Separate Amenities Act (Act 49 of 1953), mixed race audiences at events were outlawed. This negatively affected the profitability of events across all sporting codes. Furthermore, most public indoor venues were too small for the installation of segregated seating. As far as black golf were concerned, clubs lacked appropriate venues for the hosting of all their events including paid ones. In terms of the separate amenities legislation, white golf courses were off-limits to black spectators. The loss of financial income due to a limited number of spectators at establishment events were offset by the ready availability of sponsorship from the business sector. Black golf lacked similar support and could at best offer small sums of prize money to participants. In addition, event promoters with the desire to host multi-racial or integrated events such as the SA Golf Open had to negotiate with the Department of Community Development for permission. Such permission including to participate in such events, were either consistently delayed or cancelled at the last minute.[52] Papwa Sewgolum's applications for participation in the white national championship is a case in point. A regular victim of the whims of apartheid's officialdom, the frequently late permissions not only affected his competitiveness but also denied him an opportunity to compete under the most conducive circumstances. Furthermore, staging events at fit-for-purpose venues (with separate entrances for race groups), were also no guarantee for approval. Given these drawbacks, a number of black sports personalities such as Ron Eland (weightlifting), Basil D'Oliviera (cricket) and Cecil February (wrestling) emigrated in pursuit of a proper professional career.[53] From the ranks of the black golfing fraternity Edward Johnson Sedibe from Johannesburg and William Manie from East London went from caddying to participating on the professional circuit in Europe.[54]

By 1963 SASA, which over the intervening period had evolved into the South African Non-Racial Olympic Committee (SANROC) under the leadership of Dennis Brutus, replaced the demand for desegregation and called for an international boycott and the destruction of all segregated sport.[55] Its aims were to "frustrate whites, deprive their sport of stimulus and drive down standards."[56] Domestically and bolstered by the efforts of organizations such as SANROC, black wrestlers among others threatened to end the control of the all-white control boards.[57] Because of his political activities, Brutus was sentenced for a term of 18 months' imprisonment to Robben Island, apartheid notorious island prison, in 1963. This severely curtailed the activities of SASA. Thanks to the collective effort of a range of organizations, including the ANC, PAC, London Anti-Apartheid Movement (LAAM) and the Defense and Aid Fund (DAF), a SANROC Committee was established in the United Kingdom. This effectively internationalize the international sports struggle. Following persistent lobbying by the African block and the Soviet Union together with SANROC, the white South African Olympic team was formally excluded from the Tokyo Olympic Games and the World Fencing Games in 1964. South Africa, however, continued to participate in the Eisenhower Trophy, Ladies World Golf Tournament and the Commonwealth Tournament.

The situation, however, remained unaltered for black golfers. Not only were permits to compete in whites-only tournaments hard to come by, but municipalities on a regular basis denied the SA Non-European Golf Association permission to use white golf courses for its competitions. Similarly, black spectators were denied access to white sports events.[58] By 1966, Sewgolum, black South Africa's leading golfer also became the victim of the official policy that denied travel documents to black South Africans wishing to travel abroad. Overseas competition as a result became out of his reach. The apartheid authorities also remained steadfast in its commitment to segregated sport. South African Prime Minister B.J. Vorster, in a statement to parliament on April 11, 1967, declared: "From South Africa's point of view no mixed sports between whites and non-whites will be practiced locally, irrespective of the standard of proficiency of participants. We do not apply that as a criterion because our policy has nothing to do with proficiency or lack of proficiency."[59]

Against the background of this hardening of attitude, Brutus mobilized support from the Supreme Council for Sport in Africa, (SCSA), Anti-

Apartheid Movement (AAM) and others such as the American Committee on Africa in New York. He specifically urged them to support a worldwide boycott of South African athletes and all-white South African teams.[60] SAN-ROC furthermore appealed to the American Olympic Committee to support South Africa's suspension from the 1968 Mexico Olympic Games.[61] A special effort was also made to involve African American athletes such as baseballer Jackie Robinson, tennis player Arthur Ashe and elements within the Civil Rights Movement and smaller organizations such as Harry Edwards's Olympic Project for Human Rights (OPHR) into the campaign.[62] Because of a better-coordinated campaign, South African boxing, cycling, fencing, table tennis, judo, netball, pentathlon, football, weightlifting and wrestling federation's lost their international membership by 1970. Although rugby, the majority team sport among whites and golf as an individual code still maintained their foothold, the tide according to Merrett started to turn in favor of the "boycotters and demonstrators."[63]

As the decade drew to its close, the anti-apartheid movement started to focus far more closely on golf with targeted protests and demonstrations at major international tournaments. At the American PGA championship in Dayton (Ohio) in 1969, protestors specifically targeted Gary Player, South Africa's leading white golfer. Despite the severity of the protest, Player still defended apartheid and called for the world's understanding which he claimed "was intended for the betterment of all races."[64] The ensuing public anger forced tournament organizers to increase both event and Player's personal security.[65] In the aftermath of these events, the anti-apartheid organizations Halt All Racist Tours (HART) and the Campaign Against Racial Exploitation (CARE) in Australia, threatened to disrupt scheduled golfing tournaments such as the Australian Open.[66] This notwithstanding, both white amateur and professional golf succeeded to maintain their foothold in the international arena whilst neighbors Rhodesia was barred from the Eisenhower Trophy scheduled for Spain for resisting black majority rule.[67]

Transitions: From Rigid Apartheid to Multinational and Multi-Racial Sport, 1970–1978

The start of the new decade saw the continuation of the anti-apartheid fight on all levels. This forced the South African authorities to make minor policy concessions for tactical and political reasons. Among these were allowing New Zealand rugby touring teams to South Africa to include Maoris. The conservative element within Afrikaner politics for whom political concessions represented a direct attack on their political, religious and cultural way of life and which was critical to their identity, resisted these concessions. Hardliners left the governing party and formed the Herstigde National Party (Reformed National Party) in October 1969.[68]

Following victory in the general election of 1969, the National Party adopted a strategy to counter the sports boycott. The so-called "multi-national sports policy" announced on April 3, 1971, opened up the system somewhat and allowed for limited inter-racial mixing on the sports field.[69] The authorities were, however, adamant that the new direction did not constitute a move toward integrated sport.[70] They were also at pains to emphasize that the new initiative was not aimed at undermining the "traditional' policy at provincial and club level where it mattered the most."[71] Key pieces of legislation, such as the Separate Amenities Act, that outlawed shared facilities, however, ensured that tournaments remained segregated affairs.[72] During this period, Papwa Sewgolum continued to dominate black golf through the on-going capturing of titles. Among these were the national titles at the Ohenimuri Country Club in Benoni, which he won by eight shots with Vincent Tshabalala in the second and Richard Mogoerane in third place.[73]

By August 1971, the SA Non-European Golfers Association announced its intention to form a Non-White Professional Golfers Association. This development was not only universally welcomed by the white golfing fraternity, but also strongly encouraged as a step in the right direction. *SA Golf*, the official white golfing magazine, implored the different bodies to strive for maximum unity and to avoid the creation of a multitude of different and differing bodies truly representative of all golfers.[74] This was in reference to the existence of four national bodies in black rugby in addition to the two national soccer associations.

Following the announcement of the new policy, the white golfing fraternity, readied itself to engage with their black counterparts with a view to hosting joint competitions or events. This venture was frustrated by the fractured state of black golf, especially the lack of distinction between amateurs and professionals. The SA Non-European Golfing Association was essentially a federal structure that allowed the different race-based and independent affiliates to maintain both their distinctive identities and to remain within the ambit of the laws pertaining to separate amenities, membership etc. Furthermore, not all regional and professional associations were in possession of a written constitution. The SA Golf Union therefore proposed to assist with the unification of black golf, the establishment of two independent entities for amateurs and professionals respectively and to rid it from splinter groups. To incentivize the process, the SAGU also encouraged its affiliates to put their facilities at the disposal of black clubs, to assist them with the raising of sponsorship and to facilitate their participation into the new competitions.[75]

In addition to extending a helping hand to their black brethren, the white golfing fraternity announced the hosting of South Africa's first open professional and multi-racial tournament. Set for November 1971, the organizers went out of their way to promote the new goal of multi-racialism. They therefore invited entries from local black players and the likes of one of America's most exciting and emergent talents, African American golfer, Lee Elder and the Republic of China's (Taiwan), Lu Liang Huan. In the process Elder ignored pleas to decline the invitation from Gary Player. He rather justified his participation by stating that "life for blacks in South Africa isn't going to change if we segregate ourselves from them because of their government's apartheid policies."[76] To facilitate the participation of blacks both local and foreign, some aspects of apartheid legislation were relaxed for the duration of the tournament. For the duration of the tournament, Elder and Huan were granted the status as "honorary whites." In addition, Elder with the assistance of the U.S. State Department, became a roving golf ambassador prior to his departure to South Africa. In this capacity, he visited Liberia, Uganda, Nigeria and Kenya where he played in exhibition games with local golfers. This move was clearly devised as a tool to prevent a backlash from the African bloc of states who were propagating South Africa's total isolation from international sport. Elder, in what could only be described as an opportunistic political act to silence his critics, also attempted to visit Mandela in prison during his visit. Unsurprisingly, this request was denied.[77]

Hosting an all-race field, involved a cumbersome process of application for a special permit, which was further accompanied by the completion of a comprehensive set of documents to a range of government departments. Aspects that specifically had to be dealt with and which was covered by the one or other piece of legislation, was the tournament venue, opening of club houses to black players, spectators and media representatives as well as catering and the selling of alcohol to the same. These aspects inter alia involved the departments of Community Development, Bantu Affairs, Justice, Health, Sport & Recreation and Police. Given this bureaucracy and the political risks associated with the event, the *SA Golf* magazine appealed to all the relevant parties to create a conducive environment where "these players can take part with dignity, and that, although their intent is utterly professional, they are seen to derive no little enjoyment from the experience." Furthermore, the magazine noted, "this is simply, first, an exercise in human relationships in which the players themselves are well-versed and which the galleries, if they wish to maintain any sporting contact with anybody from overseas, whatever his color, must enter without reserve."[78]

Following Elder's participation, which undoubtedly gave credibility to the event, and the South Africa tours of the likes of entertainers Percy Sledge and Eartha Kitt, the pressure group, the Committee of Concerned Blacks

(CCB) started to question the morality of such visits. They also called on Americans to support the anti-apartheid forces within the USA and to make direct monetary, book or medical contributions to the liberation armies engaged in the fight for African freedom.[79] Elder, having compromised his credibility by participating in a tournament with an overt political and racial agenda, upon his return to the USA denounced apartheid and vowed never to return.[80] This notwithstanding, South Africans continued their participation in key events such as the World Cup of Golf, and the Eisenhower and Humberto de Almeida Trophy.

Confronted with the potential of the new multi-national policy to undermine the international sports boycott, the South African Council on Sport (SACOS–established in 1973) intensified resistance against multi-racial sport. Guided by the slogan of "No normal sport in an abnormal society," the organization also discouraged competition with and against white sporting bodies. This resulted in a split within the ranks of the renamed and reconstituted SA Non-European Golf Association now known as the SA Golf Association. This division was strongly motivated by their dependence on white golf courses for the survival of their sport. When the Durban Golf Club protested against the national amateur body's efforts to affiliate to the white body, they were banned from participating in the official tournaments of the Natal Golf Association. A group of Transvaal golfers who shared this sentiment was similarly treated. As a result, professionals from both groups established their own SA Professional Golf Players Association (SAPGPA) to host its own events.[81] This placed further pressure on the pro-affiliation especially when the mother body, SACOS, started to use any available means, even a gathering of the Australian Society for Sports History, as a platform for propagandizing the isolation of white sport.[82]

Despite this flurry of anti-apartheid activity, white South African golfers maintained a recognizable presence on the international scene. Their domestic organization, the SA Golf Union, also continued to host high-profile events such as the World Cup of Golf. By September 1975, Minister of Sport Piet Koornhof, in the face of all the politicking, announced the removal of all restrictions from professional golf. Both white administrators and journalists hailed this move and described golf as "the first major sport to win the battle of politics."[83] The battle, however, was far from won since the international scene was alive with the on-going mobilization of the anti-apartheid network. On the level of the United Nations, American activist, Richard Lapchick who was closely connected with the Centre Against Apartheid (UNCAA), appealed for the admission of non-racial sports federations in South Africa represented by the SA Non-Racial Olympic Committee, as members of international sports organizations.[84] This call presupposed the expulsion of any remaining white South African sports bodies.

In the wake of the Soweto Uprising in Johannesburg in June 1976, violence spread throughout South Africa. In addition to mass arrests, a State of Emergency was declared and extraordinary powers given to the security forces to restore law and order. In its wake, large numbers of people were injured, killed, arrested or exiled. Mass gatherings, including sports events and political demonstrations, fell foul to the emergency regulations. Because of being subjected to strict security controls, these events often became the site of violent confrontation between local communities and the police.[85] This coincided with the adoption of the Gleneagles Agreement by Commonwealth countries that discouraged contact with the apartheid state. It also coincided with a boycott of the Montreal Olympic Games by 22 countries following the tour of the New Zealand national team through South Africa. Against this background, Vincent Tshabalala, the new black national golf champion, won the French Open Championship to become only the second black South African golfer to win a major international title. This new era, however, started just as the anti-apartheid groups were starting to give more focused attention from various anti-apartheid groups.

Toward Non-Racial Sport, 1978–1991

The World Amateur Golf Tournament scheduled for Dublin in Ireland during February 1978 became the first victim of anti-apartheid mobilization. Faced with the possibility of mass demonstrations, the Irish Government objected to South Africa's participation in the event.[86] As a result, the tournament was shifted to Fiji, leaving South Africans in the cold. More was to follow. Following a protest by the exiled SA Non-Racial Olympic Committee, South Africa was denied entry into the next tournament scheduled for Athens in Greece. By 1980, the American Coordinating Committee for Equality in Sport and Society (ACCESS) also entered the fray when it started a campaign against the South Africa's participation in the Eisenhower Golf Tournament scheduled for October of the same year at Pinehurst, North Carolina. ACCESS specifically appealed to the USA Golf Association (USAGA) to withdraw the invitation for South Africa's participation.[87] Its members were also encouraged to write letters to the White House requesting President Jimmy Carter to deny visas to the visitors in protest against apartheid. In both cases, the requests were ignored.[88]

Beyond appeals to the White House, ACCESS also lobbied the mayor of Pinehurst and the president of the country club where the event was to take place. In addition, a letter-writing campaign targeted the event broadcaster, ABC-TV Sports and implored the station not to "become the servant of the South African Government by publicizing South Africa's veneered racial laws."[89] The USGA's declaration that withdrawing the invitation to South Africa was outside of his powers, further aggravated matters. Although the South African teams competed at Pinehurst and performed commendably, the end was in sight.[90]

Over the last two decades of the 20th century, the collective impact of a range of political events gradually pushed South African golf to the brink. The 1980s started with the publication of the United Nations Centre Against Apartheid (UNCAA) "blacklist" of more than 500 prominent sporting personalities, including golfer Nick Faldo who had visit South Africa in breach of the Gleneagles Agreement and other international resolutions. This, suggested the *Canberra Times*, threatened to derail scheduled international events. Moreover, the fear of sportspersons and organization for being labeled apartheid apologists started to scare international competitors away and turned various high profile South African sporting events into a "tame affair between local competitors."[91] In October, Tunisia banned South Africans from playing in its Open Golf Tournament. They also threatened to vet all other participants for their South African links that placed the participation of Bernhard Langer (West Germany) and Sevvy Ballesteros previous participants in the SA Open and Sun City World Challenge respectively, in jeopardy.[92] This was followed by the Irish cancellation of the World Cup of Golf at Waterville; Australian withdrawal from the Eisenhower Trophy tournament in Switzerland (1982) and a Commonwealth ban on all athletes that participated in South Africa in close succession.

As the decade progressed, the armed struggle led by the armed wings of the ANC and PAC as an extension of the anti-apartheid fight, started to make an impact within South Africa.[93] Concomitantly, the levels of domestic resistance against apartheid increased fundamentally and resulted in the formation of the United Democratic Front (UDF), a broad anti-apartheid front. This development, according to Swilling, provided the freedom struggle with both a "national political and ideological centre."[94] To counter the threat against the state, government used its time-honored tools of detentions, banning, killings and the violent repression of all internal dissent.

Realizing the futility of their efforts to maintain the status quo, the National Party announced a referendum of the white electorate to search for a mandate to implement a new constitution based on the "consociation theory of power sharing" in which power is shared among groups whose rights are constitutionally protected. It was also aimed at gaining approval for establishing a system of limited joint governance by "whites, colored and Indians" but minus the African majority.[95] Although this change was approved by two-thirds of the white electorate, new waves of anti-apartheid resistance resulted. Similarly, a backlash among reactionary and conservative Afrikaners followed. Discontented rightist Afrikaners as a result formed extremist paramilitary organizations to defend their established privileges and threatened to physically and militarily resist racial integration.[96] This was, however, not enough to prevent the implementation of a new system of limited political reform in the form of a Tri-cameral parliament representative of the white, colored and Indian population groups.

The new political order, a "peace-making device" according to Steytler, confronted white administrators with a new set of dynamics.[97] These structures in the face of the new dispensation were thus forced to find ways of including black Africans. Furthermore, the representation of black Africans, excluded from the new system but omnipresent due to their majority, posed their own particular challenges. This matter was particular vexatious given Nelson Mandela's rejection of a conditional release from prison following an offer by State President P.W. Botha to this effect. In the face of the failure of the new dispensation to deliver fundamental change, the political situation worsened. Against the background of daily mass protest, police violence and military control of civilian functions, the USA passed the Comprehensive Anti-Apartheid Act that "banned new investment and loans, withdrew landing rights and severely curbed imports of coal, uranium, iron and steel."[98] This was followed by punitive measures by the European Union. When the UN National Assembly adopted the International Convention against Apartheid in Sport (Resolution 40/64 of December 10, 1985) which called on member countries to move beyond condemning apartheid to immediate isolation, apartheid sport reached the end of the line. Over the next five years "big politics" dictated the pace, sportsmen and women in this process were reduced to the role of spectators. By 1989, with no realistic prospect of international tours, the sports establishment finally came to realize that only a political solution could bring the desired results.

Conclusion

Black golfers like other sportsmen and women, were as keen to be recognized on the international stage. Over nearly a century and despite a myriad of obstacles, they established their own clubs; associations and competitions and through sheer hard work built a strong sporting legacy. The emergence of the likes of Papwa Sewgolum and Vincent Tshabalala was therefore not a fluke but the result of a long struggle by a significant group of golf-lovers in the face of sometimes-insurmountable obstacles.

From the onset, black club administrators promoted the concept of respectability in conduct, integrity in administration and governance and adherence to the generally accepted and internationally practiced rules of the game. This was in accordance with the long-established practice of using sporting conduct and prowess in order to pass the test of respectability that at one time, appeared to offer a pathway for integration into white society. Indeed, patrons and caddie masters regularly emphasized the need for good conduct, respect for the existing rules, an apolitical stance and sound administration as part of the road toward general acceptance. Against the background of apartheid, resistance and repression, respectability came to be associated with a non-political stance. The overwhelming majority of the black golfers and their organizations based on the available evidence, steered clear from the politics and put their game first. They also attempted to use their golf clubs to do the talking and to use success on the international golf circuit as a means to establish their right for social justice.

Following a basic and essentially beneficial strategy of accommodation, they succeeded in developing a strong fraternal and friendly relationship with the white golfing establishment. To this end, black clubs almost as a rule offered patronship of their clubs to prominent white golfing personalities, both playing and non-playing. This assisted in overcoming the perennial problems posed by a lack of proper playing facilities. Depending on their patron's social standing and stature within white society and their access to the political decision-makers, these individuals negotiated access to normally reserved-for-whites golf courses. This assisted black golfers to compete and play their national tournaments under the best possible conditions, albeit on an irregular basis. It further helped them to establish credible playing records as preparations for participating in qualifying tournaments, both local and abroad.

White patrons, non-interest in liberation politics and an accommodative and compliant approach, however, did not make life easier for those in the black golfing fraternity. Like all other non-white sporting organizations, the myriad of laws underlying apartheid and institutionalized segregation and a threatening international sports boycott driven by anti-apartheid activists, equally frustrated black golfers. The need for tournament permits, bureaucracy and a long administrative procedure further complicated the lives of those that merely wanted to play their chosen game. Their timidly and aversion for politics, inevitable turned them into pawns in the larger political game. In the end, it took decades of political struggle and thousands of deaths on both sides of the ideological divide, to effect irreversible political change in South Africa.

Notes

1. R.G. Fall, 1958, *Golfing in Southern Africa*, Salt River: SA Golf Pty.
2. The *Illustrated African Golfer* was published between 1934–6 as a dedicated magazine for the white golfing fraternity. Thereafter it was rebranded as *The Illustrated Sporting Review*, a multi-sports magazine.
3. Simon Malaza, 1947[?], *The Bantu Golf*, Johannesburg: Lovedale Press.

4. See for example the works of Chris Nicholson, 2005, *Papwa Sewgolum: From Pariah to Legend*. Johannesburg: Wits University Press, Michael Vlismas, 2012, *The Extraordinary History of South African Golf*, Parktown North: Penguin, Craig Urquhart, 2013, *The Kings of Swing: Behind the Scenes with South Africa's Golfing Greats*, Cape Town: Zebra Press, and Maxine Case, 2015, *Papwa: Golf's Lost Legend*, Cape Town: Kwela.

5. Compare for example the publications of Maxine Case (2015) and Christopher Nicholson (2005) who, despite a time-span of 10 years between the books, also failed to properly situate the achievements of Papwa within the long struggle of black golfers before 1959 to make their mark on the South African golfing landscape.

6. See for example Wornie L. Reed, 1991, "Blacks in Golf," *Trotter Review* vol. 5: issue 1, article 6. Available at: http://scholarworks.umb.edu/trotter_review/vol5/iss1/6, M.P. Dawkins, 2004, "Race Relations and the Sport of Golf: The African American Golf Legacy," and E.V. Gable, 2015, *The Pre and Present Tiger Woods Effect: Blacks in Golf* (Doctoral dissertation, San Francisco State University) and Sanjeev Baidyaroy, 2011, *Blacks, Golf, and the Emerging Civil Rights Movement, 1947-1954*, honors thesis, Carnegie Mellon University, available from http://repository.cmu.edu/hsshonors.

7. Cape Archives Division (forthwith KAB): Colonial Office (forthwith CO): 4017: 287 Memorials Received—C.L. Herman, W.F. Hertzog and P. Van Breda, 23 January 1843. Members of the Society Room Good Hope, a local organization, promoted "Kolf" or "Golf" for an extended period and hosted competitions for the "Silver Kolf" or "Silver Golf."

8. Fall, 1958, *Golfing in Southern Africa*, pp. 19-22.

9. Some of the first clubs established on a national basis were Maritzburg GC (1886), Durban GC (1892), Port Elizabeth (1890), Kingwilliamstown (1892), Adelaide Queenstown, Bedford, East London, Grahamstown—all 1983, Klerksdorp (1889), Germiston (1890) Johannesburg (1891) and Bloemfontein (1888).

10. KAB, Accessions (forthwith A), 727: Golf. Copy of Minutes, 8 October 1910.

11. John Nauright, 1998, *Sport, Cultures, and Identities in South Africa*, Claremont: David Phillip, p. 43.

12. See "Sport on the 'Fields,'" 1873, *The Cape Monthly Magazine*, November, vol. V11, p. 120; and "Health and Happiness: A Lay Sermon," 1873, *The Cape Monthly Magazine*, November, vol. V11, p. 120, p. 305.

13. Andre Odendaal, 1988, "South Africa's Black Victorians: Sport and Society in South Africa in the Nineteenth Century," in J.A. Mangan (ed.), *Pleasure, Profit, Proselytism: British Culture and Sport at Home and Abroad, 1700-1914*, London: Frank Cass & Co., pp. 199-200.

14. See for example Nauright, 1998, *Sport, Cultures, and Identities*, p. 61, and Gavin Lewis, 1987, *Between the Wire and the Wall: A History of South African "Coloured" Politics*, New York: St. Martin's Press, p. 36.

15. Quoted in V. Bickford-Smith *Ethnic Pride and Racial Prejudice in Victorian Cape Town: Group Identity and Social Practice, 1875-1902*, Cambridge, 1995, p. 149.

16. "Golf and Politics," *The New Zealand Herald Supplement*, 1 July 1903.

17. Nauright, 1998, *Sport, Cultures, and Identities*, p. 61.

18. See for example"General Gossip," Saturday, 16 May 1890, *The Queenscliff Sentinel, Drysdale, Portarlington and Sorrento Advertiser*, Victoria: 1885-1894; and "Football," 27 May 1896, *The Barrier Miner (Broken Hill, NSW)*, p. 2.

19. Simon Malaza, 1947[?], *The Bantu Golf*, Johannesburg: Lovedale Press, p. 7.

20. Case, *Papwa*, pp. 42, 69-70.

21. *The Illustrated African Golfer*, vol. 1, no. 3 June, 1934, p. 93.

22. Malaza, *The Bantu Golf*, pp. 7-9.

23. *The Register* (Adelaide), "Golf," Friday, 7 March 1924, p. 5. Fotheringham was not only a five-time winner of the SA Open Golf Championship (1908, 1910-12 and 1914) and SA Open (1905 and 1909), but was also a founder member of the American Professional Golfers Association.

24. See, "Playing Golf in Matabeleland," 25 June 1910, *The North Otago Times Supplement*; "Golf Under Difficulties: The Not-to-Be-Denied Golfer,"17 January 1924, *The Auckland Star*, p. 3; and "Kaffir Toe Lies," 2 November 1933, *The Evening Post*, p. 6.

25. "Rand Natives Are Becoming Good Golfers: Regular Club Matches Played on Eight Reef Courses," 19 November 1938, *The Rand Daily Mail*.
26. Nauright, 1998, *Sport, Cultures, and Identities*, p. 62.
27. Malaza, 1947[?], p. 11.
28. KAB, 1/LSK: 2/17/10—Native Affairs: Sports & Recreation for Natives—HM Nourse: Magistrate Lusikisiki—Chief Magistrate Umtata, 23 September 1939.
29. *The Sportsman*, "Do You Know," January 1967, p. 41.
30. Malaza, 1947[?], pp. 13, 15.
31. *SA Golf*, April 1948. Available from Available from SA Golf Association website at http://history.saga.co.za/history/advancement-of-the-underprivileged-in-the-game-of-golf/?id=119 (Accessed 12 December 2016).
32. The founding members on this occasion were Eastern Cape inclusive of Eastern Province and Border/East London, Griqualand-West/Kimberley, Western Cape inclusive of Western Province and Karoo/Beaufort West, Transvaal Bantu Golf Union, Natal Golf Union and the Basutoland Golf Union. These associations were not always fully constituted as regional entities with formal constitutions and were in most cases representatives of a small number of clubs within the larger urban centres.
33. *SA Golf*, June 1961.
34. Malaza, 1947[?], p. 23.
35. *SA Golf*, September 1958.
36. *SA Golf*, October 1961.
37. *SA Golf*, November 1959.
38. KAB, 2/ OBS: N7/10/2: Bantu Welfare: Sport and Recreation for Rural Bantu—Chief Bantu Commissioner: Observatory—The Secretary: Bantu Administration and Development, 15 November 1967.
39. *SA Golf*, May 1954.
40. *SA Golf*, April 1962.
41. "Rugby Team May Tour Japan," 4 February 1950, *The West Australian*.
42. Christopher Merrett, 1996, "In Nothing Else Are the Deprivers So Deprived': South African Sport, Apartheid and Foreign Relations, 1945–1971," *The International Journal of the History of Sport*, vol. 13, no. 2, August, p. 147.
43. University of the Witwatersrand Historical Papers Archive, South African Institute of Race Relations Collection (forthwith Wits), AD 1715: D.A. Brutus (South African Sports Association—Appeal to All Olympic Councils, 1 January 1962.
44. Wits AD 1715: D.A. Brutus (South African Sports Association, the Manager: Hullett's Sugar Refinery, 16 July 1962).
45. South African Sport Book of Records, 1989, *The Allied Book of SA Sport & Sports Records 1988/89*, Randburg: SASBOR, p. 196.
46. Nicholson, 2005, *Papwa Sewgolum*, pp. 49–54.
47. South African History Online, "Sharpeville Massacre, 21 March 1960" available from http://www.sahistory.org.za/topic/sharpeville-massacre-21-march-1960, accessed on 12 December 2016.
48. *SA Golf*, February 1960.
49. Chris de Broglio (undated), "The SANROC Story," available from http://onlinelaw.co.za/docs/The_SANROC_story.pdf, accessed 13 December 2016.
50. Gary Player and Michael McDonnell, 1991, *To Be the Best: Reflections of a Champion*, London: Sidgwick & Jackson, p. 50.
51. Marc Keech, "The Ties That Bind: South Africa and Sports Diplomacy 1958–1963," *The Sports Historian*, 21(1), pp. 75–76.
52. "New Venue for Mat Tourney," 21 November 1967, *The Cape Argus*.
53. "Coloured Wrestler Excels Overseas," 19 August 1967, *The Cape Argus*.
54. *SA Golf*, July 1961.
55. Douglas Booth, 2003, "Hitting Apartheid for Six? the Politics of the South African Sports Boycott," *Journal of Contemporary History*, vol. 38, no. 3, July, p. 482.
56. Merrett, 1996, "In Nothing Else Are the Deprivers So Deprived," p.152.
57. KAB, Accessions: A.2446, Report of the South African National Wrestling Control

Board and Financial Statements for the Period 1 January 1964–30 June 1964, as well as Memorandum from the SA National Wrestling Control Board SA Police Service, 22 September 1964.
  58. Merrett, 1996, "In Nothing Else Are the Deprivers So Deprived," p. 151.
  59. Daryl Adair (ed.), 2012, *Sport: Race, Ethnicity and Identity: Building Global Understanding*, Oxon: Routledge, p. 26.
  60. American Committee on Africa (forthwith ACOA), Brochure, 1966/67, "Announcing Dennis Brutus: Poet, Teacher, Sportsman Speaking On: I Was a Prisoner on Robben Island and Topics Related to Apartheid" (Brochure).
  61. ACOA, 1967, "Statement by Dennis Brutus," 21 March 1967.
  62. Dexter Blackman, 2012, "African Americans, Pan-Africanism, and the Anti-Apartheid Campaign to Expel South Africa from the 1968 Olympics," *The Journal of Pan African Studies*, vol. 5, no. 3, June, p. 12.
  63. Merrett, 1996, "In Nothing Else Are the Deprivers So Deprived," p. 158.
  64. "Player on Apartheid," 22 November 1969, *The Canberra Times*, p. 32.
  65. Gary Player and Michael McDonnell, 1991, *To Be the Best: Reflections of a Champion*, London: Sidgwick & Jackson, pp. 54–55.
  66. See "Vigilantes Warned," 25 September 1971, *The Canberra Times*, p. 34; and "Golf Open Faces Wreckers If Player Allowed to Compete," 19 November 1981, *The Canberra Times*, p. 34.
  67. "Racialists Jibes Cost Win," 3 June 1970, *The Canberra Times*, p. 34.
  68. Nauright, 1997, *Sport, Cultures and Identities*, pp. 96–98.
  69. Juan Klee, 2012, "Multinational Sport Participation Replaces Apartheid Sport in South Africa—1967–1978: The Role of BJ Vorster and PGJ Koornhof," *New Contree*, No. 64, July, p. 165.
  70. "Clarity on Mixed Sport," *The Cape Argus*, 8 June 1971.
  71. André Odendaal, 1995, "The Thing That Is Not Round- the Untold Story of Black Rugby in South Africa," in A.M. Grundlingh, A.A. Odendaal & B. Spies, 1995, *Beyond the Tryline: Rugby and South African Society*, Johannesburg: Ravan Press, 1995, p. 58.
  72. KAB, accessions: A.2446: Minutes of the special meeting of the SA National Wrestling Control Board, 24 October 1975.
  73. South African Golf Association, "The SA Non-European Open Championships," available from http://history.saga.co.za/history/the-sa-non-european-golf-championships/?id=125 (Accessed on 12 December 2016).
  74. *SA Golf*, August 1971.
  75. *SA Golf*, October 1971.
  76. "Blacks, Whites Alike Loved Lee Elder in South Africa," 7 March 1972, *The Spartanburg Herald Journal*, p. 8.
  77. Player and McDonnell, 1991, *To Be the Best*, pp. 54–55. See also article entitled "Elder Made Bold Play in South Africa," available from http://garyplayer.com/news/news_detail/elder_made_bold_play_in_south_africa/ (accessed on 19 December 2016).
  78. *SA Golf*, November 1971.
  79. John Henrik Clarke and Louise Meriwether, 1972, "Should American Blacks Tour South Africa to Entertain Africans?" *Committee of Concerned Blacks*: Bronx, New York. Available from http://africanactivist.msu.edu/document_metadata.php?objectid=32-130-1533 (Accessed 1 July 2016).
  80. Lee Elder, 1989, "Lee Elder Sees Changes in Apartheid South Africa," *Jet Magazine*, April, p. 46.
  81. B.A. Khoapa (ed.) 1972. *Black Review*. Durban Black, Community Programmes. pp. 199–200. Available from Digital Innovation South Africa (DISA), University of Kwazulu Natal. URL: http://disa.ukzn.ac.za/sites/default/files/pdf_files/Br1972.0376.4354.000.000.1972.18.pdf.
  82. South African Council on Sport (forthwith SACOS)—*Facsimile: Y. Ebrahim: President (SACOS) to the Australian Society for Sports History*, 4 July 1989.
  83. Ted Partridge, 1975, "Golf's Breakthrough," September.
  84. Richard. E. Lapchick, 1976, "Apartheid Sport and South African Foreign Policy:

1976," *Paper Presented at the International Seminar on the Eradication of Apartheid and in Support of the Struggle for Liberation in South Africa*, Havana, Republic of Cuba, 24–28 May, United Nations Centre Against Apartheid.

85. For a comprehensive understanding of the Soweto Uprising and its aftermath, consult among others, Gary Baines, 2006, "Coming to Terms with the Past: Soweto, June 16th 1976," *History Today* 56.6; Baruch Hirson,1979, *Year of Fire, Year of Ash: The Soweto Revolt, Roots of a Revolution?* Vol. 3. Zed Press; John Stuart Kane-Berman, 1978, *Soweto: Black Revolt, White Reaction*, Raven Press South Africa; Helena Pohlandt-McCormick, 2000, "Controlling Woman: Winnie Mandela and the 1976 Soweto Uprising." *The International Journal of African Historical Studies* 33.3: 585–614.

86. March, L. Krotee and Luther C. Schwick (undated), "The Impact of Sporting Forces on South African Apartheid," available from http://citeseerx.ist.psu.edu/viewdoc/download?doi=10.1.1.840.7357&rep=rep1&type=pdf (Accessed on 1 October 2016).

87. American Coordinating Committee for Equality in Sport and Society (forthwith ACCESS), "Action Alert: Launching of Campaign Against Apartheid in Golf," 9 July 1980.

88. ACCESS, 11 July 1980, "Action Alert: ACCESS Announce Campaign to Isolate South African Golfers Playing in the United States—Eisenhower Cup to Be the First Target."

89. ACCESS, 12 September 1980, "ACCESS Announces Intensification of Campaign to Exclude South African Team from Eisenhower Cup Golf in October."

90. "Golf: Record Total in Team Event," 13 October 1980, *The Canberra Times*, p. 15.

91. "UN Blacklist 'Could Boomerang,'" 17 March 1981, *The Canberra Times*, p. 17.

92. "Golf: Tunisia Erects Barrier to Top World Golfers," 18 October 1981*The Canberra Times,*, p. 2.

93. Gay Seidman argued that the armed struggle "played a key role: it attracted popular support to the anti-apartheid movement, it demonstrated the persistence of resistance to white supremacy despite repression, and it served as a complicated badge of commitment for anti-apartheid activists." See full article (2001), "Guerrillas in Their Midst: Armed Struggle in the South African Anti-apartheid Movement,"*Mobilization: The International Journal of Research and Theory About Social Movements, Protest, and Contentious Politics*, vol. 6, no. 2, Fall, p. 111.

94. Mark Swilling, 1986, "The United Democratic Front and Township Revolt—South Africa," conference paper, March. Available from sahistory.org.za (accessed 21 October 2016).

95. David Black, 1999, "The Long and Winding Road: International Norms and Domestic Political Change in South Africa," in Thomas Risse, Stephen C. Ropp and Kathryn Sikkink (eds.), *The Power of Human Rights: International Norms and Domestic Change*, Cambridge: University Press, p. 91.

96. Klee, 2012, "Multinational Sport Participation," p. 163.

97. Nico Steytler and Johann Mettler, 2001, "Federal Arrangements as a Peacemaking Device During South Africa's Transition to Democracy," *Publius*, vol. 31, no. 4, p. 93.

98. Giliomee, Hermann, 2008, "Great Expectations: Pres. PW Botha's Rubicon Speech of 1985," *New Contree*, No. 55, May, p. 38.

National Heroes or Disgusting Nazis?

Soccer Patriotism, German National Identity and the "Gaucho Gate" Incident After the FIFA World Cup 2014

YANNICK KLUCH

Abstract

When the players of the German national soccer team entered center stage to be celebrated by the fans at Germany's *Siegesfeier* (victory celebration) after winning the 2014 FIFA World Cup, they performed a dance that overtly mocked their Argentinian opponents. The controversial nature of the dance—later termed "gaucho gate"— created major uproar in both national and international media landscapes, with Uruguayan journalist Victor Huge Morales describing the German national team soccer players as "disgusting Nazis" ("Unsere 'gaucho dancer,'" para. 15). Why did the "gaucho dance" inspire a heated discussion in Germany (and abroad)?

Interestingly, soccer remains an important source of national identification for Germans (Mutz, 2012). Zambon (2012) has argued that it was the soccer World Cup that "finally succeeded in breaking the taboo against the public expression of overt national pride," which is why "during the 2006 World Cup, the past finally 'went away,' emancipating national symbols and placing German patriotism above reproach."

I remember very vividly the day the German national soccer team won the FIFA World Cup in the summer of 2014. I had traveled through Europe with my best friend from the United States for four weeks, and after weeks on the road we had settled back into my brother's apartment in Hamburg for our last week in Europe before heading back to the United States to finish up my doctoral studies. It was one of our last days in Europe when Germany faced Argentina in the final, sparking hope in millions of Germans—including myself—to win our first World Cup title since 1990. As so often growing up in Germany, my friends and I gathered at the *Heiligengeistfeld* in Hamburg the day of the final match to join over 50,000 enthusiastic soccer fans in watching the mediated game on giant screens overlooking one of Hamburg's most iconic sites, the *Medienbunker*. This "public viewing," as Germans call the ritual in which thousands of people come together to watch such games, sure did not disappoint—and so we were at the edge of our seats through the ups and downs of the game. And when Mario Götze finally scored the winning goal in overtime, we were proudly singing our World Cup song, hugging strangers like we had known them for years, and crying tears of joy that Germany—*our team*—had won the World Cup. From fear to joy, from disappointment to pride, and from anticipation to enthusiasm, clearly the evening Germany won the World Cup was charged with many emotions that now turned into a memory that will stay with us for a long time.

I chose to open this essay with this short anecdote to share a personal example of how the mediated spectacle that is the FIFA World Cup can provide sports participants of various types with "immediate contact to and a symbolic interaction with" sport communities (Kassing et al., 2004). Despite not having stepped foot on a soccer field in years, the anecdote above shows that the FIFA World Cup as mediated mega-event provided a platform for spectators like myself to symbolically identify with the athletes on the field. On that summer night in Hamburg, I felt like I *was* part of the German team without even being in the actual stadium. The team on the screen, it became obvious to me, provided a means of identification for me—a source of national pride that seemed foreign to me at the time.

Celebrating at the Siegesfeier: *Germany's Success in the 2014 FIFA World Cup*

When Germany won the final of the 2014 FIFA World Cup against rival Argentina, the whole country was in a constant state of ecstasy. Domestic and international media alike celebrated the new soccer world champions, and hundreds of thousands of German fans attended the *Siegesfeier*, the victory celebration, at the Brandenburg Gate in the country's capital city of Berlin, Germany. Despite the general euphoric mood in the country, the actions of some of the players during the *Siegesfeier* received major media attention: When players Miroslav Klose, Andre Schürrle, Shkodran Mustafi, Mario Götze, Roman Weidenfeller, and Toni Kroos entered center stage to be celebrated by the fans, they performed a dance which was termed the "gaucho dance" in the weeks following the event. In this dance, the players overtly mocked their Argentinian opponents.

The controversial nature of the dance created major uproar in both national and international media landscapes. In his article from July 16, 2014, *Washington Post* reporter Anthony Faiola accurately described the political dimension of the dance in the country of Germany:

> With a debate already on here about the return of patriotism in a nation long uncomfortable with the notion in the years after World War II, the inference landed like a bomb. After the Germans generally held themselves with grace in victory after their 7-1 thrashing of Brazil in the semi-final, for some, the grandstanding put more than a little tarnish on Germany's glistening trophy, generating outrage as well as outright charges of racism.

One such charge came from the Uruguayan radio journalist Victor Huge Morales, who described the German national team soccer players as "disgusting Nazis" and even compared the athletes' behavior to that of Nazi Germans who discriminated against Jews and other minorities in the 1930s and 1940s ("Unsere 'Gaucho Tänzer'"). Morales resumed that the "disrespectful behavior" of the German athletes shows that "there is still a part of Germany that is very sick. These sick players show that Germany has not changed as much as it wanted to show in 2006" ("Unsere 'Gaucho Tänzer'").

This essay focuses on the media narratives dominating the German media in response to what soon became known as the *gaucho gate* incident after the 2014 FIFA World Cup. The media narratives following this incident, as well as the construction of the *Siegesfeier* as the ultimate spectacle celebrating the German nation in itself, provide great insight into what it means to be *German* during and after major sporting events in the 21st century— decades after the horrific shadow that the Holocaust has thrown over the country's national confidence and collective identity. Even more importantly, *gaucho gate* also raises questions about the importance of sport in the practice of safe patriotism in contemporary Germany. By analyzing the *Siegesfeier*, during which the controversial gaucho dance was performed, as well as the media narratives surrounding the coverage of the incident, this essay aims to unravel the underlying assumptions attached to the construct of national identity and nationhood in contemporary Germany by situating the highly controversial "gaucho dance" in the context of the country's troubling relationship to overt patriotism that resulted from Germany's horrific past.

Mediating Nationhood: Sport, Media and the Construction of the Nation

Cultural identities, as Hall (1991) reminds us, are by no means fixed or unified, but rather contingent, in process, and potentially contradictory. Similarly, national identity has long been conceptualized as a socio-historical construction and, put more eloquently, "imagined political community" (Anderson 1991, 6). Anderson (1991) argued that the nation "is imagined because the members of even the smallest nation will never know most of their fellow-members, meet them, or even hear of them, yet in the minds of each lives the image of their communion" (6). Anderson (1991) also attributes a major role of the media in this construction of a collective national identity by members of a given nation.

Applying the notion of community construction to sports media, Kassing and colleagues (2004) point to the dominance of the media in the co-creation and the communicative perpetuation of sport communities and experiences. They argue that the media is "the one communication channel that frequently and directly enables participants to have immediate contact to and a symbolic connection with the sporting community" (Kassing et al. 2004, 384). Many scholars have pointed out the beneficial contribution of mediated major sporting events in the construction of "the nation" as an imagined community (see, e.g., Steenveld and Strelitz 1998; Brencis and Ikkala 2013). When it comes to sport, the media does not only reflect national identities, but also constructs, shapes, constitutes, and transforms national identities, which necessarily means that "national identities are not just imagined once, but are continually reinvented" (Brookes 2002, 89). Crolley and Hand (2001), similarly, view the media as a "conduit for concepts of national identity" that provides powerful "points of reference that help to bind individuals into a national community" (8). As such, sport is inextricably linked to forces of nationalism and identity (Hobsbawm and Ranger 1983).

Boyle and Haynes (2009) have also argued that sport can be seen as a cultural form that is used as an indicator of certain national characteristics and that is often seen as representative of national identity, as sport can become "a symbolic extension of various collective identities" (147). Looking at the relationship between national identity and sport in contemporary England, Polley (2004) has also examined the construction of collective national identities in and through sport; he writes:

> People's national sporting affiliations are among the most public statements that they make about their identities.... The physical, competitive, supra-linguistic, and populist nature of most sports have made them the perfect media for the expression of group identities. Sports are places in which groups can find peaceful physical fora for the beliefs they hold about themselves as entities [12–13].

This expression of group identities comes not without problems. Brookes (2002) has pointed out that mediated sporting events represent celebratory images of nationalism that are used as markers of difference that distinguish one nation from another. In his analysis of national sporting stereotypes, O'Donnell (1994) further reminds us that national identity is always constructed through difference. The celebration of one country over another that is so often to be found in international media sport is, as O'Donnell (1994) argues, a process that "routinely involves downgrading other national groups" (353).

Soccer and National Identity in Contemporary Germany

To understand why *gaucho gate* inspired mixed reactions from the media, it is important to look at sport and the construction of national identity in contemporary Germany, a country that is known to have a troubled relationship with overt displays of patriotism due to its horrific past (Amsler 1995; Wittlinger 2010). Even though the country was re-unified in 1990, Germany looks back on a past that saw the country as both physical and psychologically divided for most of the 20th century. In the context of a continuous struggle for a cohesive national identity among Germans in a divided country, soccer has become central in the construction of German national identity since the end of World War II. Ismer (2011), for instance, has pointed out the immense importance of the "triad of football [soccer], rituals and emotions" (554) as a major influence on the construction of collective German national identity. Rituals, according to Ismer (2011), can act "as a frame for experiencing collective emotions" (551), which in turn are "of crucial importance for the process of constructing national identity" (551). In his analysis of the 2006 FIFA World Cup, Ismer (2011) identified the team formation segments on TV, the singing of the national anthem, and the commentary on screen as such rituals that gave Germans a sense of belonging by constructing a cohesive German national identity.

Soccer played a significant role in German national identity construction long before 2006, and many scholars have examined the importance of competing in or winning a World Cup in German history (Gethard 2006; Heinrich 2003). Heinrich (2003) analyzed the cultural significance of the win by Germany in the 1954 Soccer World Cup. He has shown that "the triumph of Bern served to make West Germans feel secure about where they were located and who they were. It signified—9 years after the end of a criminal regime and dreadful war—something like a re-entry into the world, this time in a civilized fashion" (Heinrich 2003, 1493).

The victory of the German team at the 1954 World Cup finals in Bern, as such, allowed Germans to carefully create a sense of national identity after years of terror. The win was particularly important as it helped the country find more confidence in times when all confidence was destroyed by the bombs of the war. In his essay examining soccer in post-war Germany, Gethard (2006) also states that the sport of soccer has served as "an accurate metaphor for much of what Germany has endured since the end of World War II" (51). Germany's win at the World Cup was not only important in 1954, but also in 1990, the year of German unification, because it created an atmosphere of optimism and collective national identity during a time when the country itself was struggling politically (Gethard 2006).

More recent scholarship has examined the role of both the FIFA World Cup and the UEFA championship as it relates to German national identity in the 2000s. In his examination of national identification of Germans during the UEFA championship in 2012, Mutz (2012) has found that the national team embodies the nation. As such, the German national team can be described as a major reference point for Germans' identification with their nation (Mutz 2012). Even further, Mutz (2012) shows that success of the German national team in a major tournament is an important source of national pride as well as for a positive identification of the German people with their own country. Most crucially, however, Mutz (2012) did not only identify an increase in patriotism and national identification during the tournament, but also a decrease of both only three weeks after Germany's loss. Mutz (2012) concluded that Germans were patriotic and created a collective German identity for the course of the UEFA championship and the few weeks following the mega event; he thus described Germans as "patriots for three weeks" (517).

The FIFA World Cup in 2006, hosted by Germany itself, was of particular importance for Germany, which led Zambon (2012) to describe the 2006 World Cup as therapeutic for the German people. Because Germans were able to publicly express patriotism within the context of this World Cup, their national pride was successfully rehabilitated during the World Cup (Zambon 2012). The media was particularly crucial to this development, as it "worked to create a break from the past by simultaneously omitting critical discourse about the role of nationalism in Germany's fascist past and creating collective memory of a new, unimpeachable 'soccer patriotism'" (3). As such, the mega event "finally succeeded in breaking the taboo against the public expression of overt national pride" (Zambon 2012, 1). Zambon (2012) concludes her analysis with her strong assessment that "during the 2006 World Cup, the past finally 'went away,' emancipating national symbols and placing German patriotism above reproach" (28). The question can then be asked, if soccer has become a safe space for Germans to practice patriotism, why did the *gaucho gate* incident cause such uproar within the country?

Studying Germany's Gaucho Gate *as Text(s): Method*

To assess the cultural meaning behind *gaucho gate*, particularly as it relates to the construction of national identity in re-unified Germany, two research questions guided this inquiry. Given that previous research has revealed the importance of the context in which the German national team has been celebrated, the first research question aims at placing the narratives surrounding *gaucho gate* into context by critically examining the incident itself.

> RQ 1: How did the *Siegesfeier* in general, and the "gaucho dance" as performed by players of the German national team in particular, construct a collective German national identity in the context of the 2014 FIFA World Cup?

The second research question that guided this inquiry looked at the narratives surrounding *gaucho gate*, so that greater understanding of how nationhood is constructed in the context of major sporting events can be achieved:

> RQ 2: What narratives dominated the German media's coverage of the *gaucho gate* incident in the aftermath of the *Siegesfeier*?

A multi-method qualitative approach was used to find answers to these research questions, combining both textual analysis of the actual *Siegesfeier* as well as qualitative content analysis and critical discourse analysis to examine dominant narratives surrounding *gaucho gate*.

It has been argued convincingly that sport incidents can be seen as texts that need to be read critically (McDonald and Birrell 1999). McDonald and Birrell (1999) advocate that sport scholars need to focus their "analytical attention on specific sporting incidents and personalities ... [in order to] reveal a nexus of power that helps produce their meanings" (284). To unravel the meanings attached to the *gaucho gate* incident, I have "read" this incident critically by following McKee's (2001) guide to textual analysis. McKee (2001) points out accurately that a text cannot be analyzed sufficiently without putting it into context. In order to do so, McKee (2001) identifies three ways: to look at other parts of the text, the text genre, and the "wider public context in which a text is circulated" (McKee 2001, 146). In order to do so, I not only researched media coverage of the 2014 FIFA World Cup but also paid close attention to other topics that were present in the media during the time of the World Cup. This helped to put my analysis in context, because I was able to get a clearer sense of what McKee (2001) describes as "the wider 'semiosphere' (the 'world of meaning')" (149) of the construction of national pride and collective identity through the *gaucho gate* incident.

I have gathered the text under analysis by accessing the broadcast of the

Siegesfeier through the online portal of the ARD, a major German public TV channel (www.daserste.de). My analysis includes both the *Siegesfeier* as an event itself as well as the players who participated in the "gaucho dance." In addition, I have accessed previous victory celebrations of German national teams that were held for previous participations in FIFA World Cups to get a clearer idea of the importance and most common characteristics of the event itself. I also extended my research to victory celebrations of the women's soccer team as well as the national youth soccer team. I conducted research on the players by examining their personal websites, their presentation at the clubs they had contracts with prior to the World Cup, as well as by looking at the media coverage of the players prior to the event. Finally, I watched interviews with the players on major German news networks (ARD, ZDF, RTL) to get a better sense of their character traits.

A qualitative content analysis of the media coverage following the incident was the basis for identifying media narratives that emerged in response to *gaucho gate*. Articles from the four most widely distributed German newspapers *BILD Zeitung* (16 articles), *Sueddeutsche Zeitung* (ten articles), *Frankfurter Allgemeine Zeitung* (18 articles), and *Die Welt* (eleven articles) over a time frame of three weeks following the incident (July 15, 2014, through August 5, 2014) were analyzed. A total of 55 articles were accessed through each newspaper's online archive and through a LexisNexis search by using "gaucho" and "siegesfeier" as the specified search terms, which were run separately. Narratives were identified to capture the discourse surrounding the *gaucho gate* incident. Zambon (2012) points out the significance of mediated discourse in her analysis of the 2006 FIFA World Cup:

> The mediated public sphere is a cradle of collective memory on the national scale. Press coverage establishes discursive frameworks that go beyond merely reflecting events to shape the collective conception and memory of those events. Although evidence of dominant discourses in the press cannot be taken as reflective of individual experiences of media events, press coverage must be taken seriously as a reflection of and powerful constitutive force in the national public sphere [3–4].

It is due to the ability of discourse to socially construct reality (Martinez 2007) that qualitative content analysis offers a valuable approach to the study of narratives surrounding *gaucho gate* as it related to national identity construction in contemporary Germany.

The Gaucho Gate *Incident*

The *Siegesfeier* after the 2014 FIFA World Cup was attended by 500,000 fans and was simultaneously broadcasted by Germany's two major public television stations ARD and ZDF. An inherent part of the celebrations was the welcoming of the athletes of the national team. In groups of five to eight, the players were brought on stage to be celebrated by the masses. Players Weidenfeller, Mustafi, Schürrle, Klose, Götze, and Kroos had their arms laid around each other's shoulders so that they built a straight line facing the crowd ahead. All were wearing black t-shirts with a giant "1" scripted on it. The number "1" was designed in the same way the national jerseys were designed, all of which were white with a giant black, red, and gold stripe on it.

After taking a few steps toward the front of the stage, the players split apart from each other further and took on a bent position so that their faces faced the ground of the stage, while taking further steps toward the front of the stage. Simultaneously, they collectively sang "So gehen die Gauchos, die Gauchos, die gehen so" ("This is how the Gauchos walk, the Gauchos walk like this") twice. While subsequently singing "So gehen die Deutschen, die Deutschen, die gehen so" ("This is how the Germans walk, the Germans walk like this"), the six players euphorically jumped into an upright position and started to jump up and down, stretching their arms to the sky while waving them to the tact of their chant.

The group repeated the same dance one more time before making it to the front of the stage, where the group is united by players Miroslav Klose and Mario Götze yelling "Und jetzt, alle zusammen!" ("And now, all together!"). They proceed to repeat the same chant they had done before for two more times. While the dance was harshly criticized for being inappropriate in regard to the Argentinian opponents, the dance has to be situated and analyzed in the context of a hyper-patriotic *Siegesfeier*. A close textual analysis of the players' presentation during the *Siegesfeier* reveals that the players' performance on stage reinforced and encouraged immense German national pride and constructed a collective German identity.

Mediating the Nation: The Siegesfeier *as Ultimate German Spectacle*

Several aspects of the *Siegesfeier* constructed members of the German national team as a source of national pride. First, the high degree of national pride associated with the players is signified by the cheering crowds. Second, both Klose and Götze emphasize the word "Weltmeister" ("world champion") during the break in between their chants. The use of this superlative describing the German national team as the best of the world supports the promotion of national pride. Finally, the actual dance in itself is the best signifier of national pride. As described before, the players first walk in a bent position before ultimately changing into an upright walk and jumping up and down while waving their hands to the rhythm of their "gaucho chant." This upright walk illustrates the pride each of the players has felt after winning the FIFA World Cup.

The *Siegesfeier* in general, and the "gaucho dance" part in particular, heavily relies on national symbols to safely express patriotism and to overtly underline German national pride.

Interestingly, Geisler (2005) has pointed out that "for most of the twentieth century, not a single one of Germany's national symbols ... functioned successfully as a stable emblem of German national and cultural identity" (67). Rather, Germans felt "alienated and excluded by the very symbols intended to include them" (Geisler 2005, 64). However, it is the German flag that has remained a stable symbol for Germans to identify with ideologically (Geisler 2005), which is why it is featured prominently throughout the broadcast of the *Siegesfeier*. Weidenfeller, Mustafi, Schürrle, Klose, Götze, and Kroos are all dressed in the black, red, and gold—the colors of the German flag. The t-shirts they wear have a giant "1" in the design of the German national jerseys on them, which is another signifier of German national pride. Similarly, Kroos is waving a German flag when dancing. And many flags are seen in the masses celebrating the players.

Interestingly, the location of the *Siegesfeier* in itself constructs the players of the soccer national team as national heroes as well. The victory celebrations were being held at the Brandenburg Gate, one of the most important historic sites of Germany. While the players are shown in close-ups before they start walking down the stage, the camera zooms out and reveals the Brandenburg Gate in the background. This visual alignment of the performance of the "gaucho dance" with the Brandenburg Gate creates an invisible link between the two that extends the famous site's patriotic power to that of the performance. The patriotic potential of the "gaucho dance" is herewith equated to that of the Brandenburg Gate, and the "gaucho dance" is framed as an expression of the players' patriotism and national pride.

It is for this reason that the highly controversial performance of the "gaucho dance" has to be situated as a ritual in the context of the hyperpatriotic *Siegesfeier*. Rituals, according to Ismer (2011), can act "as a frame for experiencing collective emotions" (551), which in turn are "of crucial importance for the process of constructing national identity" (551). The "gaucho dance" in itself can be classified as a ritual that relies heavily on the experience of collective emotions. While there are several moments of the "Gaucho dance" that create collective emotion through its ritualized form, it is the final chant of the soccer players that most overtly contributes to the creation of collective emotion. For the final chant, players Klose and Götze encourage the audience to join them as they continue to sing and dance to their "gaucho chant." By encouraging the fans to join the dancing and singing ("and now, all together!"), the team encourages the fans to share this moment of positive German identification by expressing their German national pride as overtly as the players do. They thus create a collective emotion based on collaboration through their song as ritual. Further, the melody of Weidenfeller, Mustafi, Schürrle, Klose, Götze, and Kroos that made up the "gaucho song" is taken from the famous German children's song *Ich kenne einen Cowboy* (*I know a cowboy*). As such, the melody itself (even though the words may be made up by the team) is emotionally charged, as it may remind the audience of a ritual from their childhood. The team herewith effectively uses a ritual as a tool to express collective emotions in order to create a sense of national unity and collective identity.

In addition to the words that are sung by the players of the national team, the physical form of the dance contributes to the creation of a collective, patriotic German national identity. By switching from the bent to the upright position when comparing the way the "gauchos" walk to the way the Germans walk, the soccer players create a collective German identity through the conscious construction of a dichotomy between the German team and their rival team. German identity, herewith, is constructed through difference from the Argentinian players. Mutz (2013) states that a positive collective identity results from a direct comparison with opposing groups who are considered inferior. In the "gaucho dance," the Argentinians are clearly positioned as being inferior to the Germans by the way the players use their bodies to walk on stage. The team members underline their rival's inferiority by walking in a bent position as well as by calling them "gauchos" rather than Argentinians. Also, the players' tone is quieter when singing "So gehen die Gauchos" ("This is how the Gauchos walk"). When singing "So gehen die Deutschen" ("This is how the Germans walk"), the players yell into the microphone. They herewith reinforce their superiority to their opponents who are framed as significantly less powerful. Both the players' way of walking and the use of their voices are herewith used to create an atmosphere of national pride and positive identification with the German nation through the inferiorization of the rival. Through their "gaucho dance," the German players not only constructed themselves as national heroes, but also promoted a collective German identity through the conscious visual construction of a dichotomy between them (as superior) and their Argentinian rivals (as inferior).

Many scholars have examined the importance of context when winning a World Cup in German history (Heinrich 2003; Gethard 2006). Both the World Cup wins in 1954 (shortly after the end of World War II) and 1990 (the year Germany was re-unified) allowed the Germans to feel a sense of national pride and optimism in times of cultural hardship (Heinrich 2003; Gethard 2006). It is this optimism during times of hardship that becomes evident in the analysis of the *gaucho gate* incident at the 2014 *Siegesfeier*. While Germany was still recovering from the economic crisis of 2009 and was simultaneously criticized for being too neutral on controversial issues like the fight of terrorism or the actions of Russia, the *Siegesfeier* became a platform to defy common criticism of Germany by signaling German dominance. The "gaucho dance" can, then, be interpreted as a way to show German confidence rooted in German national pride and collective German identity. The performance, even more importantly, shows that the climate of the FIFA World Cup in 2014, like that of previous World Cups, is perceived as a safe space for the overt expression of patriotism.

Media Narratives in Response to Gaucho Gate's *Overt Patriotism*

Indeed, the overt patriotism that was shown by the German players by mocking their Argentinian rivals was perceived with mixed feelings by the German media. Several narratives surrounding "gaucho gate" viewed the dance as not fundamentally inappropriate. One narrative, for instance, viewed the German's mockery of their opponents as a common aspect of competitive sport. Statements like the following, published by Michael Pilz in *Die Welt* on July 17, 2014, were common in the aftermath of the mocking performance: "*Fussball ist nicht nur das grösste und schönste Spiel der Welt. Im Stadion finden Stammesfehden statt, die im zivilen Leben gütlich beigelegt sein sollen*" [Soccer is not only the biggest and most beautiful game on earth. In the stadium, tribal conflicts are played out that are reconciled in civil life]. Articles like these illustrate that a clear distinction is made between the sport of soccer and civil life. The playing field is constructed as a site in which friendly competition is welcomed and in which conflicts can be fought out. The association of the soccer field as "tribal" underlines the construction of the sport as a primitive site of conflict that is clearly distinguished from the real life off the field.

A second narrative that dominated the German media argued that the "gaucho dance" was a result of the overwhelming emotions of the soccer players who, after all, had just won the soccer World Cup. The German newspaper *BILD Zeitung* wrote on July 16: "*Der Gaucho-Jubel auf der Fanmeile in Berlin nach sieben Wochen höchster Anspannung ist nur ein harmloser Freuden-Gesang*" [The Gaucho celebration on the Fanmeile in Berlin after seven weeks of tension and pressure is no more than harmless joyful singing]. In another article on the same day, the newspaper argued that "our World Champions celebrated like kids." The media, in both instances, herewith attempts to downplay the controversy of the dance by comparing the players' actions to boyish celebrations that should not be taken too seriously. Through the positioning of the dance as a harmless expression of joy and pride, these media voices attempt to decrease the political charge of the actions.

Another related narrative defending the actions of the German national team players emerged in the aftermath of *gaucho gate*. This narrative argued that the critics of the "gaucho dance" were simply overreacting. In an article from July 17, 2014, the *BILD Zeitung* writes: "*Die Diskussion um den Gaucho-Tanz ist typisch deutsch. Und aus diesem Tanz einen Skandal zu stricken, ist absurd, kleinkariert, humorless und völlig daneben*" [The discussion surrounding the gaucho dance is typical for Germany. To turn this dance into a scandal is absurd, narrow-minded, and completely inappropriate]. Here, the *BILD Zeitung* relies on German stereotypes to expose the insecurity of many Germans when it comes to being patriotic. However, it calls this insecurity "absurd, narrow-minded, and completely inappropriate" in order to restore a collective national identity that seemed to have suffered from the incident. The overreaction by the critics is herewith dismissed as being typical of a Germany that is not ready to be as patriotic as the German soccer players.

The narratives in the media approving the patriotic "gaucho dance" have one important feature in common: They all show a clear plea for depoliticizing the actions at the *Siegesfeier*. As Andrian Kreye from the *Sueddeutsche Zeitung* put it in an article published on July 17, 2014: "*Die Debatte erzählt weniger über die Gesinnung von Fussballspielern als einiges über den Stand der politischen Korrektheit in Deutschland*" [The debate tells us more about the state of political correctness in Germany than about the political attitudes of soccer players]. Here, the media outlet criticizes that being patriotic does not seem to be politically correct in Germany. However, showing national pride during sports tournaments has become very common in Germany in recent decades, which is why this narrative argues that actions in the context of sport should not be scrutinized for its political meaning.

While the majority of the media defended the actions of the German players and called for a de-politicization of the "gaucho dance" incident, some media outlets harshly criticized the performance of the players as being contra-productive in the representation of contemporary Germany. One such narrative was expressive of the fear that the "gaucho dance" jeopardized the newly created image of Germany abroad. For instance, in an article from July 15, 2014, journalist Frank Lübberding wrote for the *Frankfurter Allgemeine Zeitung*: "*Die Siegesfeier am Brandenburger Tor wird zum gigantischen Eigentor. Mit einer üblen Persiflage auf ihren Finalgegner verspielen die deutschen Weltmeister das Image der weltoffenen, toleranten Nation*" [The Siegesfeier at the Brandenburg Gate becomes a gigantic own goal. With a nasty persiflage of their final opponent, the German World Champions destroy their image as an open-minded, tolerant nation]. The *Frankfurter Allgemeine Zeitung*, as such, dispraises the "gaucho dance" due to its discriminatory nature, which according to the news platform does not represent the image of the "new Germany," which is characterized as modern, open-minded, and tolerant. The players jeopardized this image with their dance by mocking the Argentinian rivals and thus marking them as inferior.

In a similar narrative, some media voices argued that the discourse surrounding "gaucho gate" does not only jeopardize the image of the German nation abroad, but does also interrupt a collective German identity within the country. As Bertram Eisenhauer and Jörg Thomann, writers for the *Frankfurter Allgemeine Zeitung*, state in an article from July 19, 2014: "*Dann wurde unser einig Weltmeisterland von einem hässlichen Riss durchzogen: Wir sind halt doch nicht wir, sondern immer noch die einen und die anderen*" [Then our united World Champion nation was marked by a devastating disruption: We are not "we" yet, but rather still the ones and the others]. With the country's past as a both physically and psychologically divided country, this statement is charged with significant cultural meaning, for it acknowledges the inconsistency and fragility of a collective German identity in the context of the FIFA World Cup.

Conclusion: Soccer, German National Identity and "Gaucho Gate"

I opened this essay by recounting my own personal experience related to Germany's win of the 2014 FIFA World Cup in order to locate myself within my research. More importantly, however, I shared the anecdote at the beginning to underline how incredibly emotional the soccer game was for me—partly due to the overt display of patriotism for the country I grew up in that I was not used to seeing outside of the sporting world. Similarly, previous research has suggested that the FIFA World Cup has been a safe space for Germans to create and reinforce national pride, patriotism, and a collective identity free from the country's troubled Nazi past. In what has been termed the "gaucho dance," several players of the German national team attempted to contribute to an atmosphere of national pride by constructing a collective German national identity that was in alignment with the hyper-patriotic character of the *Siegesfeier*. Indeed, it was the construction of the *Siegesfeier* as the ultimate spectacle celebrating the German nation that provided a platform for the athletes to make an overtly patriotic statement. While similar patriotic sentiments have been rather common during mega sporting events like the FIFA World Cup, it was the performance of the "gaucho dance" that inspired harsh responses both within the country and abroad.

By analyzing the *Siegesfeier* itself as well as the media narratives emerging in the coverage of the incident, this essay aimed to unravel the underlying assumptions attached to the construction of national identity and nationhood in contemporary Germany by situating the highly controversial "gaucho dance" in the context of the country's troubling relationship to overt patriotism that resulted from Germany's horrific past. In contrast to previous studies, this analysis shows that, for the German people, soccer is not necessarily an area in which "safe patriotism" can be practiced, and the realm of German sport is far from being freed of the country's troubling past. It may be for this reason that the majority of the German media was defensive of the German soccer players performing the "gaucho dance" and called for a strict de-politicization of the *Siegesfeier*.

Yet, the few critical narratives in the discourse surrounding the mediated sporting event show that patriotism in Germany is not yet placed above reproach, as implied by Zambon's (2012) study of the FIFA World Cup 2006. The analysis of the narratives emerging in response to *gaucho gate* clearly imply that the taboo against the public expression of overt national pride in Germany is still in existence. Put more accurately, it is the discourse itself that shows that German soccer is far from being a safe space for overt expression of patriotism and national pride. *Gaucho gate*, then, is a glaring reminder that "in the current climate in Germany, football is always an issue of political significance" (Eggers 2006, 226).

At a time when the players were constructed as national symbols and thus a source of national identification for the viewers of the *Siegesfeier*, the responses to *gaucho gate* reveal that the players' mockery dance was a clear disruption of the supposedly safe display of patriotism in soccer. As such, *gaucho gate* provides valuable insight into the complex relationship between German national identity and overt patriotism during the 2014 FIFA World Cup, as the media narratives that resulted in response to *gaucho gate* emphasize that soccer patriotism and German national identity remains a highly scrutinized, vague, and fragile construct in 21st century Germany.

REFERENCES

Amsler, Peter. 1995. *Was Eint Und Was Trennt Die Deutschen? Stimmungs-Und Meinungsbilder Nach Der Vereinigung*. Mainz: Forschungsgruppe Deutschland am Institut für Politikwissenschaft der Johannes Gutenberg-Universität Mainz.
Anderson, Benedict. 1991. *Imagined Communities: Reflections on the Origin and Spread of Nationalism*. London: Verso.
Boyle, Raymond, and Richard Haynes. 2009. *Power Play: Sport, the Media and Popular Culture*. Edinburgh: Edinburgh University Press.
Brencis, Ainars, and Jacob Ikkala. 2013. "Sports as a Component of Nation Branding Initiatives: The Case of Latvia." *Marketing Review* 13: 241–254. Accessed February 1, 2017. doi:10.1362/146934713X13747454353538.
Brookes, Rod. 2002. *Representing Sport*. London: Arnold.
Crolley, Elizabeth, and David Hand. 2001. "France and the English Other: The Mediation of National Identities in Post-War Football Journalism." *The Web Journal of French Media Studies* 4. Accessed September 3, 2016.

Eggers, Erik. "All Around the Globus: A Foretaste of the German Football Imagination, C. 2006." In *German Football: History, Culture, Society*, edited by Alan Tomlinson and Christopher Young, 225–237. New York: Routledge.

Eisenhauer, Betram, and Jörg Thomann. 2014. "Ich Stimme Das Einfach Mal An." *Frankfurter Allgemeine Zeitung*, July 19. Accessed May 5, 2016. http://www.faz.net/aktuell/gesellschaft/menschen/gaucho-tanz-und-merkel-lied-peinliche-auftritte-13054724.html.

Faiola, Anthony. 2014. "Racist or Playful? the German Soccer Team's 'gaucho Dance.'" *The Washington Post*, July 16. Accessed July 1, 2016. https://www.washingtonpost.com/news/worldviews/wp/2014/07/16/racist-or-playful-the-german-soccer-teams-gaucho-dance/?utm_term=.9060730420e3.

Geisler, Michael E. 2005. *National Symbols, Fractured Identities: Contesting the National Narrative*. Middlebury: Middlebury College Press.

Gethard, Gregg. 2006. "How Soccer Explains Post-War Germany." *Soccer & Society* 7: 51–61. Accessed September 6, 2016. doi: 10.1080/14660970500355587.

Hall, Stuart. 1991. "Old and New Identities, Old and New Ethnicities." In *Culture, Globalization and the World-System*, edited by Anthony D. King, 41–68. London: Macmillan.

Heinrich, Arthur. 2003. "The 1954 Soccer World Cup and the Federal Republic of Germany's Self-Discovery." *American Behavioral Scientist* 46: 1491–1505. Accessed August 15, 2016. doi: 10.1177/0002764203046011003.

Hobsbawm, Eric, and Terence Ranger. 1983. *The Invention of Tradition*. Cambridge: Cambridge University Press.

Ismer, Sven. 2011. "Embodying the Nation: Football, Emotions and the Construction of Collective Identity." *Nationalities Papers* 39: 547–565. Accessed September 14, 2016. doi:10.1080/00905992.2011.582864.

Kassing, Jeffrey W., Andrew C. Billings, Robert S. Brown, Kelby K. Halone, Kristen Harrison, Bob Krizek, Lindsey J. Mean, and Paul D. Turman. 2004. "Communication in the Community of Sport: The Process of Enacting (Re)producing, Consuming, and Organizing Sport." *Communication Yearbook*, 28: 373–408. Accessed August 2, 2016. doi: 10.1080/23808985.2004.11679040.

Kreye, Andrian. 2014. "Wer Verliert, Wird Brüskiert." *BILD Zeitung*, July 17. Accessed May 8, 2016. http://www.sueddeutsche.de/kultur/gaucho-tanz-wer-verliert-wird-brueskiert-1.2049695.

Lübberding, Frank. 2014. "So Gehen Gauchos." *Frankfurter Allgemeine Zeitung*, July 15. Accessed May 2, 2016. http://www.faz.net/aktuell/feuilleton/medien/tv-kritik-empfang-der-weltmeister-so-gehen-gauchos-13047240.html.

Martinez, Dolores Fernández. 2007. "From Theory to Method: A Methodological Approach Within Critical Discourse Analysis." *Critical Discourse Studies* 4: 125–140. Accessed July 23, 2016. doi: 10.1080/17405900701464790.

McDonald, Mary G., and Susan Birrell. 1999. "Reading Sport Critically: A Methodology for Interrogating Power." *Sociology of Sport Journal* 16: 283–300. Accessed February 25, 2016. doi: 10.1123/ssj.16.4.283.

McKee, Alan. 2001. "A Beginner's Guide to Textual Analysis." *Metro* 127/128: 138–149. Accessed March 1, 2016.

Mutz, Michael. 2012. "Patrioten Für Drei Wochen: Nationale Identifikation Und Die Fußballeuropameisterschaft 2012." *Berliner Journal Für Soziologie* 22: 517–538. Accessed September 5, 2016. doi:10.1007/s11609–013–0201-z.

O'Donnell, Hugh. 1994. "Mapping the Mythical: A Geopolitics of National Sporting Stereotypes." *Discourse and Society* 5: 345–380. Accessed November 28, 2016. doi: 10.1177/0957926594005003005.

Pilz, Michael. 2014. "Wenn Die Gauchos Rückgrat Zeigen." *Die Welt*, July 17. Accessed May 4, 2016. https://www.welt.de/print/die_welt/kultur/article130240705/Wenn-die-Gauchos-Rueckgrat-zeigen.html.

Polley, Martin. 2004. "Sport and National Identity in Contemporary England." In *Sport and National Identity in the Post-War World*, edited by Dilwyn Porter and Adrian Smith, 10–30. London: Routledge.

Steenveld, Lynette, and Larry Strelitz. 1998. "The 1995 Rugby World Cup and the Politics of

Nation-Building in South Africa." *Media, Culture & Society* 20: 609–629. Accessed November 27, 2016. doi: 10.1177/016344398020004006.
"Unsere 'Gaucho-Tänzer' in Südamerika Als Nazis Beschimpft." 2014. *BILD Zeitung*, July 16. Accessed May 3, 2016. http://www.bild.de/sport/fussball/nationalmannschaft/gaucho-taenzer-in-argentinien-als-nazis-beschimpft-36840460.bild.html.
Wittlinger, Ruth. 2010. *German National Identity in the Twenty-First Century: A Different Republic After All?* Houndmills, Basingstoke, Hampshire: Palgrave Macmillan.
Zambon, Kate. 2012. "Constructing Patriotism Above Reproach: The Rehabilitation of German National Pride in the 2006 World Cup." Paper presented at the annual meeting for the International Communication Association, Phoenix, Arizona, May 24–28.

National Identities and International Sport
What About the Women?

Ali Bowes

Abstract

Historically, the nation has been considered to be made by men, for men (Gellner, 1983), and the nation as an imagined community seeming "more real as a team of eleven named people" (Hobsbawm, 1990, p. 143). As such, much research on sport and national identity has focused primarily on the role of men. However, women have a pivotal role in the nation more generally, one that is by no means confined to biological reproduction (Yuval-Davis, 1997). Yet, the relationship between women, the construction of nations, and the reproduction of national identities remains under-researched, particularly in the realm of sport. Women have been regularly excluded in literature on sporting nationalisms, and because women have been written out of the nation, and subsequently out of analyses on sport and the nation, their experiences have been ignored.

Of the wealth of research on men's sport and national identities, few research studies actually focus on those who are the embodiments of the nation in sport—the athletes themselves—and when this is the case, these very athletes are often men. Following Tuck (2003) and McGee and Bairner (2011) this essay demonstrates the need to ask those athletes who actually act as representatives of the nation about their identities and sense of belonging, and begins to address the relative absence of research on women, sport and national identity. As such, this essay centers on the complex relationship between sport, gender and nationhood, and more specifically the role of elite sportswomen in imagining the nation, by drawing upon data from interviews with 19 international female sporting representatives. It is argued here that international sport, as a site for the performance of national identities, provides an avenue whereby women can legitimately represent and actively embody the nation.

Considering the nation in relation to sport requires an initial understanding of what nations and nationalism are, and what connects them. There have been multiple approaches to explaining the development, and persistence, of national communities. Anderson proposes that the nation, nationality, nationalism have all proved notoriously difficult to define.[1] Common concerns within the study of nationalism are the lack of agreement about what nationalism is, what nations are, and how we are to define nationality.[2] There are numerous debates within the field of nationalism about the origins of nations. Smith proposes that in the past, "many scholars and most of the educated public assumed that nations and nationalism were, if not primordial, at least perennial"; nations can be found everywhere in historical record.[3] Most scholars would now appear to have abandoned this old perennialist paradigm in favor of modernism, which assumes nations were created following the industrial revolution. However, modernism has not been uncontested. In particular, it has come under attack from those historians who still regard at least some of today's nations and even their nationalisms, as pre-modern.

The modernist paradigm proposes that nationalism was "invented" in the wake of the political and economic revolutions of the 18th century in Europe. So, while Smith believes the concept of the nation predates the ideology of nationalism, modernists such as Gellner dispute this, stating that "it is nationalism which engenders nations, and not the other way around."[4] More recently, Hobsbawm's theory of "invention of tradition" and Anderson's work on "imagined communities" have been central in debates surrounding the nation.[5] While it is beyond the scope of this essay to present an in depth discussion on the quandaries of nationalism, there is one common factor that does unite the multiple sociological and historical explanations on the origins of the nation—the absence of discussion on the role that women have played.

Yuval-Davis, who has been central in feminist interpretations of nationalism, confirms that most hegemonic theorizations about nations and nationalism have treated gender relations as irrelevant.[6] Indeed, leading theorists of nations, such as the aforementioned Anderson and Hobsbawm, while mentioning gender in their works, failed to elaborate on its importance. Subsequently, Whitehead et al. explain that "nationalism is gendered—women's bodies are the boundary of the nation, and the bearers of its future."[7] The construction and naturalization of gender differences have an impact on every area of social life and, consequently, there is no reason to believe that the social organization of nations and nationalism is exempt from their influence.[8]

Pettman explains how the gender politics of nations and nationalism are complex, "including both the gendering of the nation as female and the construction of women as mothers of the nation, responsible for its physical, cultural and social reproduction."[9] Consequently, women's roles in the nation are often linked to their reproductive ability; thus, Yuval-Davis and Anthias identify five ways in which women have participated in national and nation-state processes and practices:

1. as biological reproducers of members of ethnic collectivities;
2. as reproducers of the (normative) boundaries of ethnic/national groups;
3. as participating centrally in the ideological reproduction of the collectivity and as transmitters of its culture;
4. as signifiers of ethnic/national differences;
5. as participants in national, economic, political and military struggles.[10]

This framework highlights not only the practical but also the symbolic nature of women's national positioning; fundamentally women have a pivotal role in the nation that is by no means confined to biological reproduction. Regardless of this, Nagel contends that still "the idea of the nation and the history of nationalism are intertwined with the idea of manhood and the history of manliness."[11]

Moving forward, many scholars highlight a progression into a global world. Globalization processes have been heralded as a possible catalyst for the end of nationalism, with countries on the surface appearing so similar in appearance and action. However, one social practice which serves as a reminder of nationhood is sport, and it has been claimed that "sport is clearly linked to the construction and reproduction of the national identities of many people."[12] It is thus essential to contemplate more closely the relationship between sport and the nation, considering how, when or where gendered relations intersect.

Sport, the Nation and Gender Relations

Sport plays a central role in inculcating national sentiment. As Cronin and Mayall explain, "sport is a vehicle, in a variety of ways, for the construction of individual, ethnic and national identities."[13] Allison describes how the setting of international sport is especially relevant in developing national identities; the frequently displayed flags, the sung national anthems, the wearing of national colors and emblems, all by large crowds, "are as easy and appropriate a setting for collective expressions of national identity as one could devise."[14] For important international tournaments and games, fans arrive to watch with faces painted and wearing national colors or replica kits; on special occasions flags are hung outside houses and pubs nationwide; "the most popular form of nationalist behavior in many countries is in sport."[15] Many authors on the relationship between sport and national identity highlight that the nation appears to become more "real" in the domain of sport, on the terraces or on the athletics tracks.[16] Indeed, Harris and Clayton, argue that Anderson's concept of an "imagined community" is, "in many cases, (re)created through sport."[17]

Clearly sport plays a central role in the formation of national identity. However, the sport that is central to recreating the national imagined community is often considered a male-only domain. Smith and Porter highlighted how England's sporting men play a central role in defining national identity.[18] Hobsbawm had concluded that "the imagined community of millions seems more real as a team of eleven named people," although it is hard to conceive he thought those eleven people were anything other than men.[19] Indeed, Hobsbawm argued that sport, at least for males, has proved uniquely effective in generating a sense of belonging to the nation.

Like the nation, it has long been considered that sport is "an institution created by and for men."[20] Sport orientates itself according to male values and norms, to the extent that, throughout history, women's struggles to participate in sport and be accepted as athletes has been constantly evident.[21] As a male preserve, sport has provided an avenue for the demonstration of not only national identity but also masculinity, in opposition to which femininity has been defined. In its organization, sport appears to maintain the binaries of both sex and gender, despite various social theorists moving to look at gender in more multiple, fluid ways. Notably, Judith Butler's contestation that the categories of sex, gender and desire are the products of particular power formations, rather than natural in formation.[22] Butler discusses the performative nature of gender identity, and illustrates the way in which these categories are produced and maintained through a variety of social practices including sport. Butler challenges those distinctions between sex and gender which see sex as the biological basis upon which gender is simply inscribed. Instead gendered subjectivity is acquired through repeated performance by the individual of discourses of gender. Thus rather than being a gender, we "do" a gender. Butler notes that "gender proves to be performance—that is, constituting an identity it is purported to be," thus gender is an act that brings into being what it names—masculine men or feminine women.[23]

Women who participate in the masculine domain of competitive sport are often seen to be going against the gender norm. With this in mind, female athletes are often under pressure to look feminine and display feminine behavior (as such, performing heteronormative femininity) in order to compensate for their "unfeminine" actions when playing sport. As Cox and Thompson explain, "female athletes, who deviate from the 'norms' of femininity by having ... athletic bodies, are challenged overtly or covertly about their sexuality."[24] Subsequently, Hargreaves noted that "women athletes feel the necessity to conform to dominant images of heterosexual femininity because female muscularity is treated as a sign of masculinization."[25] The continued stigmatization of athletic women helps to maintain sport as a male domain, with the labeling of sportswomen as homosexuals further problematizing the relationship of the nation's women (as supposed reproducers) to sport.

A limiting factor for women's capabilities in sport is the association of female athleticism and female sex appeal.[26] Central to this discourse is the media and popular press, which have played an integral role in stereotyping female athletes in accordance with heterosexual femininity. Representations of women in sport portrayed to us by the media restrict our imagination about women's sport and what women can achieve. Birrell and Theberge explain that "media images misrepresent, distort, trivialize, marginalize and heterosexualize women athletes rather than presenting them as serious, talented and hardworking."[27] More recently, Bruce describes how the sports media can simultaneously challenge and reinforce dominant assumptions that sport is primarily a male domain.[28] Ultimately, sport is overwhelmingly constructed in the mass media as a male domain, with professional male sport represented as the pinnacle of sporting value and achievement.

When women do find themselves represented on the sports pages of the popular press, they are represented in notably different ways from men. Bruce explains that when women receive media coverage, "extensive international research has shown that the media have historically used five techniques to represent women in line with cultural ideas about femininity," as identified initially by Wensing and Bruce.[29] In *gender marking*, an event is presented as a women's event, with the men's version as *the* event, and the implication that women's sport is inferior. The technique of *compulsory heterosexuality* means that journalists present female athletes as sex objects, or portray them in heterosexual roles such as wife/mother/girlfriend. The emphasis of *appropriate femininity* focuses on traditional notions of acceptable feminine physical or emotional characteristics or behaviors. *Infantilization* presents sportswomen as girls, thus undermining their sporting achievements. Finally, the *downplaying of sport*, which focuses on non-sport-related aspects such as appearance, family, personal life, alternative careers and comparisons to male athletes, demeans female performance and reinforces the idea that, for women, sports performance and success and secondary to other things, including male sporting success. It was also noted that while evidence of these five rules remain, in many cases this approach appears to have given way to a framing technique they have termed *ambivalence*, by which positive descriptions and images of women athletes are juxtaposed with descriptions and images that undermine and trivialize women's efforts and successes.

However, Wensing and Bruce described the ways in which media coverage of international sporting events may be less likely to be marked by gendered discourses.[30] These "media rules" are "bent" when presenting international sportswomen who are representing and, more importantly, winning for the nation. Thus, national identity becomes important in these moments of sportswomen's success, with nationalism overriding the usual ways that the sports press report on female athletes. However, these situations are limited and it remains that women are often still subjected to the trivialization of their achievements.

National Sporting Women

Women continue to make inroads into traditional male sports and, in so doing, they are actively redefining readings of women's sports by blurring the boundaries between the traditional binary of masculinity and femininity. It is debatable the extent to which society accepts and celebrates women's participation and achievements in sport, particularly on the international stage. Willis questioned over twenty years ago how it is that "the meanest local fifth division, male works" team gets more respect, in popular consciousness, than a women's national team?[31] Not surprisingly, the relationship between women, the construction of nations, and the reproduction of national identities remains generally under researched. Furthermore, women have been systematically excluded from literature on sporting nationalisms, and as a result, their experiences have seldom been directly addressed. Much of the research that is concerned with national identity in sport utilizes a methodological approach which analyzes the role of the media in (re)producing a sense of national identity.[32] However, few research studies actually focus on those who embody the nation in sport—namely, the athletes themselves. This is confirmed by Holmes and Storey (2004: 95) who write, "little research into professional sportspeople's attitudes to issues of national identity has been undertaken." However, when such research has been conducted, the athletes in question have tended to be men.[33]

The research methodology used for this study involved a series of in-depth, semi-structured interviews with English sportswomen from cricket, football, netball and rugby union, conducted in 2011 and 2012, alongside articles from the popular press collected at the same time. The relatively unusual aspect of this research project is the participants are identifiable.

Flick explains that "the issue of confidentiality or anonymity may become problematic when you do research with several members of a specific setting."[34] It is much easier to identify the "real" person from the context information included in quotations, particularly in a setting such as elite, international level sport. In line with McGee and Bairner, and following institutional ethical approval, it was established with the participants that they would feature in the research as themselves, they would be named, and the personal details about their sporting lives would be retold in full.[35] Whilst anonymity can protect the participants, it can also deny them "the very voice in the research that must originally have been claimed as its aim."[36] Following Tuck and Maguire, "this collection of emotions, attitude and feelings provides some original evidence for viewing national identities 'at play' through the eyes of elites sports[wo]men."[37]

Sport and National Identity

> BETH MORGAN: "I think it is really important for national identity I guess, and something that unites the country. Probably like nothing else, I'm not sure there is an equivalent to sport."

The participants, as national representatives, perhaps unsurprisingly noted the importance of sport in the imagining of a sense of national identity. Specifically, sport proved to be one arena where England appeared real.[38] For most of the women interviewed, sport provided an important avenue through which they could express their national identification and not surprisingly, the participants believe that sport plays an important role when attempting to imagine a national collectivity:

> CHARLOTTE BARRAS: "I think it is because of national identities, because of national competition, because you are showcasing yourself, showing off to the world."
>
> KAREN CARNEY: "It's like a religion.... It's massive, it kind of gives an identity to certain countries, especially England."

A persistent theme throughout the narratives of the participants was the idea that the national dimension of sport enables the nation to come together in support of national teams. International sport was then seen to foster a sense of community within a nation. Sport was also understood to provide a platform from which a nation can display its culture and "show off," or perform, to the rest of the world. In particular, it seemed that football was the sport that was central to imagining the English nation:

> HARRIET MILLAR-MILLS: "I think it's important because, I don't know, it brings people closer together and stuff. Like in the [football] World Cup, everyone

just, when you are winning, everyone is so much happier, I don't know why it is, it's like England as a whole, it's like you're winning if England win."

OLIVIA MURPHY: "At different times I think it's massively important, obviously something like, the [football] World Cup ... when England are being represented ... there is a massive feel good factor ... although its short lived, I think from a nation's point of view it's the one time that people do seem to get together or feel quite passionate about something. I know not everyone likes sport but I think for those people that do it is a tie that they are brought together."

Here, some of the sportswomen alluded to the ways in which success in sport can reflect back upon the whole national society. In a sense, therefore, sport acts as a way to dull the people's awareness of the state of their society, through the "feel good factor." Sport is also a catalyst for bringing people together.

Others also identified rugby, as well as football and cricket, as symbolic of England:

BETH MORGAN: "What do you think of when you think of England ... well I immediately think of kind of the England football team ... cricket, rugby, whatever. So I think it is really important for national identity I guess, something that unites the country, probably like nothing else."

Tuck notes how particular sports often come to symbolize the nation, with rugby, cricket and football tied to particular types of Englishness.[39] Indeed, Smith and Porter claim:

Having once made the requisite leap and accepted that the eleven men who appear in white shirts at Wembley, or the fifteen at Twickenham, are "England," the possibilities for defining and redefining what it means to be "English" are inextricably linked to what happens on the field of play.[40]

Often, participants described the ways in which (male) athletes become representative of the nation:

SOPHIE RUSSELL: "Sport is like, possibly the only thing that brings everyone together, because of the national identity; even if you aren't interested in sport you want to know if England won the football. It's the one thing that brings everyone together, you know the time England were in the football World Cup, everyone in the country was interested in England and wanted to support England and then it's really important that England play well and the team itself represents well.... So yeh, it's really important ... the teams are representing the country on a world stage.... In football that's eleven people standing up for all of the country."

Sophie Russell highlights the eleven people standing up for all of the country, in a similar vein to Hobsbawm's contestation that the national community seems real in sport, embodied into the 11 people (read men) representing their nation on the pitch.[41] Despite both Hobsbawm and Sophie Russell using the term people, it remains likely that they both meant eleven men, rather than eleven women as representative of the whole nation.

Thus, on the sports field it is clear that it is men who are imagined as actively embodying the nation during international competition. Maguire and Poulton describe the ways in which male footballers, during major international tournaments, become embodiments of the nation in the popular press, with Tuck offering us the term "patriots at play."[42] It is evident that for the participants in this study too, male sport is symbolic of the nation and can help to foster a sense of togetherness and community. The participants allude to the sense of national pride that can be fostered through (men's) sport. As such, male athletes can become active embodiments of the nation. However, what about the role of women's sport in the national imagination?

Women's Sport and Nationalism

It is quite clear that many sportsmen, such as David Beckham, are often described as representatives of the English nation.[43] It was interesting to understand how the participants as national representatives themselves articulate the place of women's sport in the national imagination, and subsequently shed light on their own positioning within the nation.

> SARAH HUNTER: "I think if it was on TV more, and more publicized, people would get behind it.... When it becomes in the public eye people are interested and it's important to them. But until it gets to that point people don't even know it's happening, which is sad. It's like the women's cricket when they won ... everything they could have won, but because it wasn't really in the news or in the public eye, it wasn't important to people that didn't know about it. Which is, well, if it had been the men ... they would have been so proud."

The disappointment at the ways women's sport is represented in England, specifically the lack of media coverage of women's sport, is identified as key to its apparent subordination. Given the lack of publicity, women's sport in England cannot be seen as of similar importance to men's within the national consciousness, and as a result, it would appear that England's female athletes are perhaps not considered as embodiments of the nation in the same way or to the same extent as the men.

The lack of media attention was further highlighted as problematic:

> BETH MORGAN: "I think it should be exactly the same and as important as the men, obviously. I think realistically, I think if you asked a random person on the street, you know, what do you think of if you think of English sport, I think they would say the football team and the England rugby team and the cricket. Maybe the Olympic athletes. I think you may get the individual females, but I don't think people would ever think of the women's football

team bringing the nation together. And I think it's purely because of the coverage and the awareness of the public really.... I think it is difficult for female teams ... to get the same kind of recognition as the male teams."

It seems that for the women involved in international sport, the issue of recognition through media coverage is very significant. In this sense, it is worth critiquing media articles written about these very women. Many of the media reports that were collected centered on major international sporting events: the women's football team's appearance in the European Championship (EC) final in 2009, the women's football World Cup (FWC) in 2011, and the women's rugby team's appearance in the World Cup (RWC) final in 2010.

Media Representations of Women's Sport

It is often noted that the popular sports media persist in underreporting women's sports throughout most of the year. Wensing and Bruce confirm that "analyses of the western media conducted over the past 20 years have discovered consistent patterns of low coverage and inconsistent quality in women's sport, particularly in everyday sports reporting."[44] In 2011, Charlie Wyett explained that women's football in the UK "is no longer ridiculed but it is hardly taken seriously. Equally the game is not well supported."[45] His article in *The Sun* newspaper, titled "Hope 'n' Glory," features an interview with the current manager of England's women's football team, Hope Powell, who is quoted as saying:

> People are aware women's football exists. But does it get the kudos it deserves? Probably not. Do we get the air-time we deserve? Probably not. Generally, women's sports get a raw deal. Our women's cricket team is really successful but they do not get the airtime. Even women's tennis does not get as much coverage. Women's sport is not as valued as men's sport. Fact. Everyone needs to take it more seriously.[46]

Amol Rajan ran a feature in *The Independent*'s "Opinion and Debate" section, posing the "Big Question," "How did Britain's sportswomen become such world-beaters?" highlighting recent successes in football, cricket, cycling, swimming and athletics by England and/or Team GB.[47] Rajan notes that "despite improved representation in sports pages, women's success doesn't get the coverage of their male counterparts," before going on to state that "true parity will only come when the likes of our women cricket and football teams are in the headlines because of their lack of success, rather than the opposite."[48] Unsurprisingly, the lack of media coverage of women's sport compared to men's sport was something of which the participants were acutely aware:

OLIVIA MURPHY: "It's splashed across the papers that most of the sport that is represented is male-dominated."

KAREN CARNEY: "When you turn on the telly you know what the football score is for the men because it's in your face but for the women you've got to go and find it."

HARRIET MILLAR-MILLS: "I don't think they get as much media coverage, nowhere near as much as men, but then I don't think there is a following there. Like if there was a woman rugby player on the back page of the *Daily Mail*, I don't think a guy would want to pick it up."

Here Harriet identifies the ways in which the sports pages are written about men, for men, confirming what Billig emphasized in his work on banal nationalism.⁴⁹ The media plays a strong role in maintaining sport as strongly aligned with notions of masculinity, and the ignoring of women's sport maintains and reinforces the notion that sport is a male preserve. Throughout the period of data collection, media articles that were collected displayed the six techniques identified by Wensing and Bruce: gender marking, compulsory heterosexuality, appropriate femininity, infantilization, the downplaying of sport and ambivalence.⁵⁰ These six techniques will be discussed alongside extracts from the interviews with the participants.

In most media articles collected during the research process, gender was a dominant framing device. It was clear that articles reporting on women's sport were gender marked, whilst those on men's sport were not. In all articles, the headline, subheading and main body of text contained "women's" as a descriptor before the name of the sport or event (women's football, women's rugby, women's World Cup etc.). A Jonathon Brown article titled "The stars of Germany 2011* (*That's the Women's World Cup)," had the following subheading: "Their salaries and egos may be smaller, but they're ready to take on a man's world—and the England team could even win."⁵¹ Robin Scott-Elliot was given the following subheading for his article on the women's rugby World Cup: "As the Women's Rugby World Cup makes its live television debut, England's center tells Robin Scott-Elliot about life in a man's game."⁵² The identification of sport played by women as women's sport, compared to sport played by men as simply sport, highlights the ways in which women's sport participation can be marginalized and trivialized by the media. The infantilization of women's sport was also evident in some of the media articles analyzed. Following England's defeat in the EC final in Helsinki, the *Sun* ran an article with the title: "Hellsinki: Girls crushed by old enemy."⁵³ The front page of *The Daily Telegraph* the day after England lost the RWC final read: "Fearsome encounter for England rugby girls."⁵⁴

The downplaying of women's sport results in a focus on women's looks, relationships, sexual orientations and lives outside of sport that devalue their sporting identities. This was evident in two articles published on June 25,

2011, one in *The Sun* and one in *The Independent*. Both newspapers had decided to run a feature on the forthcoming women's World Cup, highlighting facts, figures and pictures of the women who were about to compete at the pinnacle of their sport. Rory Davidson's article, titled "USA will fly solo to win it," was noticeably smaller than *The Independent*'s article, but featured a summary of ten things their readers should know about women's football.[55] These included only three facts that were explicitly relevant to football: "best team," "best star," "best stats." Whilst also covering topics such as "best bruv," "best name" and "best muddle," "best riddle" draws attention to hearsay that "three players are suspected of being blokes." Furthermore, the "best ref" stat was included because of an incident where the referee in question was "famously accidently groped by an absent-minded player during a game." The subject of the article, obviously, had not been taken all that seriously by Davidson or *The Sun*.

Jonathon Brown's article, titled "The Stars of Germany 2011* (*That's the Women's World Cup)," again could be seen to downplay women's sport.[56] This article featured facts and pictures of 11 people involved in the women's football World Cup. Of these, there were four women in football kit, three of these were of the footballers in action, with the ball. Five of the pictures were of the footballers in non-sports clothes, with one picture of a player's husband, and another of a psychic octopus. The eleven categories were, similarly to those in *The Sun*, not always focused on the football event, despite the title of the article. Featured for their footballing ability were: Abby Wambach "The Tough Girl," Birgit Prinz "The Villain," Faye White, "The Tough Girl II," and Marta Viera da Silva, "The Special One," "dubbed Pelé in a skirt." Then there was Eniola Aluko, "The Intellectual," who was featured because of her first class law degree; Kelly Smith was presented as "The Hero," as the article focused on her struggle with alcoholism as well as her expected starring role for the England national team; and then "The Golden Girl" Jessica Landstrom, labeled "the sports original pin-up." After that there is Nadine Angerer, "The Bisexual Trailblazer"; "The Especially Controversial One" Genoveva Anonma, a footballer from Equatorial Guinea who has undergone a sex test; "The Male WAG" Adam Feely, an NFL footballer whose presence is seemingly more important than his wife's, who is a member of the U.S. national team; and "The Psychic Cephalopod" Lola the Octopus. It appears that the event itself had not really been taken seriously by the media in either article, with a focus on the lives, sexuality and careers of many of the women. Furthermore, there is evidence of ambivalence toward women's sport. As Wensing and Bruce explain, and what is clear here, is that positive descriptions and images of women in sport (such as the active photos and descriptions of the star players) are juxtaposed with descriptions and images which undermine and trivialize women's sport.[57]

It is often noted that journalists present women in ways that align with compulsory heterosexuality. Birrell and Theberge note, "media images ... heterosexualize women athletes."[58] Again, examples in the media articles collected provide evidence of the heterosexualization of female athletes, in some cases through the rejection of alternative forms of sexuality. Andrew Dillon wrote an article about the England's women's football team the day before their EC final match.[59] Instead of focusing on the importance of the game ahead, this article was rather trivial in nature. Initially discussing the television singing contest X Factor, Alex Scott, a senior member of England's squad, was then quoted as saying: "We don't have the equivalent of WAGs [wives and girlfriends], either. Some of us have boyfriends and they are at home working."[60]

Two members of the England women's rugby World Cup squad, in interviews with the media, describe occasions where there is surprise at their sporting careers due to their appearance not fitting in with perceptions of rugby players. In response to the question, "how do people react to you being a rugby player?," Rachel Burford responds: "The classic response from men is: 'you don't look like a rugby player.' 'What does one look like?' I always reply. It's been a long time since I heard any of the old stereotypes concerning women and rugby."[61] Not looking like a rugby player was also highlighted in an interview with Emily Scarratt: "When people ask me what I do and I tell them they say 'You don't look like a rugby player.' But it doesn't bother me what the wider population think."[62]

In an interview with rugby player Rachel Burford, Joanna McGarry asks: "Do you ever worry about being seen as butch?" This question highlights exactly how "butchness," and therefore lesbianism, is othered by the media, demonstrating how heteronormative femininity is the only appropriate gender performance for women whether they are in sport or not. Rachel's response was: "I am happy with how I look. Before Nike became our sponsor, we used to train in oversized men's shirts. Now we have fitted rugby kit designed specifically for women that feels much more feminine."[63] It is not only the media that presents sportswomen in a particular way, then, but the women who are interviewed are also complying with, and performing, notions of appropriate femininity and compulsory heterosexuality, often through a rejection of the butch stereotype and, by implication, lesbianism and homosexuality.

Media Framing of Women's International Sport

The sports media play an integral role in fostering national identity through sport. Newspapers can act to "remind" readers of their own nation and who they are, through what Billig termed "national flagging."[64] National flagging is often evident in reporting on men's sport, with words such as "we," "our" and "us" being used to link the men's national sports teams to national populations. However, the relationship between the media, women's sport and national identity is rarely researched. As Billig explains, "all the papers, whatever their politics, have a section in which the flag is waved with regular enthusiasm. This is the sports section."[65] These sporting pages define and repeat national stereotypes, which are distinctly masculine. As such, the "we" that the popular media presents to us is narrow and male, reinforcing the stereotype of who dominates the national sporting arena.

Nonetheless, Wensing and Bruce note that coverage of female representatives during international sports events "may be less likely to be marked by gendered discourses or narratives than reporting on everyday sports."[66] For this reason, it was important to try to incorporate, where possible, examples of media representations of England's sportswomen at this time, given the importance of the media in constructions of national identity, and their role in strengthening the relationship between national identity and sport with men and masculinity. In Bruce's media analysis on female athletes in New Zealand, the focus was on gender ideologies and the positioning of sportswomen who have represented their nation on the international stage.[67] She describes how coverage during major sports events demonstrates that "women who win for the nation are highlighted as worthy of attention."[68] Indeed, Bruce found that "in stark contrast to gender ideologies of female weakness, they were represented in ways that emphasized physical power, strength and domination."[69] She further states:

> Thus, from this analysis of print media coverage, it became apparent that the concepts of gender marking, compulsory heterosexuality, appropriate femininity, infantilization, downplaying sport and ambivalence, provided very little help in understanding the way that these female athletes were represented. In this case, nationalism almost completely overrode the usual ways that the sports media report on female athletes.[70]

Furthermore, Wensing and Bruce found how "generally accepted rules for media coverage of female athletes may be challenged under particular circumstances."[71] They note how it "appears that media conventions may be 'bent' to accommodate nationally important female sports stars."[72] It is certainly the case that in some media articles, England's sportswomen are highlighted as worthy of attention, and represented in ways that do not focus on their gender, but on their sporting performance for the nation.

Despite the women's football team losing 6–2 to Germany in the EC final, and the women's rugby team losing 13–10 to New Zealand in the RWC final, their appearance in a final was considered a success. Arguably, this was due, in part, to the failings of the men's football and rugby teams in major international tournaments in recent years (The England men's football team have not progressed past the quarterfinal stage of either the World Cup or the European championship since 1994, whilst the England men's rugby team did not make it out of the group stage during a home rugby World Cup in 2015). As a result, instead of focusing on femininity and sexuality, in the match reports of the two final appearances there was little or no evidence of gendered reporting. In stark contrast to gender ideologies of female weakness and passivity, the women were represented in ways that emphasized physical power, strength and domination:

> "England showed their resolve with some fearsome defending, one thumping tackle from Danielle Waterman on Brazier preventing what seems a certain try."[73]
>
> "When the final whistle went, England's rugby women slumped to the turf at The Stoop, battered and bruised, physically and mental shattered, having given 100 percent to wrest the World Cup from New Zealand."[74]
>
> "[England's] defeat was the stuff of legend. Heroic defense, last-ditch tackles made without a thought for personal safety, every ounce of effort left on the pitch."[75]

These three extracts highlight the ways in which England's rugby women were reported in the British press. Before the tournament, the media often focused on the lives of the women outside of sport, appearing to not take women's sport seriously. However, the immediate pre- and post-match reporting on the RWC final demonstrates a "bending of the rules," as described by Bruce.[76]

Given the importance of sport to national identity, most sports fans (with the help of the media) cast their sporting heroes in the role of "proxy warriors" for the nation.[77] Garland and Rowe identified how, during major international (men's) football tournaments (such as the World Cup), journalists seem to embrace George Orwell's characterization of (men's) sport as "war minus the shooting" by frequently drawing on military references to dramatize their accounts.[78] The use of such rhetoric by the media further links sport with war and national identity. There was some evidence of war metaphors in the match descriptions of women's sport. This was similar to the ways in which the sports media usually present male national athletes, and highlights how sportswomen can on occasion also assume the role of proxy warriors for the nation:

> "Battling England narrowly failed to dethrone the all-conquering Kiwis who have ruled women's world rugby for 16 years…. New Zealand had to fight every inch of the way."[79]
>
> "Against a team who were fast, accurate and crunchingly brutal, England did not hide from the physical battle from before the start, when they advanced in a line towards New Zealand as they performed the haka, to the final whistle…. England continued to put everything into the tackle…. Nothing illustrated their never-say-die attitude more than McGilchrist."[80]

These two extracts evoke war-like connotations in their descriptions of the match, using words such as "battle," "fight" and the imagery of advancing in line. Likewise, in an article titled "Overpowered: England can't halt the mighty Germans," the coach of the women's football team was quoted as saying "we didn't lie down and die," implying that the women carried on fighting until the very end.[81]

Furthermore, descriptions of the players themselves adopted war-like imagery:

> "Their bravery had been extraordinary, the strength of their willpower almost scary.... England's valor in defeat was magnificent.... Emily Scarratt put her body on the line to spectacular effect.... Barras's try ... was stunningly brave."[82]
>
> "Those who cannot comprehend that women have the same relish as men for the physical, the confrontational and the gladiatorial aspects of the game can be referred to Amy Garnett, a 34-year-old Metropolitan Police officer, England's hooker through two World Cups and a grueling 86 caps. 'It is definitely the battle up front that is the attraction.'"[83]
>
> "England have a fierce pack in which Rochelle Clark is an imposing scrummager and Amy Garnett a warlike hooker."[84]

Defining the sportswomen in this way allows them to be imagined as national, sporting "proxy warriors," in the same way that national sportsmen are presented in the press. However, this presentation is contextual, and only apparent in these exceptional circumstances, such as major championship final appearances.

Despite the positive presentation of the sportswomen, there were a few examples of reporting during this period that perhaps did not consistently take the sportswomen as seriously, even in special circumstances.

> "That Pocock subsequently left the field on a stretcher was unfortunate but, in a way, strangely reassuring. Had she bounced straight back to her feet it would have been definitive proof that women's rugby has not merely smashed through the glass ceiling of male indifference but entered a whole new stratosphere of concrete-limbed super-women."[85]

An article in the *Daily Mail* described the haka, performed at the RWC final by New Zealand, in less complimentary ways:

> "The New Zealand haka, or should that be hakette, was also more pleasing on the eye, a beguiling fusion of tribal challenge and South Sea island welcome committee."[86]

The haka is "one of New Zealand's most identifiable national sporting rituals," performed before entering the "battlefield of sport" to demonstrate a "unity of passion, commitment, and assertiveness."[87] Because the haka is used to intimidate the opposition, to describe the women's attempt as a "welcome committee" seems rather demeaning. However, comments like these were few and far between. Far more journalists were positive about the possibilities for women's sport:

> "Regardless of the outcome, the popular notion that women's rugby is but a pale imitation of the men's version has been lain to rest this past fortnight."[88]
>
> "Whoever wins today, England, the Ferns and the other teams must be congratulated for obliterating what convention, chauvinism, or maybe their own psyche, once saw as the limits of the sex."[89]

On the whole, during the reporting of important international events such as the RWC and EC final, it appeared that nationalism overrode the usual ways in which the sports media present women athletes. It seems possible that some women's sport can be symbolic of the nation. Vincent, Kian and Pederson note how "the national soccer team is central to both national and masculine identity in England," explaining that "it has traditionally been associated with an ethos of high physical work rate, honest endeavor, commitment and the notion of fair play."[90] The presentations of the women in this way open up a space for them in the English national consciousness. Through the media discourse, the English women were presented as the (almost) national heroines, embodying a specific type of (masculine) Englishness during the eighty or ninety-minutes of play. This is made possible when nationalism overrides gender in the reporting of events. This idea of the "almost" national heroines, somewhat in the shadow of the men, was something that resonated with the participants themselves, in their discussions on what it meant to be a sportswoman.

Being Sportswomen

Being a sportswoman appeared to be a defining part of the participants' identities. As Collinson and Hockey state, "the concept of identity *per se* has of course been highly problematized within postmodernist writings, with their focus on the fluidity of subjectivities."[91] Consequently, it is important to realize the fluid and contextual nature of subjectivity. Not surprisingly, given the performance level of the participants, as well as the amount of time, dedication and commitment these women have put into their sporting careers, their sporting identity was indeed central to their sense of self, and integral to how they defined themselves.

> SERENA GUTHRIE: "I like being [a sportswoman] ... I've never had anyone tell me I couldn't do it because I'm a woman.... I always say I don't know what I'd do if I didn't play a sport really, if I didn't play netball.... Just because it's such a big part of our lives."
>
> STACEY FRANCIS: "I think it's massively part of my identity at the moment, because although I'm also a student I think I would say I was an athlete first,

and that's the first thing that most people would identify me for ... so yeh, I think, yeh I think being an athlete for me is quite important."

Sophie Russell explains that for her, being a woman can offer the "best of both worlds," as "it's alright for women to play sport and be strong and to display more masculine features than they could before." So for Sophie Russell, the progression of women's sport represents a positive development for women. According to her, playing sport allows these women to actively redefine who women are and what they are capable of, and for these women that often meant on a national stage. Claire Allen answered: "I think for me it's quite a lot to do with, I'm not like a feminist or anything like that but I'm quite into doing everything on equal. So, like doing the same things as blokes, so in work, training wise.... I like to be seen as an equal almost." Similarly to Sophie, for Claire, sport represents an avenue where women can prove themselves, and be seen as equals in the man's world of sport. However, for some participants, being a woman represented a stumbling block to their ambitions:

> CHARLOTTE BARRAS: "I don't think it actually matters whether I was, whatever. Yeh, I have achieved what I wanted to achieve so I don't think it matters. Obviously I am extremely disappointed that I'm not a man in the sense that I can't be paid to do my sport...."
> KATHERINE BRUNT: "It sucks [laughs]! What does it mean? I don't know. Well in my life it sort of means that you get a step down from everything. With me being an athlete, you get less pay, less facilities, less treatment.... I'd say it means less."

For Charlotte, despite the initial insistence that sex does not matter, being a woman in sport clearly raised issues, as it did for Katherine. For these participants, being a woman in sport simply means facing inequality. History tells us that women's involvement in sport has been characterized by inequality and discrimination, and what is evident here is perhaps the England's sportswomen still regard that to be the case.

Concluding Remarks

Bowes and Bairner highlighted the importance of the "summer of 2015" for women's national sport in England.[92] The netball and football teams picked up bronze medals in their respective world championships, following the cricket team's second place finish during 2014 in the Twenty20 world championship format. The rugby team, however, went one better and collected the rugby World Cup trophy after a convincing win over Canada. Results such as these thrust England's sportswomen into the national popular consciousness. Whilst these successes were celebrated by many across England, there were still timely reminders of their positioning within the national sporting arena; a "tweet" by England's football association on social media website Twitter stating "our lionesses go back to being mothers, partners and daughters today, but they have taken on another title—heroes."[93]

Clearly, women have a pivotal role in the nation, but it is one that is by no means confined to biological reproduction.[94] Despite this, the relationship between women, the construction of nations, and the reproduction of national identities remains under researched, particularly in the sociology of sport. Women have been systematically excluded in literature on sporting nationalisms, and because women have been written out of the nation, and subsequently out of analyses on sport and the nation, their experiences have largely been ignored. By attempting to address this imbalance, this essay seeks to highlight the experiences, and representations, of international sportswomen.

In the player's eyes, men's sport is an important source of national pride, and a central part of English national culture. However, as for women's sport, the participants describe that a persistent lack of media attention dulls public awareness of their achievements. This leaves the majority of the nation's sportswomen on the sidelines, and perhaps not considered as national sporting heroines. It is clear, however, that the relationship between women, sport and the nation is much more complex than this.

Given that sport is identified as a male-domain that valorizes masculine-defined characteristics, it appears obvious that it does not represent an arena in which femininity is appropriate, as the participants explained. However, as sportswomen who represent England at the highest possible level, these women can negotiate what Krane highlighted as the female/athlete paradox, through the performance of different types of femininities.[95] These performances are contextual and highlight the fluidity of gender identities. Women representing their nation in sport are women who actively push the limits of their bodies and also the boundaries of femininity.[96] Malcom confirms that "female athletes no longer downplay the traditionally masculine traits of aggression and toughness as they relate to the athletic competition."[97] This is certainly the case with the women who were interviewed—proud of their dedication, their determination and their toughness in the sporting environment. They understand that being weak and passive will not help them to succeed especially in the male-dominated arena of competitive team sports and, in particular, during international representation. Similarly, media representations of women's national sporting success align with the ideas that perhaps our female sports stars do not have to be feminine too.

On June 22, 2011, Hope Powell was quoted as saying, "let's not make it a gender issue. Let's talk about football, not whether someone's male or female."[98] However, success in major international competitions seems to open up an avenue for sportswomen to be presented as legitimate national representatives, rather than discussed in terms of their femininity and heterosexuality. Edensor argues that one of the most powerful forms of popular national performance is to be found in sport.[99] As sporting representatives, these women have a role in the nation that is distinct from those identified by Yuval-Davis and Anthias.[100] As Wensing and Bruce revealed, success in major international competitions opens up an avenue for sportswomen to be presented as legitimate national representatives, rather than discussed solely in terms of their femininity and heterosexuality (and subsequently as the nation's mothers).[101] As Bowes and Bairner highlight, international sportswomen on the international sporting field can become active embodiments of their nation.[102] Their reflections (and their representations) demonstrate that in sport, those who represent the nation, and who are the embodiments, heroes, and proxy warriors of their nation, need not always be men.

Notes

1. Benedict Anderson, *Imagined Communities* (London: Verso, 2006).
2. David McCrone, *The Sociology of Nationalism: Tomorrow's Ancestors* (London: Routledge, 1998).
3. Antony Smith, *The Nation in History: Historiographical Debates About Ethnicity and Nationalism* (Cambridge: Polity, 2000), 27.
4. Antony Smith, *Nationalism: Theory, Ideology, History* (Cambridge: Polity, 2001); Ernest Gellner, *Nations and Nationalism* (New York: Cornell University Press, 1983), 55.
5. Eric Hobsbawm, "Introduction: Inventing Traditions," in *The Invention of Tradition*, eds. Eric Hobsbawm and Terrance Ranger (Cambridge: Cambridge University Press, 1983): 1–15; Anderson, *Imagined Communities*.
6. Nira Yuval-Davis, *Gender and Nation* (London: Sage, 1997).
7. Anita Whitehead et al., "Nationalisms and National Identities Editorial," *Feminist Review* 44, no. 1 (1993): 1.
8. Graham Day and Andrew Thompson, *Theorizing Nationalism* (Basingstoke: Palgrave Macmillan, 2004).
9. Jan Pettman, *Worlding Women: A Feminist International Politics* (Sydney: Allen Unwin, 1996): 187.
10. Nira Yuval-Davis and Floya Anthias, *Woman-Nation-State* (London: Palgrave Macmillan, 1989).
11. Joane Nagel, "Gender, Sexuality and Nationalism," in *Nations and Nationalism: A Global Historical Overview*, eds. Guntram Herb and David Kaplan (California: ABC Clio, 2008): 900.
12. Alan Bairner, *Sport, Nationalism and Gloalization: European and North American Perspectives* (Albany: State University Press, 2001): 1.
13. Mike Cronin and David Mayall, "Sport and Ethnicity: Some Introductory Remarks," in *Sporting Nationalisms: Identity, Ethnicity, Immigration and Assimilation*, eds. Mike Cronin and David Mayall (London: Frank Cass & Co., 1998): 1–2.
14. Lincoln Allison, "Sport and Nationalism," in *Handbook of Sports Studies*, eds. Jay Coakley and Eric Dunning (London: Sage, 2000): 351.
15. James Kellas, *The Politics of Nationalism and Ethnicity* (London: Palgrave Macmillan, 1991): 21.
16. Grant Jarvie, "Sport, Nationalism and Cultural Identity," in *The Changing Politics of Sport*, ed. Lincoln Allison (Manchester: Manchester University Press, 1993): 58–83.
17. John Harris and Ben Clayton, "David Beckham and the Changing (Re)presentations

Part Two: Sport and National Identity

of English Identity," *International Journal of Sport Management and Marketing*, 2, no. 3 (2007): 209.

18. Dilwyn Porter, "'Your boys took one hell of a beating!' English Football and British Decline," in *Sport and National Identity in the Post-War World*, eds. Adrian Smith and Dilwyn Porter (London: Routledge, 2004): 31–51.

19. Eric Hobsbawm, *Nations and Nationalism Since 1870: Programme, Myth, Reality* (Cambridge: Cambridge University Press, 1990): 143.

20. Michael Messner and Don Sabo, "Introduction: Towards a Critical Feminist Reappraisal of Sport, Men and the Gender Order," in *Sport, Men and the Gender*, eds. Michael Messner and Don Sabo (Champaign: Human Kinetics,1990): 9.

21. Jennifer Hargreaves, *Sporting* Females (London: Routledge, 1994).

22. Judith Butler, *Gender Trouble: Feminism and the Subversion of Identity* (London: Routledge, 1990).

23. Butler, *Gender Trouble*, 25.

24. Barbara Cox and Shona Thompson, "Multiple Bodies: Sportswomen, Soccer and Sexuality," in *International Review for the Sociology of Sport*, 35, no. 1 (2000): 5–20.

25. Hargreaves, *Sporting Females*, 169.

26. Amanda Roth and Susan Basow, "Femininity, Sports and Feminism," in *Journal of Sport and Social Issues*, 28, no. 3 (2004): 245–265.

27. Susan Birrell and Nancy Theberge, *Feminist Resistance and Transformation in Sport* (Champaign: Human Kinetics, 1994): 341.

28. Toni Bruce, "Women, Sport and the Media: A Complex Terrain," in *Outstanding Research About Women and Sport in New Zealand*, eds. Camilla Obel, Toni Bruce and Shona Thompson (Hamilton: Wilf Malcom Institute for Educational Research, 2008): 57.

29. Bruce, *Women, Sport and the Media: A Complex Terrain*, 60; Emma Wensing and Toni Bruce, "Bending the Rules: Media Representations of Gender During an International Sporting Event," *International Review for the Sociology of Sport*, 38, no. 4 (2003): 387–396.

30. Ibid.

31. Paul Willis, "Women in Sport in Ideology," in *Women, Sport and Culture*, eds. Susan Birrell and Cheryl Cole (Champaign: Human Kinetics, 1994): 35.

32. Jason Tuck, "The Men in White: Reflections on Rugby Union, the Media and Englishness," *International Review for the Sociology of Sport*, 38, no. 2 (2003): 177–199.

33. Jason Tuck and Joe Maguire, "Making Sense of Global Patriot Games: Rugby Players' Perceptions of National Identity Politics," *Football Studies*, 2, no. 1 (1999): 26–54; Tuck, *The Men in White*; Darragh McGee and Alan Bairner, "Transcending the Borders of Irish Identity? Narratives of Northern Nationalist Footballer in Northern Ireland," *International Review for the Sociology of Sport*, 46, no. 4 (2011): 436–455.

34. Uwe Flick, *Introduction to Qaulitative Research (3rd ed.)*. London: Sage (2006): 50.

35. McGee and Bairner, *Transcending the Borders of Irish Identity*.

36. Ian Parker, *Qualitative Psychology: Introducing Radical Research*. Maidenhead: Open University Press (2005): 17.

37. Tuck and Maguire, *Making Sense of Global Patriot Games*, 26.

38. Jessica Robinson, "Tackling the Anxieties of the English: Searching for the Nation Through Football," *Soccer and Society* 9, no. 2 (2008): 215–230.

39. Tuck, *The Men in White*.

40. Adrian Smith and Dilwyn Porter, "Introduction," in *Sport and National Identity in the Post-War World*, eds. Adrian Smith and Dilwyn Porter (London: Routledge, 2004): 2.

41. Hobsbawm, *Nations and Nationalism Since 1870*.

42. Joseph Maguire and Emma Poulton, "European Identity Poitics in Euro 96," *International Review for the Sociology of Sport* 34, no. 1 (1999): 17–30; Tuck, *The Men in White*.

43. Harris and Clayton, *David Beckham and the Changing (Re)presentations of English Identity*.

44. Wensing and Bruce, *Bending the Rules*, 387.

45. Charlie Wyett, "Hope 'n Glory," *Sun*, March 24, 2011, 60.

46. Ibid.

47. Amol Rajan, "How Did Britain's Sportswomen Become Such World-Beaters?," *Independent*, September 9, 2009, 26.
48. Ibid.
49. Michael Billig, *Banal Nationalism* (London: Sage, 1995).
50. Wensing and Bruce, *Bending the Rules*.
51. Jonathon Brown, "The Stars of Germany 2010* (*That's the Women's World Cup)," *Independent*, June 25, 2011, News 11.
52. Robin Scott-Elliot, "People Say I Don't Look Like a Rugby Player…," *Independent*, August 20, 2010, 51.
53. Vikki Orvice, "Hellsinki: Girls Crushed by Old Enemy," *Sun*, September 11, 2009, 74.
54. "Fearsome Encounter for England Rugby Girls," *Daily Telegraph*, September 6, 2010, 1.
55. Rory Davidson, "USA Will Fly Solo to Win It," *Sun*, June 25, 2011, 73.
56. Brown, "The Stars of Germany 2010* (*That's the Women's World Cup)," 10–11.
57. Wensing and Bruce, *Bending the Rules*.
58. Birrell and Theberge, *Feminist Resistance and Transformation in Sport*, 341.
59. Andrew Dillon, "Our Girls Have Really Got the X Factor," *Sun*, September 10, 2009, 67.
60. Ibid.
61. Joanne McGarry, "How I Make It Work: Rachel Burford," *Sunday Times Style Magazine*, September 5, 2010a, 49.
62. Scott-Elliot, "People Say I Don't Look Like a Rugby Player…," 51.
63. McGarry, "How I Make It Work: Rachel Burford," 49.
64. Michael Rosie et al, "Nation Speaking Unto Nation? Newspapers and National Identity in the Devolved UK," *The Sociological Review* 9, no. 2 (2004): 215–230; Billig, *Banal Nationalism*.
65. Ibid., 119.
66. Wensing and Bruce, *Bending the Rules*, 393.
67. Bruce, *Women, Sport and the Media: A Complex Terrain*.
68. Ibid., 62.
69. Bruce, *Women, Sport and the Media: A Complex Terrain*, 66.
70. Ibid., 67.
71. Wensing and Bruce, *Bending the Rules*, 389.
72. Ibid., 388.
73. Gavin Mairs, "England Unable to End New Zealand Monopoly," *Daily Telegraph*, September 6, 2010, Sport 17.
74. Stephen Jones, "Wonder Women," *Sunday Times*, August 15, 2010a, Sport 12.
75. Ivan Speck, "Heartbreaker: England's Heroines Lose Final Nail-Biter," *Daily Mail*, September 6, 2010, 74.
76. Bruce, *Women, Sport and the Media: A Complex Terrain*.
77. John Hoberman, *Sport and Political Ideology* (Austin: University of Texas Press, 1984).
78. John Garland and Mike Rowe, "War Minus the Shooting? Jingoism, the English Press, and Euro 96," *Journal of Sport and Social Issues* 23, no. 1 (1999): 80–95.
79. Harry Talbot, "Brazier Boot Helps Ferns Beat Roses," *Sun*, September 6, 2010, 53.
80. Patrick Kidd, "English Hearts Left Broken by the Speed and Ruthlessness of Champions," *Times*, September 6, 2010, 66.
81. Ashley Gray, "Overpowered: England Can't Halt the Mighty Germans," *Daily Mail*, September 11, 2009, 105.
82. Robert Kitson, "Heartbroken England Rue Missed Opportunities as New Zealand Rule Again," *Guardian*, September 6, 2010a, Sport 8.
83. Stephen Jones, "World in Her Hands," *Sunday Times*, August 15, 2010, Sport 15.
84. Jones, "Wonder Woman," Sport 12.
85. Robert Kitson, "England Look to Raise Roof After Shattering Glass Ceiling," *Guardian*, September 4, 2010, Sport 8.

86. Speck, "Heartbreaker: England's Heroines Lose Final Nail-Biter," 74.
87. Steven Jackson and Brendan Hokowhitu, "Sport, Tribes and Technology: The New Zealand All Blacks Haka and the Politics of Identity," *Journal of Sport and Social Issues* 26, no. 2 (2002): 127.
88. Kitson, "England Looks to Raise Roof After Shattering Glass Ceiling," *Sport* 8.
89. Jones, "Wonder Woman," *Sport* 12.
90. John Vincent, Edward Kian and Paul Pederson, "Flying the Flag: Gender and National Identity in English Newspapers During the 2006 World Cup," *Soccer and Society* 12, no. 5 (2011): 621.
91. Jacquelyn Collinson and John Hockey, "'Working Out' Identity: Distance Runners and the Management of Disrupted Identity," *Leisure Studies* 26, no. 4 (2007): 383.
92. Ali Bowes and Alan Bairner, "England's Proxy Warriors: Women, War and International Sport," *International Review for the Sociology of Sport* (2016): 1012690216669491.
93. Laura Bates, "Sport's Woman Problem: The FAs Tweet Is Just the Tip of the Iceberg," *Guardian*, July 8, 2015: http://www.theguardian.com/football/womens-blog/2015/jul/08/sports-woman-problem-the-fas-tweet-is-just-the-tip-of-the-iceberg.
94. Yuval-Davis, *Gender and Nation*.
95. Vikki Krane, "We Can Be Athletic and Feminine, but Do We Want To? Challenging Hegemonic Femininity in Women's Sport," *Quest* 53, no. 1 (2001): 115–133.
96. Bowes and Bairner, *England's Proxy Warriors*.
97. Nancy Malcom, "Constructing Female Athleticism: A Study of Girl's Recreational Softball," *American Behavioural Scientist* 46, no. 10 (2003): 1388.
98. Bim Adewumni and Ben Kingsley, "A Whole New Ball Game," *Guardian*, June 22, 2011, 8.
99. Tim Edensor, *National Identity, Popular Culture and Everyday Life* (Oxford: Berg, 2002).
100. Yuval-Davis and Anthias, *Women-Nation-State*.
101. Wensing and Bruce, *Bending the Rules*.
102. Bowes and Bairner, *England's Proxy Warriors*.

PART THREE

Athletes and the Global Spectacle

A Fatwa for German Soccer

BRUCE S. BURNSIDE

Abstract

In the fall of 2009, three professional soccer players in the German Soccer League were suspended by their team for fasting during the Islamic month of Ramadan. A key German Islamic organization, the Central Council for Muslims in Germany, stepped in to help arbitrate the ensuing dispute over the suspension. The following summer, just after the 2010 World Cup, the Central Council, in coordination with the German Soccer League and the team, presented a fatwa, an Islamic legal opinion, on the issue which gave permission to the players to forgo fasting during Ramadan in the soccer season. In this essay, drawing on legal anthropological theory and German and religious studies among others, I track the various actors that helped enact what became a national drama in the media, including the Council, the League, the player's union, the team, and Al-Azhar University in Cairo which issued the fatwa. I argue that the Central Council for Muslims in Germany used a relatively benign religious issue (fasting) intersecting with a professional sport with strong links to ongoing identity formation in Germany, to position Islam as compatible with professional German sports and thus with German identity writ large. I map the deeply intertwined history of German nationalism and sport as well as the more recent policy changes that have opened up citizenship paths (since 2000) of those with Muslim backgrounds and the contentions issues that Islam should play a role in regarding German social and legal life. This demographic shift was evident in the 2010 World Cup German soccer team where 11 of 22 players had migration backgrounds. The fatwa, I contend, marshaled the power of that shift, of German soccer and the authority of Al-Azhar University to reconcile and make the case for a "German Islam."

In October of 2009, news media widely reported that three Muslim players were reprimanded by their professional soccer team in Germany for fasting during the holy month of Ramadan. The reporting seemed to suggest an intractable mismatch between the players' faith and the beloved sport of a nation. But the story quickly disappeared into the grist mill of the news cycle. It was to the surprise of many that in the following summer the incident was brought back into the limelight with great fanfare in conjunction with the World Cup. A major German Muslim association, along with the key operators of professional German soccer, and the players' team trumpeted a solution to the previous year's reprimands. The answer was a fatwa, an Islamic legal opinion, which the promoting parties presented as a just reconciliation of the players' Islamic faith and the needs of German soccer. This was the latest public voice in an ongoing debate of what it means to be a European or German Muslim. Islam's role in German social and legal life is a hotly contested issue, especially within German media and politics. In the year of the fatwa's issue, 2010, the German Interior Minister, Hans-Peter Friedrich of the ruling conservative party (CDU), stated that Islam is not a part of a German "way of life" ("How Can Germany's Interior Minister Do the Job?" 2011). But that same year at an event celebrating twenty years of German unification, the German president, Christian Wulff, also with the CDU, made two remarkable declarations to the opposite effect. First, Islam, "like Christianity and Judaism," is a part of Germany and not a foreign element; and second, the "integration" of Germany's migrant communities would be Germany's "second unification" (Warner 2010).

In this essay I consider the appearance of this single fatwa in German and international news media, which considered the permissibility of active professional soccer players in Germany to forgo fasting during the month of Ramadan. To the surprise of many, the fatwa gave permission to professional soccer players to *not* fast on game days during Ramadan, with certain provisions. I ground the understanding of this fatwa in an exploration of the context for Ramadan and its relationship to soccer in Germany exemplified by mainstream media in this period. It is this context which gave this particular fatwa its potency and which in turn is illuminated by asking in what world would such a fatwa matter? In tracing the "life" of this fatwa in Germany, I argue that it represented a powerful opportunity to pair Islamic jurisprudence and practice with soccer, a sport which has been intertwined with German national identity, and for its proponents to position Islam for positive inclusion in the discourse on national belonging—as something *also* German—or at least compatible with a major German cultural practice.

Following a short discussion of the theoretical framework and methodology underscoring this essay, I proceed by exploring the context for understanding Ramadan's place in Germany in 2009 when the initial controversy erupted. I also show the conditions for the issuing of the fatwa a year later as Germany's national team competed in the World Cup in South Africa. Examining this fertile ground is key to understanding why the fatwa emerged when it did. I examine the Central Council for Muslims in Germany (ZMD) and the professional soccer organizations' co-press release about the fatwa to the German media. To situate the ZMD's motivation in packaging the fatwa as they did in a major press release (in which the fatwa itself was often obscured or lost in further reporting), I inspect their "Islamic Charta," a declaration of principles they issued in 2002. The "Charta" explicates their understanding of Islam and Islamic law within German society. I then discuss the fatwa as a document in its German and Arabic versions and trace the fatwa back to its issuing body, the Dar al-Ifta, the official fatwa issuing body in Egypt, and show that the same fatwa had in fact had a previous "life" and had been in existence since 2008. Finally, I situate the fatwa in the larger discourse of Islam in German society and argue that this the "failure" of an Islamic practice and German society to (temporarily) co-function (namely the reprimanded players), provided the impetus for the ZMD and the professional soccer representatives to create a moment for a "German" Islam to emerge and showcase an integration success.

Framework

The case examined here is built on the continuing centrality and importance of soccer's potential for articulating national understanding in Germany. Such potential is deeply intertwined with German history. In broader strokes, scholars link this association's emergence to the "Turnen" movement of the Napoleonic era, which intensified following imperial unification in 1871. It underscored the link of the health of the nation's morals to its citizens' fitness (Goltermann 1998). By the Weimar period (1918–1933) soccer had taken a prominent place in the relationship between the nation and the bodies of its citizens (Eggers, 2001). During the subsequent decade and half of National Socialism, scholars have argued that this link with sport, including soccer, and the nation reached an apex (Fischer 1999, Bitzer 2003, Ewing 2008). Even following the repudiation of Nazi principles, soccer continued to play a major part of the national consciences in the two German states that emerged from the war's aftermath, as it did in many other countries (Meier and Mutz 2016; Quiroga 2013). Particularly heightened moments of concern for soccer concentrated around the World Cup championships, including in recent decades (Brüggemeier 2004). This particular study hinges on the 2010 World Cup. The "multicultural" (as it was described) make-up of the team was apparent like never before, following a change in citizenship laws in 1999. This change excited comment in major news media around the world (as shown below) as well as a range of scholarly attention in the years that followed (Stehle and Weber 2013; Dubin 2011; Majer-O'Sickey 2006; Young 2013; Hicks 2014).

Additionally, this essay aims to build on the ways in which Muslims and Islamic practices have come to figure in the discourses of national belonging in Germany and Europe, and more particularly by means of their interaction with sport and fitness. Indeed, fatwas regarding sports have received detailed attention, showing a "mushrooming" in number as well as a wide range of concerns, from players' salaries to the suitability of being a spectator or an Islamic militant who loves the game, and arguably show the contours of a "struggle between modernity and tradition" (Shavit and Winter 201, 280; see also Dorsey 2016). In Germany, legal challenges have garnered both mainstream and scholarly attention, in particular to the challenges brought by students to issues with their schools' sporting programs (Rohe 2008). The cases, from mixed-gendered swimming to the suitability of a headscarf, have often been perceived as an attack on German values and even its polity, as many mistakenly believe school sports to be enshrined in the German constitution (Ewing 2008). However, anthropologists in particular have drawn attention to the ways such issues, when they are out of the limelight, have been "solved" at the neighborhood or at the city level (Kuppinger 2014), even if such solutions are often misinterpreted when disseminated to a wider audience (Shavit and Wiesenbach 2012). Like many of these studies, I aim to contribute to the understanding of what "integration"—that oft deployed term—comes to mean in the complexity of "socio-religious realities" (*ibid.*, 59)—specifically here in the life trajectory of this fatwa born of a momentary failure to reconcile Islam and German soccer.

In examining the fatwa, I follow Jakob Skovgaard-Petersen (1997) method for understanding fatwas. He argues that we must look beyond the language and content of the fatwa to understand how they work in the world: "A fatwa is part of a complex world where different interests and ideologies will compete to make use of it for their own purposes" (*ibid.*, 20). This method is echoed in the anthropological treatment of objects as socially constructed. Simultaneously de-fetishizing (observing the social and other labor put into an object's creation) and re-fetishizing an object methodologically (by "following" the object), an object's "biography" or "life," just like a human's, could reveal in its trajectory social forms and construction of the human worlds which conjured forth such an object (Appadurai 1988; Kopytoff 2013). Therefore I treat this fatwa not only as a set of words, but also as an object whose "life," in particular in the portion where it appeared couched in a major press release, can tell us something about the ongoing position of Islam in the discourses over national belonging in Germany. The scholarly work on belonging and Islam in Germany is wide and deep. It examines such discussion and action at the level of the street and neighborhood (Kuppinger 2014), in education and policy, from legal cases (Rohe 2014) to food regulation (Çağlar 1998). As will become evident in this analysis, I keep my examination at the level of national and international media attention, largely focused on newspapers. I do not measure the impact of the fatwa in the lives of everyday professional players who fast (though we will see hints that the impact is limited), nor do I attempt to evaluate the success (or failure) of integration into national belonging. For my purposes, national belonging is a discursive action taken by participants and I intend for this to serve as a case for *how* such an action unfolds in newspapers and other related media as well as some of the tangled complexities that tracing its trajectory can reveal. In particular I attempt to show why such a fatwa came to such a prominent phase of its life in Germany in 2010.

The Frankfurt Three

In October 2009 a second division professional soccer team in Germany, Fußballsportverein (FSV) Frankfurt, reprimanded three of its players for fasting during Ramadan. According to the team, the three players—Soumaila Coulibaly, Pa Saikou Kujabi and Oualid Mokhtari—fasted during the month of Ramadan without notifying the team's management. A press release from FSV explained that the reprimand was not due to the "fact of fasting," but arose instead from the players' violation of their contracts, which the team claimed required them to disclose information that might put the players' health and performances at risk. The press release added: "The actions of FSV Frankfurt in no way constitutes a violation of religious freedom, the rules apply just as well to the Christian Lent before Easter" ("Drei Fussballer Wegen Ramadan Abgemahnt" 2009). The FSV management tried to avoid a controversy over religion in their reprimands, but many others saw this action exactly as such.

The news of the reprimands was reported widely in the German and international newspapers ("FSV Frankfurt: Ramadan-Klausel!" 2009; Bossaller 2009; Chawla 2009). The Union of Contracted Soccer Players (VDV) represented reprimanded players in the controversy. The VDV counsel, Frank Rybak, responded to the reprimands in a statement labeling them a "novelty" and as "absolutely illegal" ("Ramadan-Fasten" 2009). He suspected that fasting might not have been the real problem, that there might be other reasons for the reprimands, hinting at an anti–Muslim bias. The German

Football League (DFL), the organization that oversees operations for the first and second division teams in Germany, insisted that the problem was between the FSV team and its players. Though the DFL had provided a model contract (with no references to fasting) for FSV to issue its players, FSV had added the specific clauses mandating that fasting be disclosed. FSV's legal department defended its reprimands and alluded to possible "doping problems" that could be caused by fasting players' nutritional supplements (that they would presumably take to keep performing), which might be on the prohibited list (*ibid.*). Despite FSV's insistence that the fasting itself was not the problem, the VDV, the players' union, claimed that the opposite was true. The VDV managing director, Ulf Baranowsky, insisted there was no direct proof of how fasting affects player performance. But the medical advisor for the German Soccer Association (DFB), which co-hosts the German professional leagues with DFL, claimed that "Ramadan becomes a problem for players due to possible circulation problems, weakness of concentration and muscle injury" that result from the absence of food and drink before games (Bossaller 2009). Ultimately the reprimand caused no direct consequences for the players. They were not benched or released from their contracts. Yet it was this reprimand, this failure to reconcile Islam and soccer, that would become an opportunity to showcase the inherent *compatibility* of Islamic law and a key German cultural practice—soccer. This arrived a year later in the form of the fatwa wrapped in a press release. That fatwa would attempt to authoritatively answer the question for Muslim soccer players in Germany of how exactly religion—here in the case of fasting and Islamic law—should situate itself professionally and personally in the German context. But that fatwa did not enter a void. In an examination of the practice of Ramadan in Germany and the discourse on Ramadan and professional soccer in German media outside of these reprimands and fatwa, we can already see a complicated engagement with the issue of fasting and negotiating belonging as a Muslim in Germany.

German Ramadan

Ramadan awareness and discussion in Germany in the years around the fatwa went beyond soccer players, of course. Close to the month of Ramadan, German newspapers often supplied general guides to explain to their readers the meaning and practice of fasting during this lunar month (Rössler 2010). Such articles also featured highlights of interesting intersections, like Ramadan and diabetes (Lenzen-Schulte 2009) in addition to soccer and Ramadan, discussed in detail in the next section. Before Ramadan 2010, RTL 2, a major private television channel, announced that it would include "tips" about Ramadan in its German broadcasts, including start and stop times.

RTL 2's press officer Carsten Molis said, "one could theorize about integration, but we wanted to send a clear signal" ("Islam: RTL II Sendet" 2010). Aiman Mayzeck, the general secretary of the Central Council of Muslims in Germany (ZMD), one of the largest Islamic organizations in the country (and the one that would arbitrate the soccer dispute), praised RTL 2's decision as showing "societal responsibility" and as setting "a good example for other major channels" (ibid.). Articles like these reflect the importance of Ramadan in German society writ large, but also its importance to the Muslim community in Germany, especially in comparison to other religious practices, like prayer or visiting the mosque.

There is an indication of fasting at Ramadan being less controversial than other Islamic practices in Germany. The newspaper *Kristeligt Dagblad* reported that Ramadan is of growing interest to Germans. Whereas "previously the *iftar* feast was only for Muslims" now Christian mayors and political parties in Germany are inviting Muslims to celebrate the breaking of the Ramadan fast, *iftar*. This tradition began with the Christian Democratic Union (CDU), but other parties soon followed. The CDU's integration policy spokesman Kurt Wansner said "that our invitation is a sign of respect to all Muslims living in this country." The article adds that "several studies show that up to 80 percent of Germany's Muslims will observe Ramadan" (Dachs 2010). It does not specify which studies this claim refers to, but it does reflect a trend among German Muslims shown in two surveys conducted in the 2000s. These show that in addition to being a more acceptable religious practice for Muslims in Germany as far as German politicians are concerned, it is also a more common practice in comparison among Muslims, especially among the young.

The Foundation Centre for Studies on Turkey conducted the first of these in October 2000. The survey focused on Turkish immigrants in Germany and the "religious influences" that affect their "daily lives." Two-thirds reported that they feel themselves "religious," 7 percent "strongly religious" and 25 percent "not religious at all." The trend is for the younger generation to feel less religious than their parents' or grandparents' generations (Şen 2008, 39). But the survey shows in the frequency of "performed religious acts" that fasting, along with dietary practice, almsgiving and the Eid al-Adha feast, are popular acts among all age groups, but especially the young. The study concludes that for the young, fasting, almsgiving, dietary laws and Eid are "not considered religious matters" (unlike mosque visits, prayer or pilgrimage), but instead are seen as "traditional practices" and part of their cultural identity (Şen 2008, 40). However, the separation of culture and religion in relation to Islam is ambiguous in Germany.

In a second survey in 2005 of young Muslims (including non-Turks) in the northern city of Kiel, a similar pattern is recorded. Eighty percent observe the fast compared to 35 percent who pray daily (Eilers et al. 2008, 102). The Kiel study does not distinguish Ramadan from other practices as more or less religious, but it does conclude similarly that the practices are part of identity performance. This may be part of the shift they note in the increased self-identification as "Muslim" or "religious" in the aftermath of the September 11, 2001, attacks in New York City (Eilers et al. 2008, 113).

Ramadan's benign mainstream presentation in Germany, in comparison to more controversial Islamic practices like headscarves, as well as its appeal to young Muslims, made it a more attractive issue to leverage in promoting a positive image of Islam. Even before the fatwa, this was often taken up by pairing it discursively with professional soccer, a sport that for Germany, as for many countries, plays a significant role in the daily lives of its people and their national imagery. It provided sympathetic newspapers a particular moment once a year to observe the ongoing notion of what it means to be Muslim in Germany and laid the fertile ground for the fatwa packaged in a press release considered here to make an impact in 2010. Notably, this presentation in mainstream media, examined next, is generally free of so much of the anxiety in German discourse on Islam, which becomes entangled with highly charged concepts from honor killing to feminism to terrorism.

Ramadan and Soccer

Leading up to the beginning of Ramadan in August of 2009 (the year of the reprimand) there were numerous stories in German media about Muslim soccer players dealing with the fast. The various articles painted a complex picture, which showcased multiple practices and solutions for the players in the Ramadan month. They also show a relatively sophisticated understanding of Ramadan's sources, including Quranic citations, and the possibility for varying interpretations. In a piece in the Zeit newspaper, a "German-Turk" player, Berkant Goektan, simply said that he did not fast at all. The coaches for the professional teams from Hamburg and Duisburg maintained that there is "a rule of exception" for soccer players and that the "Quran allows" for the fast to be moved to breaks between games. The Zeit notes that this point is controversial and cites the Quranic sura (chapter) 2 verse 185, noting that "previous Quran-interpretations allow exceptions for travelers, sick people, pregnant women, small children or those who do hard manual labor." The article elaborates that it is "interpreted a little differently" for each regarding who qualifies as a "hard worker." The Augsburger striker Momo Diabang sought counsel with an imam in his homeland of Senegal, who reportedly told him "'If the job from which your livelihood stems does not allow the fast, it is okay to forgo it'" (Aumüller 2009).

Many of the articles in the German press around Ramadan in 2009, like the Zeit piece, framed Ramadan and soccer as a question or a conflict for the players, but crucially a resolvable one, either through personal choice or consultation with an authority. Franck Ribery is a frequently mentioned player in these articles. His star status, combined with his French citizenship, his conversion to Islam and playing for one of Germany's most famous teams, Bayern München, makes him a popular focus. An article from the Welt begins cheekily that "with all due respect to the Archangel Gabriel: He couldn't know what kind of difficulty he would bring to the soccer player Franck Ribery when he revealed the Koran to the Prophet Mohammad in a cave in Mount Hira in 610 AD" (Lüdeke 2009). It goes on to explain that this "conflict of conscience" is something that all Muslim pro-sport players around the world face once a year. It also cites the previously mentioned Qu'anic Sura 2 verse 185 and tells us that all believers must not eat or drink during Ramadan between sunrise and sunset. This article, like the others, reports that Ribery found a compromise: on the days he plays games, he forgoes the fast, but when not playing, he attends to his religious duty and fasts. Interestingly, the article goes on to interpret that this "path is certainly allowed at away games, because the Koran allows explicit exceptions for 'travel.'" It notes that the Egyptian team, before it played Rwanda the previous Saturday, "allowed a legal opinion (fatwa) to be made. This came a few weeks ago—and 1399 years after the Koran's revelation—to the conclusion that the team is 'on a national mission' and for that reason the players do not have to comply with Ramadan" (Lüdeke 2009).

A similar portrayal of the professional player Ümit Korkmaz, (an "Austrian with Turkish roots"), who explained to the *Frankfurter Allgemeine Newspaper* (*FAZ*) in 2009 that "fasting from a sporting perspective is too difficult. In the end I want to have fuel for practice" (Beister 2009). He further elaborated that for each day he does not fast during Ramadan he donates alms to the poor in Turkey. The *FAZ* article explains that the Quran exempts hardworking people from the obligation to fast. A doctor affiliated with the newspaper explains the dangers of fasting, especially to metabolism and says that he advises his patients who engage in hard labor or high performance to forgo fasting (Beister 2009). In a different *FAZ* article from the previous year on fasting, the newspaper explained that for Muslim players Ramadan is a "long time of discord" where they must "decide between health and belief and therein find a personal compromise." The article claims that ten Muslim players in the German League, including Franck Ribery, will not fast on game days due to health reasons. It says that they "interpret the Quran to their favor" by associating soccer with hard work, as accepted in the Koran, and allowing them "a way out from their discord." In contrast, the article presents Abdelaziz Ahanfouf, a second division player for Wehen Wiesbaden. This "Moroccan with a German passport" says he cannot look to others, but for him "fasting his very important for his belief." He adds that of the eight teams he's played for in Germany not one had forbidden him to fast. In fact, his only hat trick came during the month of Ramadan while he was fasting ("Fasten und Fußball" 2008).

The religious aspects of Ramadan, its sources and interpretation, are noted to a degree in all the articles, but some present a deeper analysis of these issues. Revier-Sport, cites verses 183 and 187 in sura 2 of the Quran to explain the command to fast during Ramadan. It says that these verses do not give much detail, but one must look to other religious texts, such as the hadith of Abu Dawud, Book 13: "The month consists of 29 days. Fast only when you first see the crescent moon (Hilal) and break the fast only when you see it again" (Redemann and Zwaagstra 2009). The article says that though opinions vary on exceptions for fasting, "generally an exception can be made for those whose hard work places a burden on their bodies and those who are ill." But notes that "to the extent that soccer players can invoke this privilege, like many rules in Islam, comes down to interpretation" (Redemann and Zwaagstra 2009). Stefan Rommel reports for Spox that Sami Khedira, the "son of a German and a Tunisian and who believes in the Koran," makes an exception to fasting for his occupation, but that other players must decide for themselves. Rommel explains that this issue comes down to a "small loophole in the Koran." He writes that the Prophet Mohammed could not have imagined his teachings coming into conflict with "the glossy product of soccer." However, there is favorable "hole in the wickerwork" from the Quran sura 2, verse 185 (once again) regarding the exceptions including those doing hard labor. As to whether professional soccer players qualify for this latter category, it is interpreted a little differently by everyone. The prominent imam from Morocco Sheihk Mohammad al Taweel, according to Rommel, opines that "soccer is a game and the fast cannot be broken because of a game." The "somewhat more moderate" General Secretary of the Islamic Council for the Federal Republic of Germany says, "Performance sports and Ramadan are combinable. One must prepare oneself, nourish oneself and take breaks." He notes that several Muslim players fast and that many of them give top performances. But ultimately the General Secretary wants for his fellow Muslims to decide for themselves (Rommel 2009).

Explicit health concerns are frequently presented as a deciding factor for players. The player Demba Ba, a "devout Muslim" says he fasts except for his game days with his team 1899 Hoffenheim. His coach Ralf Rangnick says he takes no particular consideration of the fasting time because Ba has practiced during Ramadan and is used to it. Stuttgart's national player Serdar Tasci explains that fasting during game days is "just too dangerous. I am just as devout as others, but [fasting] bothers me because of my occupation." Mesut Özil a professional player for Werder at the time with "Turkish roots," (who we will discuss below in his role with the national soccer team) does not fast any longer, due to an experience in the youth league that left him with headaches and feeling limp. Fatmire Bajramaj, a player for the Women's German National soccer team, says that she eats normally during this time, otherwise she simply couldn't make it through the practice and games. Fasting is for her too exhausting (Puck 2009). The striker for the Borussia Monchenglad team, Karim Matmour, says during Ramadan that "as a professional in Germany it doesn't work any other way. I try, so far as possible, to not eat during the day. But only when there is no risk to my health. On game days I eat just as I would normally" (Krümpelmann 2009). He also notes that when he traveled to Algeria to train with the national team there, their practice schedule is moved to the middle of the night (beginning at 11pm) to accommodate Ramadan. Interestingly, Matmour mentions in this article that his former teammate Coulibaly tried fasting completely for two days the previous season and was unable to practice for three days afterward. This is the same Soumaila Coulibaly who would be reprimanded for fasting that year (2009) at his new team, FSV Frankfurt (*ibid.*). This is the incident that would spark the fatwa.

These articles show a willingness for German media to understand Ramadan as a complex issue that can vary from player to player. They attempt to take a matter-of-fact look at the sources and differing interpretations of Ramadan as well as to listen to the players' explanations. The authors try to balance the religious prescriptions with health concerns. Interestingly, rarely does an article presents the view of any Muslim authority in the form of a person; instead the Quran is cited. Most notably, Ramadan and soccer are presented (almost) entirely as reconcilable issues. I argue that this context—this relative openness to and curiosity about Ramadan in mass media and its relationship to the national pastime of soccer—combined with the lack of an authoritative religious voice in that media, allowed for a moment of intervention in the story about the three players reprimands. This temporary failure of integration was taken up by the ZMD and the German Soccer League and they would use the fatwa to make the case for repairing this breach with a new integrative opportunity a year later in the summer of 2010. It was that summer in the full hype of the World Cup that the "multicultural"—and Islamic—character of the new national German men's team debuted to the world and would set the perfect backdrop for a fatwa of reconciliation.

Weltmeisterschaft 2010 and a Fatwa in Germany

In the first games of the World Cup in South Africa in the summer of 2010, a new soccer star was born on the German squad. The 21-year-old Mesut

Özil led the team to victory over Australia and the international press took note. Frequently remarked on was Özil's "Turkish descent" and how he celebrates his heritage. Özil noted in *The Guardian*, "my technique and feeling for the ball is the Turkish side to my game," whereas, "the discipline, attitude and always-give-your-all is the German part" (McCarra 2010). It was not only Özil's heritage which proved interesting for the media, but the heritage of many of the team's players. Eleven of the squad's 22 athletes had a least one immigrant parent. A different *Guardian* article by David Hytner stated that Germany was the most "ethnically diverse" team in the tournament. The makeup of the team in part reflected the dedication of the coach Joachim Löw who made a concerted effort to recruit young players from immigrant backgrounds, including Özil (Hytner 2010). However, it was Germany's 1999 citizenship eligibility laws, which made it easier for the children of immigrants to become citizens that made such a recruitment scheme possible. The German Soccer Association (DFB), one of the co-hosts of the professional leagues, appointed a "dedicated immigration officer" to facilitate the new team, and to ensure that the players did not play for other national teams they might be eligible for as well. The "poster boy" for Germany's team, Sami Khedira, said about his teammates, "We are aware that it's something new to have German national players with Turkish, Ghanaian, Nigerian or Tunisian roots, but for our generation it's very normal. We have some players called Khedira and some called Müller. We don't know any differently" (Hytner 2010). The *New York Times* columnist Roger Cohen, in a piece gushing over Özil and the multicultural squad of Germany, likened the "new Germany of Özil and Aogo" to no less than a "victory over the Big Man [Hitler] who destroyed Europe" (Cohen 2010). It was in these heady days of German soccer in summer 2010 that the story of the three reprimanded FSV players from the previous year reentered the mass media discussion. This time, the question posed by their fasting and reprimand and the compatibility of Islam with German soccer came with an answer: a fatwa.

On July 28, 2010, just before the beginning of Ramadan, a joint statement was released by Central Council of Muslims in Germany (ZMD), the German Soccer Association (DFB), the German Football League (DFL), and the players' team, FSV Frankfurt, whose message was unambiguous in its headline: "Professional Soccer Players May Break the Fast During Ramadan" ("Profifußballer Dürfen" 2010). The statement goes on to explain that, following the reprimand of the three players the year before, the ZMD offered confidential talks to the players, their union and leading functionaries from the DFB, DFL, and FSV Frankfurt. They all agreed to a mutual statement during a meeting at the DFL-Central. ZMD et al. found agreement also with the "collection of theological legal opinions." These included ZMD's own religious advisors, the legal opinion of Al-Azhar in Cario (who ultimately issued the fatwa) and the leading authorities of European Council for Fatwa and Research (ECFR). Al-Azhar came to a "conclusion" [*Schluss*] (which ECFR agreed with and so did not issue a further legal opinion), that

> the work contract between the player and the organization compels the player to a specific performance, and when this work—which is contract based (not for amateurs—hobby soccer)—is his sole source of income, and if he must play a soccer match in the month of Ramadan, and the fast influences his performance, then he may break the fast ["Profifußballer Dürfen" 2010].

This remarkable statement from ZMD et al. was accompanied in the press release by supporting statements of the various parties involved in the talks. The DFL managing director Christian Seifert and the ZMD general secretary Aiman Mazyek commented jointly that "the associations' and also the players' 'legal security' are achieved likewise in worker's rights and in the sense of theological law." The ZMD elaborated that this "opinion" from Al-Azhar allows for professional players to follow their "occupation and religious duties without incorrect feelings of guilt." Mazyek added that players can make up missed fasting days later. He also noted though this opinion is in contrast to some judgments, it once again makes clear that "work and faith are interdependent and are not in conflict with one another." The general manager of the FSV team, Bernd Reisig, affirmed that he was happy that FSV could help contribute to this solution and that it is clear that players could achieve "professional high performance in sport and fully live their faith" (*ibid.*). In addition to the ZMD's website, the press release was included in full on many of the other parties' official websites. Though notably, the ZMD was the only one with the actual Arabic and German versions of the fatwa available for download at the end of the press release, which I discuss more in detail below.

The "conclusion" contained in the press release relating the fatwa was picked up and interpreted in the German press and around the world. It is in this truncated form (that is without the bulk of its text) that the fatwa traveled. The German news magazine *FOCUS* presented a straight-forward reporting of the press release next to a photo of Mesut Özil praying in his German national team uniform. Although the *FOCUS* article mentions that talks had been held between ZMD, the players and the functionaries, it says that a theological opinion was agreed on—without mention of Al-Azhar or ECFR (*FOCUS* 2010). An Associated Press wire published on Fox.com however explained in its report about the fatwa that Al-Azhar is the "pre-eminent theological institute of Sunni Islam" and it is to Al-Azhar that the ZMD "sought advice." It describes the statement from Al-Azhar as a "ruling," but presents the announcement overall as something the ZMD and "German soccer authorities determined." It also noted that Ramadan is when "devout

Muslims" fast from dawn until dusk ("German Muslim Group" 2010). The *Mitteldeutsche Zeitung*, in its article, quotes the German coach for Azerbaijan's national team, Berti Vogts, blaming Ramadan for his team's poor performance in a match against Germany. The article notes that the sick, the old, children, travelers and pregnant women are excepted from the commandment to fast during Ramadan. However, now one more exception has been "approved" by the ZMD: professional soccer players, who may postpone their fast. This article, like the *FOCUS* one, does not mention Al-Azhar or the ECFR ("Hintergrund" 2010). The *Thüringer Allgemeine* newspaper quotes the RWE striker, Fikri El Haj Ali, as saying that the decision is "important for me. I no longer have to hear complaints about eating and drinking." He noted he would make up the fast days later and that his family understands (Fritz 2010). An article on the announcement titled "Permission to Break the Fast" appeared in the *Süddeutsche* newspaper. It claimed that many players, like Özil and Tasci "worry how they can reconcile the commandments of their religion and competitive sport with one another" (2010). It suggests that "this should now change" because the players have received "important guidance" (*ibid.*). The article cautions however that the ZMD does not speak for all Muslims living in Germany, but is one of many umbrella organizations and not even the largest. Nonetheless their position has a special weight because the "legal opinion" was asked for and attained from Al-Azhar University, "one of the most important authorities in the Islamic world." After examining the announcement, the author claims that "to follow the logic of the argument put forth and put professional soccer players under the category of 'hard worker,' like a worker in a blast furnace, might be difficult for some" (*ibid.*). The ZMD secretary Aiman Mazyek responded that "We are certainly going to hear minority views." The article notes that when Ramadan begins, that despite the ZMD opinion, a "small number of players may want to stick to the narrow fasting rules." It singles out the player Jawhar Mnari who would be switching to FSV that summer, and who had fasted the previous year. The FSV coach Bernd Reisig responded that he would accept it when a player decided to fast anyway: "I have great respect for him, because he is a very religious man." He mentions that he has spoken with Mnari, and that if he decides to fast, he only has to tell the coach (Aumüller 2010). Mnari was not the only "minority opinion" that the announcement would spark.

The "soccer culture" magazine *11Freunde* interviewed the second vice-chairman of ZMD, Yakup Tufan and shows that final decision must have been made despite internal disagreement. When asked how he responds to the "ruling," Tufan says that he cannot condone what has been agreed, and the solution presented in the joint statement is "no solution of dialog." Instead, he believes the situation of each individual player should be assessed by talking together. Such dialogs should include the "scholars of Islam." After explaining his understanding of Ramadan, based on the Qur'an, Tufan claims that every player should ultimately decide for himself whether to fast or not, but there should be no general rule. Fasting should be made easier, not impeded. However, Tufan, argues despite the "choice" he wishes for the players, that there is not a true possibility of finding a compromise at the expense of fasting. Players should fast, as "devout Muslims hold their *ibada*, their commitment, regardless of their profession." He says this is not for soccer associations to decide, but for the scholars of Islam to "judge" ("Muslimische Spieler" 2010). It is not clear in the article what Tufan makes of the fatwa from Al-Azhar, though he does not like the general solution-touting message from the ZMD et al.

Background for the ZMD

The Central Council for Muslims in Germany (ZMD) formed in 1994 in response to heightened debate in Germany over "foreigners," including millions of Muslims. The umbrella organization defined its primary goal as "achieving recognition for the religious needs of Muslims in Germany" (Tietze 2008, 220). Though ZMD only represents a minority of Muslims in Germany in terms of membership, its ambition is broader than many similar groups, which though larger, tend to represent specific ethnic groups, like Turks (Şen 2008, 36–37). The ZMD revealed this ambition in early 2002 with the publishing of a remarkable document, the "Islamic Charta: Fundamental Declaration of the Central Council of Muslims in Germany on the relationship between Muslims, their State, and their Society." Many other Islamic organizations accepted this Charta, despite some its more controversial positions (Tietze 2008:216). The Charta's opening statement declares that most of the 3.2 million Muslims who now live in Germany will stay and "identify with Germany" and hopes that the Charta will contribute to "dispassionate debate on the political and social level" ("Islamic Charta" 2002). The Charta's preamble explicitly explains it is in response to the debates in Germany on Muslims in German society following the September 11, 2001, attacks. Its first article states that "Islam is a religion of Peace" and the first nine articles in general explicate the tenants of Islam, including fasting. The tenth article however affirms that "Islamic Law is Relevant for Muslims in the Occident." It notes that although Muslims can live anywhere in the world, they should meet their religious duties, while respecting the "local legal order." Article 11 goes further to state that "Muslims accept the basic legal rights guaranteed by the Constitution." Regardless of citizenship, the Charta states that Muslims represented by the ZMD accept the German Constitution and its legal order, including democracy and freedom of religion ("Islamic Charta" 2002).

The freedom of religion in the German Constitution (Article 4, Paragraph 1 and 2 GG) (Tietze 2008, 232) has been used as a successful legal tool for Muslims seeking to practice their religion in public in Germany. In a judgment handed down by the Higher Administrative Court in response to a case brought by several Muslim school girls who wanted exemption from co-educational swimming at school, the court said that part of the freedom of religion involves "the external freedom to manifest one's beliefs in public" (Tietze 2008, 230). These challenges to Germany's courts have acted as "unobtrusive promoter of the inclusion of Islam in Germany systems of social order" (Tietze 200, 231). As mentioned above, the FSV management insisted immediately following its three players' reprimands, that it in no way violated their religious freedom, despite suggestions otherwise. Freedom of religion, especially in the very public space of professional soccer—and free from a discussion of gender or other contentious topics—can act as a powerful message of inclusion. The ZMD's entry into the controversy should be seen in this context. The "failure" represented by the Ramadan reprimands is in this sense resolvable and powerful.

The ZMD limits its own understanding of Islamic Law (Sharia) that should be practiced in Germany to anything not contradicting local legal norms, pledging in Article 13 ("Islamic Charta" 2002) its full acceptance of German civil and criminal law, including marriage and inheritance laws. This necessarily then excludes a great part of the traditional Sharia, which held range over most criminal and civil matters. This winnowing down of Sharia's role in the modern era is widespread, including in Muslim-majority countries (Hallaq 2009). But it is this remaining realm of so-called private sphere or personal practice (prayer, pilgrimage, fasting, almsgiving and belief) that the constitutional freedom of religion mostly protects in Germany. In this personal realm then, we can understand the ZMD's seeking an inclusion of the fatwa in its arbitration and as part of the solution. On one hand the fatwa acts as a supporting text for the ZMD's statement as integrating these two systems (Islamic and German), underlining its authority by noting its origins in an "Islamic" country, Egypt. This "authority" came to stand in for the fatwa itself in the reporting. They referred to Al-Azhar and its authority often (but not always), however, they rarely mentioned the connecting fatwa directly (which was only attached to the ZMD version of the press release), and only quoted from the part of the fatwa that the press release itself had quoted. Though a fatwa is at the center of this reconciliation, it often remained obscured or even hidden as it was spread.

The Two Fatwas

In its role as a supporting text, there are actually two versions of the fatwa, one in German and one in Arabic. The German language version is about half the size of the Arabic, three paragraphs to the latter's six paragraphs. The German version's short length is explained by its exclusion of most (but not all) of the quotes and reasoning from the *fiqh*, the human legal doctrine, that are in the Arabic version and often are included in the opinions. The German fatwa is a pdf document. At the top, the title reads "Fatwa of Al-Azhar for the Pro-Soccer Player in the Month of Ramadan." This is followed by a boxed text: "Question: we have heard that many soccer players do not fast during the month of Ramadan, with the reason that due to the performance that is expected of them, they cannot fast. What does the Sharia say in this case?" The three paragraphs that follow are under the heading "Answer." The first paragraph begins with the quote in full reproduced above in the press release: "The work contract between the players" (etc.). It continues with a more general argument about employees who are contract bound to do hard work during the fast and that if so, "as the Hanafi fiqh allows," may break it ("Profifußballer Dürfen" 2010). The second paragraph extends the general argument without reference to soccer per se. It notes first that the scholars of many law schools have given their opinions on the issue, including Ibn 'Abidin al-Hanafi, al-Hattab al-Maliki, Ibn Hajar al-Haytami al-Shafi, Ibn Abd al-Hamid Shrawany. It goes on to refer to the noted exceptions like the sick and those who are nursing. But it notes that breaking of the fast is permitted also for those farmers who must harvest the wheat and laborers whose livelihoods would be affected by fasting and make them reliant on the alms of others. The third and final paragraph returns to the issue of soccer specifically. It says that if the soccer games need to be played in the day, then the practices should be moved to the nighttime. However, if this does not happen, then "the sin is ascribed" to those responsible for not moving them. The fatwa answer ends here with a Qur'an citation and quote, "Allah says: (But whoever is forced [by necessity], neither desiring [it] nor transgressing [its limit], there is no sin upon him. Indeed, Allah is Forgiving and Merciful) 2/173." The answer is followed by "Secretariat of the Fatwa Al-Azhar" and the date of 08/21/2008. The document ends with a note that it was translated by Omar Soufan on 7/23/2010 ("Profifußballer dürfen" 2010). Tracing the Arabic version of this fatwa's life will explain the discrepancy in these dates.

The Arabic fatwa from the ZMD website is a Word document and begins with the same title as the announcement. There are two pieces of additional information. The first notes the "following questions were sent to the Public Administration of Al-Azhar Journal answered under the section 'Fatwa for the Readers.'" The second piece explains that the "fourth question" (the other questions are not included) was sent from "Mr. R.M.N." The question is the same and the six paragraphs that follow cover the same ground as the German version, only in more detail. Both versions follow a standard question-answer formulation that Muftis, a category of Muslim jurist who issues these non-binding legal opinions, have been following for centuries (Messick 1996, 140). Each of the legal scholars mentioned in the German version is here given more space and their individual works and arguments are addressed. For example, Ibn 'Abidin al-Hanafi work *The Response of the Puzzled to Many Choices*, is quoted "What must be said for the professional dilemma is: if he has sufficient support for himself and his family (children) it is not permissible for him to break fast; because it is forbidden to beg, then breaking fast would be permissible and foremost in this situation…" (420/2). Likewise Al-Maliki's *Brief Friendly Explanation for the Great Talents*, Ibn Hajar al-Haytami "masterpiece" *The Needy*, and the "masterpiece on" al-Shrawany are all quoted from as supporting arguments, some of which had been summarized in the German version. The last paragraph is virtually the same as the German, with one additional line following the Quran citation: "Therefore, the sin is lifted or suspended if there is no desire of transgression." Additionally, just below the text, before the "Secretariat of the Fatwa Al-Azhar" line, is a final note: "And Allah the Almighty and Exalted Knows More." The date of 8/21/2008 ends the document ("Profifußballer dürfen" 2010).

The answer to why the date for the "Fatwa for the Soccer Player" predates the FSV controversy by a year, and the ZMD et al. press release by two years is straight forward: The Egyptian State Mufti "often copies his own previous fatwas on the subject, so that in practice he operates with a set of stock answers which may then be elaborated if special circumstances are involved" (Skovgaard-Petersen 1997, 33). Though the press release from ZMD et al. referred to the fatwa issuer as "Al-Azhar," in fact it was the Dar al-Ifta, the State Fatwa Office in Egypt, which issued it. The Dar al-Ifta is now closely intertwined with Al-Azhar (for example, the latter's journal publishes many of the fatwas issued by the former as well as trains many students in a curriculum designed by Dar al-Ifta). However, the two organizations have had a long rivalry since the Dar al-Ifta's founding in 1895, with a particularly low point in the early 1990s (*ibid.*, 289). Al-Azhar, or parts of it, have always had competing fatwa-issuing Muftis and bodies (*ibid.*, 257). But the two institutions have sought to collaborate as well. In 2007, Al-Azhar officials claimed that the Dar al-Ifta was "the only legally recognized organization authorized with issuing religious edicts," at least on the national television channels and through governmental institutions (Saleh 2007). Though this caused an uproar in certain circles, it placed the Dar al-Ifta more thoroughly at the center of discussions in Egypt about the role of Islam in society. This push began in 1978 with the inspired leadership of Jadd al-Haqq to minimized "trivial" fatwas (on inheritance disputes, for example) and moved toward "novel and important social phenomena" like politics, medicine and economics (Skovgaard-Petersen 1997, 378). At the time of the soccer fatwa being issued, the Dar al-Ifta was headed by the Grand Mufti Ali Gomaa, who himself trained and worked as a professor at Al-Azhar ("Biography" 2010). After being appointed in 2003, Dr. Gomaa had accomplished several notable achievements for Dar al-Ifta. He began by forming a fatwa council that would seek to find "collective ijtihad (en: Personal Reasoning)" and work under the guidance of the Grand Mufti to issue fatwas. He also established more independence apart from the Ministry of Justice, of which it is still formally a part (Webb 2009). As part of the Dar al-Ifta's intention to respond to concerns of not just Egypt, but the whole world, Dr. Gomaa set up multiple channels for people to ask fatwas, including an international call center, a postal mail center, a fax center and most notably an attractive and sophisticated website in Arabic, English, French, German, Russian, Turkish, Urdu and Indonesian. On the website one can submit a question in any of these languages and await an email response, follow Dar al-Ifta on Facebook or Twitter and search for previous answers.

If one searches for the Soccer Fatwa on the website, it is not available in English (initially) or German. However, a search in Arabic brought up fatwa number 1202 with the same text as available from the ZMD website fatwa, but with a slightly different date. This time it gives the date of the question's submission and answer as August 10, 2008 ("Fatwas" 2008). As alluded to above, this fatwa was ironically making waves in late summer 2009 during Ramadan in its Egyptian context as the three German players were reprimanded and a year before it would do so in Germany. News reports from September 2009 about the fatwa in that context quote what is almost certainly the same text: "a player who is tied to a club by contract is obliged to perform his duties and if this work is his source of income and he has to participate in matches during Ramadan and fasting affects his performance then he is allowed to break the fast" ("Egypt Fatwa Exempts" 2009). An article from *The National* titled "Fasting exemption for football team kicks off debate in Egypt" explains that this fatwa was posted to the front page of Dar al-Ifta's website just before Ramadan. This action set off a flurry of responses. It was seen as directed toward the Egyptian national team's upcoming match against Rwanda. The Egyptian Football Association responded by claiming that the players would not fast on that game day because of the fatwa. However, the team's star midfielder Mohammed Aboutrika immediately said he would stick to the fast even on the game day. The national coach added that many other players would do the same. Sheikh Farahat el-Mongy, a senior Al-Azhar scholar, called the fatwa "rude," and said that though God allows the sick, the pregnant, breastfeeding and menstruating women to fast, "God said nothing about allowing football players to break their fast." Khaled Tawhid, the editor of Al-Ahram's sport's magazine said that he opposes the fatwa, "as do most religious scholars." Karam Gabr, who sits on the board of the government daily, Roselyoussef, called the fatwa "confusing," and asked: "Does it apply to all matches or only the upcoming match? Does it apply to handball and basketball matches as well? What happens if, God forbid, the national team lost while its players are not fasting?" The Rwanda match was seen as very important to qualify for the World Cup. The cartoonist Amr Selim drew one Dar al-Ifta sheik telling another that "this fatwa 'is better of two evils: When 11 players break their fast is better than 80 million losing their faith while watching the match'" ("Fasting Exemption" 2009). This is to underscore Skovgaard-Petersen's point that when studying fatwas, context matters. For when the fatwa is loosed on the world, it "is not simply an outcome of the stringency of its argumentation [...] the fatwa is part of a complex world where different interests and ideologies will compete to make use of it for their own purposes" (1997, 20). There was an Egyptian context in 2009 for how the fatwa was asked for and received in a different context and reaction in Germany in 2010. So for the latter, why did the ZMD go to al-Azhar at all?

I argued in part above that we should understand the ZMD's appeal to an authority that would be beyond debate, to a certain extent. Al-Azhar's authority was almost never challenged in the German press however much the idea of a pro–Soccer player exemption to fasting was debated. Though the ZMD does not state specifically why it consulted al-Azhar and not, say, a Turkish fatwa body (considering Germany's large population of Turkish-descent), we do know that al-Azhar has loomed large in Muslim Germany. In a study of German imams, Melanie Kamp reports that when faced with more complex questions from their communities that they usually consult outside bodies, including al-Azhar (Kamp 2008, 151), a place where many of them studied, including some Turkish imams (*ibid.*, 42, 153, 155). In the mid–1980s, when the German school system developed curriculum for Islamic classes, it submitted it for evaluation to "theological faculties in Turkey and the al-Azhar faculty in Egypt" (Sovik 2008, 246). A 2002 Federal Constitutional Court made a landmark decision to allow halal slaughter in Germany, and partially appealed to a fatwa issued by the Egyptian State Mufti and al-Azhar in the 1980s. The ZMD general secretary attended the Annual Islam Conference from 2005 to 2009 in Cairo, partly under the auspices of the Honorary Chair and Grand Sheik of al-Azhar Dr. Muhammad Sayyid Tantawi ("Zentralrat Der Muslime" 2009). So though al-Azhar (and the Dar al-Ifta) is not the only authority that the ZMD could have consulted, it was one with a certain pedigree in Germany and the Islamic world at large, one which underlines the impact they hoped to have. As we saw in the reporting of the fatwa, it was an authority that went unchallenged in mainstream press. Not least, Al-Azhar already had an agreeable fatwa ready for the taking.

German Islam?

In conclusion, what exactly is the *quality* of this effort at integration, which utilizes the power of German football to position Islam as a part of German life? The ZMD Charta's Article 15 declares that "it is necessary to form a European Muslim identity." It goes on to claim that Islam has been "saved from any serious clash between religion and science" due to its underlying rationality. It is this "tradition" that supports "a contemporary reading of the Islamic sources which takes into account both the particular problematics of contemporary issues and the development of a properly European Muslim identity" ("Islamic Charta" 2002). Article 16 further specifies Germany as the focus of the ZMD's activity and, by extension, other German Muslims: "For the local Muslim population Germany is the focal point of their lives, interests, and activities" ("Islamic Charta" 2002). For this reason I argued that the ZMD choice of collaborators—the German soccer organizations—in finding a solution to the players' reprimands; their presentation of the fatwa as a major press release to Germans international news organizations well beyond the sport world as well as touting its origin at Al-Azhar; and especially the topic of choice for their intervention—Ramadan and soccer—are all specific to the German context and contribute to understanding of what they suggests it means to be a Muslim in Germany, or indeed a German Muslim.

Tariq Ramadan, the Swiss Muslim scholar and philosopher, in discussing the issue of European Muslim identity, posed a similar problematic to our fatwa: the feeling among some European Muslims (especially young ones) that the "only appropriate answer [to a question of Islam] is a legal one as if *Fiqh* alone can solve all their problems [and the] unhealthy development of a complex whereby they discredit themselves and think that the right responses should come from abroad, from great *ulama* residing in Islamic countries" (Ramadan 1999). As to the first part of this statement, our examination of German reporting on Ramadan in 2009 showed many players like Ozil and Ribery, who seemed to have come up with their own solutions to soccer and Ramadan without any apparent recourse to *fiqh*, or indeed fatwas. This was despite how the articles about the reprimands frequently tried to frame the issue as one of inherent conflict to the players. For many of the players the ulema of Islamic countries mostly did not come into play in their decisions. This is also true among amateur league players in Germany, of which a much greater number are Muslim—and to whom of course the fatwa would not technically apply as non-professionals. Though a deeper study of these leagues is beyond the scope of this study, it is apparent that ad hoc solutions to the issue of fasting and soccer are the rule on team and individual bases (Tricarico 2010). However, overall the actions of many German soccer players must allay some of Ramadan's worries. Ramadan's greater concern is how Islam is presented in Europe. A negative presentation of Islam can put European Muslims in a "reactive and defensive posture and this prevents them producing an original and serene attitude." Negative presentations of Islam are still frequent in Germany especially in connection to contentious issues such as the headscarf, as noted above. However, the Ramadan fast and professional German soccer seems to be an intersection where the presentation is not predicated on its inherent negativity, although concerns about health were especially present. Perhaps then Özil's serene attitude on the field and in front of a microphone, talking about his faith, speaks to this opening in the German discourse on Islam, that the ZMD assertively enjoined. In this limited scope, from our three soccer players in Frankfurt, to the fatwa a year later, I suggest a tactile German *and* European *and* Islamic possibility emerged. The ZMD and its allies seized upon a valuable and opportune "failure" of integration and conjured a distinctly German Islamic moment in the mainstream discourse, where one could imagine a player both confidently German and assertively Muslim.

REFERENCES

Aumüller, Johannes. 2009."Religion Und Sport: Fußball Im Fastenmonat." *Die Zeit*. October 16, sec. Sport. http://www.zeit.de/online/2007/37/ramadan-fussball.
Aumüller, Johannes. 2010., "Erlaubnis Zum Fastenbrechen." *Süddeutsche Zeitung*, July 29, sec. sport. http://www.sueddeutsche.de/sport/muslimische-profifussballer-erlaubnis-zum-fastenbrechen-1.980981.
Beister, Christian. 2009. "Sport Im Ramadan: „Richtig Schwer Fallen Mir Die Letzten Zwanzig Minuten." *Frankfurter Allgemeine Zeitung*, September 21. http://www.faz.net/aktuell/rhein-main/sport/sport-im-ramadan-richtig-schwer-fallen-mir-die-letzten-zwanzig-minuten-1859709.html.
"Biography." 2010. Ali Gomaa—Grand Mufti of Egypt. https://web-beta.archive.org/web/20120417162317/http://www.aligomaa.net/bio.html. [Original site http://www.aligomaa.net/bio.html deleted ca. 2012]
Bitzer, Dirk. c2003. *Stürmen für Deutschland: Die Geschichte des Deutschen Fussballs von 1933 Bis 1954*. New York: Campus.
Bossaller, Matthias. 2009. "Ramadan: Zweitligist Mahnt Fastende Spieler Ab." *Die Zeit*. October 16, sec. Sport. http://www.zeit.de/sport/fussball/2009-10/ramadan-abmahnung-fsvfrankfurt.
Brüggemeier, Franz-Josef. c2004. *Zurück Auf Dem Platz: Deutschland Und Die Fussball-Weltmeisterschaft 1954*. München: Deutsche Verlags-Anstalt.
Çağlar, Ayşe Ş. 1998. "McDöner: Dönerkebab Und Der Kampf Der Deutsch-Türken Um Soziale Stellung." *Sociologus* 48, no. 1: 17–41.
Chawla, Suresh. 2009. "German Football Club in Row Over Ramadan Fasting Warning." *Top-News*, October 13. http://www.topnews.in/german-football-club-row-over-ramadan-fasting-warning-2224000.

Cohen, Roger. 2010. "Özil the German." *New York Times*, July 1. http://www.nytimes.com/2010/07/02/opinion/02iht-edcohen.html.
Dachs, Heidi. 2010. "Ramadanen Fylder I Tyskland." *Kristeligt Dagblad*, August 19. https://www.kristeligt-dagblad.dk/udland/ramadanen-fylder-i-tyskland.
Dempsey, Judy. 2011. "Muslims' Role in Germany Questioned by Interior Minister." *New York Times*, March 6. http://www.nytimes.com/2011/03/07/world/europe/07germany.html.
"Drei Fussballer Wegen Ramadan Abgemahnt." 2009. *Berliner Zeitung*, October 13. http://www.bz-berlin.de/artikel-archiv/drei-fuballer-wegen-ramadan-abgemahnt.
Dubin, Steven C. 2011. "Imperfect Pitch: Pop Culture, Consensus, and Resistance During the 2010 World Cup." *African Arts* 44, no. 2: 18–31.
Eggers, Erik. 2001. *Fussball in der Weimarer Republik*. Kassel: Agon Sportverlag.
"Egypt Fatwa Exempts Footballers from Ramadan." 2009. Al Arabiya News, August 25. https://www.alarabiya.net/articles/2009/08/25/82891.html.
"Egypt's Dar Al-Ifta—About Us." 2017. *Egypt's Dar Al-Ifta*. Accessed January 27. http://dar-alifta.org/Module.aspx?Name=aboutdar&Home=1&LangID=2.
Eilers, Kea, Clara Seitz, and Kondrad Hischler, 2008. "Religiousness Among Young Muslims in Germany." In *Islam and Muslims in Germany*, edited by Ala Al-Hamarneh and Jorn Thielmann, 103–115. Leiden: Koninklijke Brill NV.
Encyclopaedia of Islam, s.v. 2017. "Ramaḍān" by M. Plessner. Accessed January 30. http://www.brillonline.nl/subscriber/entry?entry=islam_SIM-6208.
"Erlaubnis Zum Fastenbrechen." 2010. sueddeutsche.de, July 29, sec. sport. http://www.sueddeutsche.de/sport/muslimische-profifussballer-erlaubnis-zum-fastenbrechen-1.980981.
Ewing, Katherine. 2008. *Stolen Honor: Stigmatizing Muslim Men in Berlin*. Stanford University Press.
"Fasten Und Fußball: Hattrick Im Ramadan." 2008. *Frankfurter Allgemeine Zeitung*, September 12. http://www.faz.net/aktuell/sport/fussball/bundesliga/fasten-und-fussball-hattrick-im-ramadan-1699617.html.
"Fasting Exemption for Football Team Kicks Off Debate in Egypt." 2009. *The National*, September 4. http://www.thenational.ae/news/world/africa/fasting-exemption-for-football-team-kicks-off-debate-in-egypt.
"Fatwas—Professional Soccer Players Refraining from Fasting in Ramadan." 2008. *Dar Alifta*, October 8. http://dar-alifta.org/ViewFatwa.aspx?ID=1202&text=1202.
Fischer, Gerhard. 1999.*Stürmer für Hitler: Vom Zusammenspiel Zwischen Fussball und Nationalsozialismus*. Göttingen: Die Werkstatt.
FOCUS. 2010. "Profifußballer Dürfen Im Ramadan Fasten Brechen." FOCUS Online, July 28. http://www.focus.de/sport/fussball/fussball-profifussballer-duerfen-im-ramadan-fasten-brechen_aid_535456.html.
Fritz, Thomas. 2010. "RWE-Stürmer Darf Trotz Ramadan Fasten Unterbrechen." *Thüringer Allgemeine*, August 14. http://www.thueringer-allgemeine.de/startseite/detail/-/specific/RWE-Stuermer-darf-trotz-Ramadan-Fasten-unterbrechen-%20894793549.
"FSV Frankfurt: Ramadan-Klausel! Abmahnung Für 3 Profis, Weil Sie Gefastet Haben." 2009. *Bild*, October 12. http://www.bild.de/sport/fussball/ramadan-klausel-abmahnung-fuer-drei-profis-weil-sie-gefastet-haben-10077114.bild.html.
"German Muslim Group: Professional Soccer Players Can Break Fast During Ramadan." 2010. *Associated Press*, July 28. http://www.foxnews.com/sports/2010/07/28/german-muslim-group-professional-soccer-players-break-fast-ramadan.html.
Goltermann, Svenja. c1998. *Körper der Nation: Habitusformierung und die Politik des Turnens 1860–1890*. Göttingen: Vandenhoeck & Ruprecht.
Hallaq, Wael B. 2009.*Sharī'a: Theory, Practice, Transformations*. Cambridge University Press.
Hicks, Gavin M. 2014. "Soccer and Social Identity in Contemporary German Film and Media." Ph.D., University of Pittsburgh.
"Hintergrund: Fußball und der Islamische Fastenmonat Ramadan." 2010. *Mitteldeutsche Zeitung*, September 10. http://www.mz-web.de/hintergrund-fussball-und-der-islamische-fastenmonat-ramadan-7515370.
Horeni, Michael. 2010. "Integration im Fußball: Der Ball Ist Bunt." *Frankfurter Allgemeine*

Zeitung, October 11. http://www.faz.net/aktuell/feuilleton/reportagen/integration-im-fussball-der-ball-ist-bunt-11051178.html.

"How Can Germany's Interior Minister Do the Job?" 2011. *New York Times*, March 8. http://www.nytimes.com/2011/03/09/opinion/09wed3.html.

Hytner, David. 2010. "World Cup 2010: Germany Reap the Rewards of the Liberation Generation." *The Guardian*, June 17. sec. Football. https://www.theguardian.com/football/2010/jun/17/world-cup-2010-germany-liberation.

"Islam: RTL II Sendet Ramadan-Hinweise für Muslime." 2010. *Die Welt*, August 10. https://www.welt.de/fernsehen/article8921695/RTL-II-sendet-Ramadan-Hinweise-fuer-Muslime.html.

"Islamic Charta." 2002. *ZMD—Zentralrat der Muslime in Deutschland*, February 20. http://zentralrat.de/3037.php.

Kamp, Melanie. 2008. "Prayer Leader, Counselor, Teacher, Social Worker, and Public Relations Officer—On the Roles and Functions of Imams in Germany." In *Islam and Muslims in Germany*, edited by Ala Al-Hamarneh and Jorn Thielmann, 133–160. Leiden: Koninklijke Brill NV.

Kopytoff, Igor. 2013. "The Cultural Biography of Things: Commoditization as Process." In *The Social Life of Things: Commodities in Cultural Perspective*, edited by Arjun Appadurai, 11. print. Cambridge: Cambridge University Press.

Krümpelmann, Dirk. 2009. "Gladbachs Karim Matmour: Mein Leben als Ramadan-Profi." *Bild*, August 25. http://www.bild.de/sport/fussball/mein-leben-als-ramadan-profi-9507074.bild.html.

Kuppinger, Petra. 2014. "Flexible Topographies: Muslim Spaces in a German Cityscape." *Social & Cultural Geography* 15, no. 6 (August 18): 627–44. doi:10.1080/14649365.2014.882396.

Lenzen-Schulte, Martina. 2009. "Diabetes: Risiko Ramadan." *Frankfurter Allgemeine Zeitung*, August 28. http://www.faz.net/aktuell/wissen/medizin-ernaehrung/diabetes-risiko-ramadan-1839324.html.

Lüdeke, Steffen. 2009. "Islam: Ramadan Stürzt Sportler in Gewissenskonflikte." *Die Welt*, September 3. https://www.welt.de/sport/fussball/article4457102/Ramadan-stuerzt-Sportler-in-Gewissenskonflikte.html.

Majer-O'Sickey, Ingeborg. 2006. "Out of the Closet? German Patriotism and Soccer Mania." *German Politics & Society* 24, no. 3 (80): 82–97.

McCarra, Kevin. 2010 ."World Cup 2010: Wizardry of Mesut Ozil Marks Out Germany's Next Star." *The Guardian*, June 15. http://www.guardian.co.uk/football/2010/jun/15/mesut-ozil-germany-world-cup, accessed April 22.

Meier, Henk Erik, and Michael Mutz. 2016. "Sport-Related National Pride in East and West Germany, 1992–2008: Persistent Differences or Trends Toward Convergence?" *SAGE Open* 6, no. 3 (September 1): 2158244016665893. doi:10.1177/2158244016665893.

Messick, Brinkley Morris. 1996.*The Calligraphic State : Textual Domination and History in a Muslim Society*. Berkeley: University of California Press.

"Muslimische Spieler im Fastenmonat Ramadan: 'Es Ist Unsere Pflicht.'" 2010. 11FREUNDE. de, August 5. http://www.11freunde.de/node/131885.

"Profifußballer Dürfen im Ramadan Fasten Brechen." 2010. *ZMD—Zentralrat der Muslime in Deutschland*, July 28. http://zentralrat.de/16130.php.

Puck, Kristina. 2009. "Fußball Mit Leerem Magen: Ramadan als Härtetest." N-Tv.de, September 2. http://www.n-tv.de/sport/Ramadan-als-Haertetest-article486312.html.

Quiroga, Alejandro. 2013. *Football and National Identities in Spain: The Strange Death of Don Quixote*. New York: Palgrave Macmillan.

Ramadan, Tariq. 1999. *To Be a European Muslim: A Study of Islamic Sources in the European Context*. Markfield: The Islamic Foundation.

"Ramadan-Fasten Bringt FSV-Trio Abmahnung Ein." 2009. Sport1.de, October 13. http://www.sport1.de/de/fussball/fussball_bundesliga2/artikel_162254.html.

Redemann, Elmar, and Steffie Zwaagstra. 2009. "Ramadan: Gesundheitsrisiko Oder Extra-Kick." RevierSport Online, September 8. http://www.reviersport.de/93574-ramadan-gesundheitsrisiko-oder-extra-kick.html.

Rohe, Mathias. 2004. "The Formation of European Shari'a." In *Muslims in Europe: From the Margin to the Centre*, edited by Jamal Malik, 161–184. Muenster: LIT Verlag.
Rohe, Mathias. 2008. "Islamic Norms in Germany and Europe." In I*slam and Muslims in Germany*, edited by Ala Al-Hamarneh and Jorn Thielmann, 49–82. Leiden: Koninklijke Brill NV.
Rommel, Stefan. 2009. "Ramadan: Die Fünfte Jahreszeit." *Spox*, September 2. http://www.spox.com/de/sport/fussball/bundesliga/0909/Artikel/ramadan-islam-koran-muslime-bundesliga-profis-leistungssport-tasci-khedira-mnari-ahanfouf.html.
Rössler, Hans-Christian. 2010. "Ramadan: die Fasten-Zeiten der Fastenzeit." *Frankfurter Allgemeine Zeitung*, August 11. http://www.faz.net/aktuell/gesellschaft/ramadan-die-fastenzeiten-der-fastenzeit-11023711.html.
Saleh, Yasmine. 2007. "Al Azhar: Only Dar Al Ifta Can Issue Fatwas." *Daily News Egypt*, January 5. http://www.dailynewsegypt.com/2007/01/05/al-azhar-only-dar-al-ifta-can-issue-fatwas/.
Şen, Faruk. 2008. "Euro-Islam: Some Empirical Evidences." In I*slam and Muslims in Germany*, edited by Ala Al- Hamarneh and Jorn Thielmann, 33–48. Leiden: Koninklijke Brill NV.
Skovgaard-Petersen, Jakob. 1997. *Defining Islam for the Egyptian State: Muftis and Fatwas of the Dar-al-Ifta*. Leiden: Brill.
Sovik, Margrete. 2008. "Islamic Instruction in German Public Schools: The Case of North-Rhine-Westphalia." In *Islam and Muslims in Germany*, edited by Ala Al-Hamarneh and Jorn Thielmann, 241–266. Leiden: Koninklijke Brill NV.
Stehle, Maria, and Beverly M. Weber. 2013. "German Soccer, the 2010 World Cup, and Multicultural Belonging." *German Studies Review* 36, no. 1 (February 26): 103–24.
Tietze, Nikola. 2008. "Muslims' Collective Self-Description as Reflected in the Institutional Recognition of Islam: The *Islamic Charter* of the Central Council of Muslims in Germany and Case Law in German Courts." In *Islam and Muslims in Germany*, edited by Ala Al-Hamarneh and Jorn Thielmann, 215–239. Leiden: Koninklijke Brill NV.
Tricarico, Tanja. 2010. "Ramadan: Härtetest für Muslimische Amateurkicker." Evangelisch.de, August 10. http://www.evangelisch.de/inhalte/101136/10-08-2010/ramadan-haertetest-fuer-muslimische-amateurkicker.
Warner, Mary Beth, and Josie Le Bond. 2010. "The World from Berlin: 'Integration Is the Second German Unification.'" *SPIEGEL*, October 4. http://www.spiegel.de/international/germany/the-world-from-berlin-integration-is-the-second-german-unification-a-721119.html.
Webb, Suhaib. 2009. "Exciting News at Dar Al-Ifta from the Grand Mufti of Egypt Dr☒Ali Gomaa." *Virtual Mosque*, February 8. http://www.virtualmosque.com/islam-studies/exciting-news-at-dar-al-ifta-from-the-grand-mufti-of-egypt-dr-%cc%94Ali-gomaa/.
Young, Michael A. 2013. "Cultural Performances of German National Identity: Popular Music, Body Culture, and the 2006 FIFA World Cup." M.A., Indiana University. http://search.proquest.com.ezproxy.cul.columbia.edu/docview/1346229080/abstract/8AAA1BD55F984C8FPQ/1.
"Zentralrat der Muslime War Zum 4. Mal Konferenzteilnehmer des Obersten Rat für Islamische Angelegenheiten in Kairo/Ägypten." 2009. *ZMD —Zentralrat der Muslime in Deutschland*, March 17. http://zentralrat.de/11732.php.

A Cause Without a Rebel

In Search of a Palestinian Sporting Hero

Jon Dart

Abstract

The Israel/Palestine conflict is one of the most contentious, longest running and divisive conflicts in the modern era. Sport is increasingly becoming a battleground with Palestinians recognizing the possibilities of sport to bring attention to their national identity and "nation." Increasing attention has been given to the Palestinian men's national soccer team and the presence of a six-person Palestinian team at the Rio 2016 Olympics. This essay assesses the likelihood of Palestinian athletes emerging whose visibility might advance their call for human rights. Attention is given to Mahmoud Sarsak who, as a young Palestinian footballer, was arrested when he tried to travel from Gaza to the West Bank to sign a professional contract. Accused of involvement in violent anti–Israeli actions, he was held for three years before being released without charge. The essay discusses how calls for social justice for the Palestinians have come primarily from non–Palestinian sports men and women, such as footballers Eric Cantona, Cristiano Ronaldo and Joey Barton, and English cricketer Moeen Ali, who was reprimanded for wearing wristbands embossed with the phrases "Save Gaza" and "Free Palestine" during a match. The highest profile support has come from beyond the world of sport, including that shown by the musician Roger Waters and film director Ken Loach. The essay assesses the claims that the Israeli state are deliberately seeking to suppress Palestinian sport by targeting Palestinian individuals (through restricting their movement) and destroying its sporting infrastructure. The essay considers why there has not (yet) been a high-profile Palestine spokesperson, linked to sport, and considers the prospects of one emerging from within to advocate for social justice for Palestinians.

The 70-year conflict between Israel and Palestine is one of the longest running and most brutal conflicts in the modern era. International sport has become one of the proxy battlefields upon which the Palestinians, and their supporters, are using to bring attention to their struggle for nationhood. The Rio 2016 Olympic Games saw the greatest expression of Palestinian sporting identity when they fielded their largest ever Olympic team with the activities of the Palestinian men's national soccer team also making an important contribution to a sense of Palestinian national identity.

Nationalism has long been inextricably linked with international sport. National and international sporting competitions act as important sites in establishing, maintaining and celebrating expressions of national identity and nationhood. This essay explores Palestinian national identity and sport, the significant difficulties faced by Palestinian athletes, and the likelihood of a Palestinian athlete emerging to shine a spotlight on the Palestinian struggle for a homeland. The essay begins with a brief outline of the origins of the Israel/Palestine conflict and of Palestinian national identity. It then summarizes the literature on sport and national identity before briefly outlining the history of Palestinian sport, focusing on soccer and athletics. The essay discusses contemporary problems within Palestinian sport, before examining the actions of the Israeli state in limiting its development. I then consider whether the Israeli state is deliberately suppressing Palestinian sport by targeting individual athletes and destroying its physical sporting infrastructure. Support for the Palestinians from non–Palestinians and non-athletes is noted before the essay concludes with an explanation as to why there has not (yet) been a high-profile Palestinian sporting hero able to advocate for the Palestinians.

Nationalism and Sport

Nationalism is a highly contested concept with signs of an increasing polarization of nationalism in practice. On the one hand, progressive nationalism (read "good/acceptable") is posited on universalism and human rights, seeing itself as adapting to a more fluid, multicultural, pluralist society and a post-national ideology supportive of immigration. On the other hand, there has been a rise in populist, chauvinistic nationalism (read "bad/unacceptable"), which has become increasingly visible in expressing skepticism/hostility toward multiculturalism and seeks "managed migration" and the introduction of ID cards to address national security concerns. The political left has traditionally viewed expressions of nationalism and patriotism in a negative light, interpreting such manifestations as atavistic and sinister. However, those who advocate for benign nationalism, claim it is "natural" for people to love their country, and that promoting loyalty to one's country generates a greater sense of belonging, allegiance, and gratitude.

Greater levels of national consciousness have been informed by increased movement of people. This has, arguably, led to the rise of populist, politically conservative movements in Western Europe, exemplified in the British voting for Brexit and election of Donald Trump in the USA. Clearly, the rise of aggressive, neo-fascist forms of nationalism which "blame the immigrant" are divisive and dangerous, but other forms of nationalism and national identity can be used for constructive activities. Since nationalistic sentiments have wide appeal and durability, in some cases it might be necessary to cultivate this kind of nationalism than to attempt to move beyond it. For the Palestinian people, an expression of their national identity is essential in their struggle to secure their human rights and a homeland.

Hobsbawm and Ranger (1983) and Anderson (2006) have shown how the nation is a "community writ large," which cultivates and celebrates its civic rituals and symbols, history, landscape, architecture, food, music, art, literature, flag, national anthem, statues, shrines and coinage, and the honoring of military and national heroes. While there is the suggestion that mainstream commentators on nationalism often paid little attention to sport (Smith and Porter, 2004), Bairner (2015) suggests sport offers multiple opportunities to create and foster a sense of nationhood with greater interest being shown in how sports events can act as sites for the construction, expression or (re)imagining of national identity and national heroes (Allen 2013; Hassan 2013; Holt and Ruta 2015; Hunter 2003; Tomlinson and Young, 2006; Wenner and Billings 2017).

The relationship between national identity and sport is multi-faceted and complex (Smith and Porter, 2004), with a growing recognition of international sport offering an effective stage for those "without a country" and/or those seeking recognition for their small or nascent nation (Sterchele 2013; Brentin 2013; Menary 2007). Smith and Porter (2004) conclude that certain sports are more effective than others in serving as cultural signifiers of national identity and where there is a minority and/or oppressed group, sport offers a unique platform around which to mobilize.

Anderson (2006) proposed that all nations are imagined or constructed upon a sense of national identity which combines invented traditions and popular mythologies. A national sports team can act as an important display of/for such "invented traditions" and unrealized fantasies. Hobsbawm (1990) applies Anderson's work to sport and claims the cultural production of soccer seizes the popular imagination more effectively than other activities in the realms of political and cultural construction. Sport produces powerful nationalistic tendencies with Hobsbawm (1990: 143) suggesting that

> What has made sport so uniquely effective a medium for inculcating national feelings, at all events for males, is the ease with which even the least political or public individuals can identify with the nation as symbolized by young persons excelling at what practically every man wants, or at one time in his life has wanted, to be good at. The imagined community of millions seems more real as a team of eleven named people.

For Palestinians, the embodiment of their nation in a national sports team, especially its soccer team, competing at an international sports event, is an essential ingredient in their sense of nationhood. Research on international sport as an expression of "90-minute patriotism" (Vincent, Kian, and Pedersen 2011; Ward 2009) cannot be applied to the Palestinians, because their nation's sport activities, especially its successes, represents much, much more than a mere 90 minutes.

The Origins of the Palestine/Israel Conflict

It is beyond the scope of this essay to offer a full explanation of historical issues that surround the fractious relationship between the Israeli state and the Palestinians. The fluidity of national boundaries, the invention of the nation-state and nationalism as a 20th-century phenomenon led Sugden (2008, 2010) to note that the deep-roots of the Israeli and Palestinian conflict make it necessary to offer an objective outline of only those socio-political and demographic features which pertain to the issue/s under discussion. As historian James Joll (cited in Bregman 2014) has advocated, including a narrative history is important as it reminds the reader of the sequence of events and provides a chart with which to navigate stormy seas.

From the time of the Assyrians before the Christian Era, through Greek, Roman, Byzantium and Ottoman administration, for over 3000 years the region known as Palestine has been at a crossroads, with a long history of invasion, occupation, migration and "foreign" rule. The region was named "Palestine" by Roman rulers with the appellation remaining to modern times despite there never having been a well-defined, nation-state (in the modern sense) called "Palestine." Jewish refugees and Zionist settlers began to arrive during the British Mandate of Palestine (or Mandate Palestine) at the end of the 19th century to join a small, long-established Jewish community (Yishuv).[1] Antisemitism in Europe saw Jews subject to repeated discrimination and pogroms which culminated in the 19th and 20th centuries. Many left to seek a new life in North America, with some attracted to the ideology of Zionism and the promise of a "safe haven" for the Jews in the Middle East (Morris 1999; Segev 2000, 2001; Stanislawski 2016).

After the defeat of Turkey in World War I and the collapse of the Ottoman Empire, Britain and France "carved up" much of the Middle East, created new borders and appointed their preferred administrators to run the newly created nations (Barr 2012; Rogan 2016). Britain took control of Palestine and governed it under a mandate until 1948. They then failed to appease either the Arab and Jewish populations (Schneer 2011; Segev 2001) and became increasingly mired in the politics of the region before passing responsibility to the United Nations (UN). In 1947 the UN drew up a partition plan that divided Palestine into two states.[2] The day after the UN Resolution was approved a civil war began which ended in victory for the new Jewish state. The declaration of the State of Israel on May 14, 1948, is viewed by the Palestinians as "Al-Nakba" (the catastrophe).

In 1949 a ceasefire was established but there continued an exodus of Palestinian refugees to neighboring countries, the Gaza Strip and the area to the west of the River Jordan (i.e., the West Bank).[3] Those who fled during the conflict were, and remain, unable to return to their homes (Pappe 2007). The arrival of large numbers of Jews ("Aliyah") to the new state took place against ongoing expulsion, exclusion and oppression of the remaining Palestinian population. This situation was compounded by the 1967 ("Six Day") war and the continued colonization of Palestinian land (Abunimah 2014; Pappé 2007 2011). What is without doubt is that the situation is nuanced, complex and multi-dimensional.

The Palestinians

Palestinian national identity is a passionately contested question with attempts by Zionists to deny the existence of a distinct Palestinian identity based on the claim there has never been a Palestinian state, and thus neither a "Palestinian." There is a widely-held, biblically-informed narrative that claims "the Jews" lived on the eastern shore of the Mediterranean until their expulsion by the Romans in the first and second century CE ("the Jewish Diaspora"); however, recent archaeological evidence has begun to challenge this narrative (Rose 2004; Sand 2012). There is also the suggestion that today's Palestinians are the biological descendants of Jews from Biblical times, but a process of assimilation and conversion away from Judaism make them more likely to be biologically closer to Moses and Jesus than those Jews who recently emigrated from the USA, Russia or Ethiopia (Sand 2014).

There are many different Palestinian communities, be they based in Israel, in the OPT, or living as refugees in neighboring countries or in the wider Palestinian diaspora.[4] There has been extensive debate about whether the Palestinians constitute a defined ethnic group with Palestinians often portrayed in Western media as Muslims, although they might be Christian or Druze (Said 2003). There have been attempts by Zionists to define the Palestinian as either "Arab" (on the grounds that "they can go and live in another 'Arab' country") or as Muslims (making it easier for the Israeli state to align with "the West" against Muslim/Islamic extremism).[5] There are just under three million Palestinians living in the West Bank and two million in the Gaza Strip.[6] Between 17 percent and 20 percent of the country's population is identified as Israeli-Arab, depending if one includes Palestinians living in East Jerusalem and the Druze in the Golan Heights. This particular demographic occupies a very different position to non–Arab Israelis and Palestinians living in the West Bank or Gaza (Shor and Yonay, 2010; Sorek, 2005; 2007).[7]

The Palestinians moved away from an unsuccessful armed struggle to civil protests, *Intifadas* (Uprising), between 1987 and 1993 and 2000 and 2005. This change in tactics saw increased international public support and the emergence in 2005 of the nonviolent Boycott, Disinvestment and Sanctions (BDS) movement (Bakan and Abu-Laban 2009; Barghouti 2011; Lim, 2012; Wiles 2013). As various governments and international agencies try to bring both parties together, "facts"—in the form of Israeli settlements—continued to be built across occupied Palestinian land making a "two-state solution" increasingly impossible. In such a climate, symbols are essential in creating and maintaining a sense of national identity. For the Palestinians this has traditionally included their food and music (Hass 2013), heroes and heroines (Khalili 2009; Tobin 2016) with sport becoming increasingly important in their struggle for greater international support and recognition.

Palestinian Sport

Palestine has never been a defined nation in the modern, Westphalian sense, with the written history of recent sport in Palestine primarily couched within Israeli state-building narratives. Sport, as a 20th century phenomenon, has its history in "Palestine" as originating in the "Yishuv" (Harif & Galily 2003; Kaufman & Galily, 2007, 2009). The available history of Palestinian sport is limited, due in part to the systematic destruction of historical and cultural records linked to the Palestinian people, with Chomsky (1999) suggesting there has been a deliberate attempt to render Palestine and Palestinians invisible. Whilst some source material was available in the press from the 1930s and the 1940s this was neglected until relatively recently (Sorek, 2000, 2013). Seeking to address the lack of scholarly interest in Palestinian sport Khalidi (2012) has identified some 65 social athletic clubs operating in

Palestine prior to 1948, most of which were affiliated to the Arab Palestine Sports Federation.

Palestine, Soccer and FIFA

The global, mass appeal of soccer is due in part to it lacking the restrictive class-based influences of other sports. This "classlessness" makes it more inclusive and allows greater legitimacy for it to be viewed as a nation's "national sport." Soccer will be argued to be the only national institution that unifies the Palestinians with this section focusing on soccer because of its centrality to Palestinian identity on an international sporting stage.

Khalidi (2012) has shown how soccer in Palestine has a long (albeit partially hidden) history with wider political events leading to the closure of many (non–Jewish) Palestinian soccer clubs. A Palestinian Football Association (PFA) was founded in Mandatory Palestine in 1928 with the Zionist Maccabi sports organization applying for and securing membership of FIFA (Mendel 2017).[8] This Palestinian Football Association operated a local league structure comprising nine Jewish clubs and one British (police) club in the top-tier with Arab clubs restricted to the secondary league. Arab soccer clubs participated in this league until 1934, when they established a parallel Arab soccer league. The two leagues operated separately until 1948 ("War of Independence"/"Al Nakba") when hundreds of thousands of Palestinians were displaced and the Arab soccer league collapsed. A new Palestine Football Federation was established in 1952 and was subsequently reformed as the Palestine Football Association (PFA) in 1962. It obtained provisional member status to FIFA in 1995 and was accepted into FIFA in 1998 after the creation of the Palestinian Authority.

The PFA operated two leagues, one in the West Bank (since 1977), the other in the Gaza Strip, but, due to the Israeli occupation and internal disputes, seasons were often incomplete.[9] In 2000 the second *Intifada* began and since then teams from Gaza have not played against teams from the West Bank. The leagues suffered from repeated interruptions and restrictions on player and fans' ability to travel due to encirclements and blockades, in addition to damage to sports facilities. Soccer players, as young men, participated in the second *Intifada* (2000–2005), with many of them either injured or imprisoned. The 2005 season was interrupted four times and only officially ended in 2007 (Mendel 2017), although in more recent years the West Bank League has been able to complete its season (Montague, 2015). Over the years, the league has taken many different forms with the West Bank structure currently the larger and more professional than the league structure in Gaza.[10] In addition to better living conditions (regularly supplies of electricity, clean water and freedom of movement, see Tawfiq 2016), West Bank players are able to earn an income from playing soccer, partly due to television coverage. The West Bank League is also a popular destination for Palestinian citizens of Israel, many of whom can earn more money than they would playing for a club in the Israeli second or third tier (Ali Khaled 2015). The PFA has responsibility for the Palestine women's national soccer team (established in 2003) who played their first game in West Bank against Jordan's national team in 2009 (Montague, 2009) with a women's league formed in 2011 (Al Arabiya News 2014). The ongoing tension in Gaza, the political division between Gaza and the West Bank, and the lack of free movement of players and teams have all conspired to prevent the establishment of a national Palestinian football league structure (Mendel 2017).

With FIFA's recognition of Palestine in 1998[11] the men's national team played friendlies against Lebanon, Jordan and Syria in the same year. They subsequently entered the Pan Arab Games in 1999 (Henry, Amara and Al-Tauqi, 2003) and sought to qualify for the finals of the 2000 Asian Cup and FIFA 2002 World Cup. Shortly thereafter, the Israeli authorities refused to issue exit visas (travel permits) for half the squad to participate in the 2006 World Cup qualifying matches; in 2007 and 2008 members of the team were similarly prevented from traveling to play in international fixtures. Palestine did not play an official fixture at home until 2008 when they played Jordan: "The political situation took its toll on the event since at least four players—including the team's captain, Saeb Jundiyeh, from Gaza and others from refugee camps in Lebanon and Syria—could not get Israeli permission to enter the country" (Wheeler, 2008). In 2011 Palestine played its first ever competitive home game in a 2012 World Cup qualifier against Thailand; later that same year, six members of the Palestinian team were refused permission to leave Gaza to play against Mauritania. Since then, FIFA have repeatedly had to intervene to resolve issues of player movement and the Israeli's refusal to issue travel permits.

Soccer has become an important expression of Palestinian national identity. The global nature of the sport makes it essential for them to field "a team of 11 shirts." However, it is not just through soccer that the Palestinians are seeking to assert their national identity; they are also using the other global sporting mega event, the Olympic Games.

Palestine and the Olympics

Despite the professed claim of the International Olympic Committee (IOC) to keep politics and sport separate, their lavish opening and closing ceremonies, and medal events are replete with symbols of national identity

(Traganou 2017; Thomas and Antony 2015). While there has been criticism of expressions of nationalism at international sports events, for some, especially smaller and/or emerging nation states, such events are important platforms upon which they can express their national identity.

The Palestine National Olympic Committee (PNOC) was formed in 1933 and although recognized by the International Olympic Committee the following year, did not enter any Olympic Games. Whilst nominally representing all those living in Mandatory Palestine (i.e., Jews, Muslims and Christians) the PNOC was controlled by Maccabi sports organization (Galily and Ben-Porat 2008) with neither their rival Jewish sports organization, Hapoel, nor non–Jewish sports organizations part of this organization. The Olympic Committee of Israel (OCI) secured IOC recognition in 1952 and debuted as the Summer Olympics in Helsinki that same year. The PNOC should thus be seen as a precursor of the OCI rather than the Palestine Olympic Committee (Khalidi, and Raab, 2017; Mallon and Heijmans, 2015).

Palestine (via the Palestinian National Authority) became a recognized member of the Olympic Council of Asia in 1986 and first competed in the 1990 Asian Games. It then secured recognition from the IOC in 1995 and sent its first team, comprising two competitors, to the Atlanta 1996 Olympic Games. Since then, Palestine has sent two athletes to Olympic Games in 2000; three athletes in 2004; four in 2008; five in 2012, and six in 2016.[12] Palestine first competed in the Paralympic Games in Sydney 2000 when they sent two athletes (with the same number of athletes appearing at the Olympic Games in 2004, 2008 and 2012).

Similar to the experience of soccer players [noted above] Paralympian athletes were adversely affected by the second *Intifada* and the Israeli attack on Gaza in 2008–2009. During these periods many sports clubs across the OPT were closed; European Union funding has since helped to re-establish these clubs, develop leadership training and regular sport practices for youth with disabilities (Ma'an News Agency 2010). In the London 2012 Olympics, Maher Abu Rmeileh became the first Palestinian to qualify for the Olympic Games on merit. At the time, Abu Rmeileh avoided commenting on the Israeli-Palestinian conflict, but stated he was "very happy I will be going as an ambassador for the Palestinian people. I will be carrying the Palestinian flag ... (and) ... it is enough for us to be able to tell the whole world that we Palestinians exist" (quoted in Sherwood 2012).

Rio 2016 Summer Olympic Games

Rio 2016 offered the Palestinian team an important platform on which to assert their national identity and attract positive attention to their "country" (Monier 2016). The 2016 Palestinian team was the nation's largest ever delegation to the Games, comprising six athletes, two of whom were born in OPT and four in Germany. Two athletes qualified on the basis of sporting merit, with the remaining four "invited" to Rio. The IOC is aware that athletes from developing nations often lack access to the necessary sports infrastructure (including training, equipment and facilities) which would allow them to meet Olympic qualification standards and thus operate a program that allows those affected to compete without qualifying on merit. The six athletes were:

- Mary al-Atrash: 50-meter freestyle Swimmer. Resident of Bethlehem. The lack of an Olympic-sized pool in the Palestinian territories meant that she had to train in a 25-meter pool. Various 50m pools are within easy distance of Bethlehem, and she could have applied for access (to Israeli pools), but acknowledged that Palestinians were rarely granted access. Due to water shortage and restrictions imposed by the Israeli state, al-Atrash's training was restricted and her first encounter with an Olympic-sized pool was in pre–Olympic training in Algeria [cited in Bernish 2016].
- Ahmed Gebrel: 200-meter freestyle Swimmer. Egyptian mother and Palestinian father; raised in Cairo, living and training in Spain. Competed at 2012 Olympics in London and the only Palestinian athlete to have participated in two Olympics. Holds various Palestinian swimming records but was an invitee after failing to meet qualification times.
- Mohammed Abu Khoussa: first Palestinian to compete in the 100-meter event. Born in Gaza and reportedly lives with a poor eight-member family in Gaza City. His family immigrated to Gaza from Egypt in 1948 [Lieber 2017].
- Mayada Al-Sayad: the first Palestinian athlete to run in the 42km Olympic marathon. Born and raised in Berlin, German mother and a Palestinian father. Qualified for Rio 2016 on merit.
- Simon Yacoub: Born and raised in Leipzig, Germany by Palestinian father and German mother. As a youngster was part of the German Judo national team, but had to stop training due to a serious illness. When he recovered "he knew he could not qualify for the German national team" and chose to represent Palestine. Invitee to 2016 Games.
- Christian Zimmerman: A German-Palestinian with dual citizenship and resident of Cologne; first Palestinian to compete in the Olympics in dressage.

The athletes competing in Rio varied in their willingness to speak to the media about wider political events. The athletes must have recognized the symbolic importance of Palestinian representation on international sporting stages with the equestrian Christian Zimmerman stating how he "want(ed) to prove that we are an independent entity and that we are represented in the international scene even if on a small scale" (quoted in Monier 2016). Mary al-Atrash acknowledged the "responsibility of highlighting that we are living under great difficulties" (quoted in Bernish 2016), with Mayada Al-Sayad (quoted in Bernish, 2016) less forthcoming stating only that "I don't have political but only sporting reasons to compete for Palestine" (quoted in Bernish 2016).

Although much of the mainstream press coverage is given to soccer and the Olympic Games, other sports form part of the debate about the occupation and Palestinian sporting identity. Examples include individual athletes such as Sani Sakakini, a professional basketball player (Carpenter 2015), and examples from grass-roots activities which are often viewed through a "sport-for-development" lens or viewed as "participation as resistance." Among such sporting activities are surfing (Mutch 2016), parkour (Thorpe and Ahmad 2015), baseball (Associated Press 2017) and bike riding (Suleiman 2016). The establishment of the first women's sports academy was proposed in 2017 with the aim of producing professional athletes. Private funds were sought as women's sports in Gaza was not a priority for the Hamas government, who stated they were more focused on building hospitals and schools (Abou Jalal 2017). While the focus of this essay is on international sport and Palestinian national identity, sport at a local level can contribute to greater social inclusion and social integration and improve "quality of life" indices. However, all is not well in Palestinian civil society with significant and varied factors conspiring to limit the emergence of elite athletes, ones capable of representing Palestine on an international sporting stage.

Complications Faced by Palestinian Athletes

Shor and Yonay (2010) have explored how sport can bring together different groups and build bridges between the Arab and Jewish communities. At the same time, soccer was shown to reflect and maintain the dominance of the wider Israel-Jewish society. They found Israeli Palestinian soccer players were consistently monitored and silenced by the Jewish-dominated media discourse. A particular ethno-Jewish discourse dominated in Israeli media which was coupled to an expectation that "foreign" athletes, particularly if they were not Jewish, should continually express their loyalty to the Israeli state. As a result, although Palestinians played in Israeli teams, as "sport stars" they were blocked from using their sporting success to express the public presence of Arabs in Israel (Shor and Yoney, 2010; see also Sorek 2007).

In contrast to the modest participation of Palestine and its athletes, Israel has participated in 19 Olympic Games since 1952 with some 338 athletes competing. Although there is no official policy which states that Arab Israeli athletes cannot be selected, only two Arab-Israelis have ever participated for Israel: weightlifter Edward Maron (Rome, 1960) and soccer player, Rifat Turk (Montreal, 1976). As noted earlier, despite forming 20 percent of the population of Israel no Israeli-Arab has attended the Olympics since Turk's appearance in 1976 (Sinai 2016). Reasons for this include the very poor sporting infrastructure in the OPT, specifically the lack of funding, facilities and coaching, which limits the development of Palestinian sport at both the grassroots and elite levels. In soccer, despite a growing level of racism among sections of the country's soccer fans (Ben-Porat 2008, 2016), Arab-Israelis have played for the Israeli national team and made an important, if not always respected, contribution (Gilmore 2005). For Palestinian sports fans an uneasiness exists if they support Israeli teams with Sorek (2016) noting the Israeli national soccer team (and its kit colors, shirt badges, national anthem) cannot be isolated from the other state symbols that contain Zionist symbolism.

"One man's freedom fighter..."

The phrase "one man's terrorist is another man's freedom fighter," might be dismissed as a hackneyed cliché, but it is relevant when discussing those who were once seen to be on the "wrong side." Nelson Mandela and Steve Biko in the struggle against South African apartheid, and Martin McGuinness and Gerry Adams in the Northern Ireland troubles are exemplars of this cliché. Without wishing to get into the semantics of what constitutes "terrorism" (Richardson 2006), the cliché is apposite when looking at how soccer is used for remembering national heroes. In 2015 teams in a Palestinian youth soccer tournament were accused of supporting terrorism after they named their squads after heroes/terrorists who had been linked to the deaths of Israeli citizens (Times of Israel 2015). In 2016 Israeli police charged a Palestinian soccer coach with inciting terrorism after he and his team, Jerusalem-based Hilal Al Quds (who played in the West Bank Premier League), posed with a banner portraying an image of Mesbah Abu Sabih who, two days previously, had killed two Israelis before being shot by police officers (Times of Israel 2015). Supporters of Hilal Al Quds took the banner to the club, taking photos of the team posing with the banner and circulating them on social media, before the images were taken down on the grounds that they contravened FIFA regulations.

It is not possible to offer a meaningful distinction between who is a freedom fighter and who is a terrorist given how the term "terrorist" is used flexibly, often negatively and pejoratively by those seeking to denigrate and discredit the actions of others. Adopting the tactic of refusing to talk to moderates, an unwillingness to negotiate and/or offer meaningful progress and/or assassinating leaders who do emerge, successive Israeli governments have long-practiced a tactic of "divide-and-rule" and of discrediting and delegitimizing those who emerge to speak for the Palestinians (Chomsky 1999; IMEU 2013). Any leader who does emerge will, if they are to have any credibility among the Palestinians, be likely to have a history of activism, something the Israelis typically describe as "terrorism." The latest example is the *ad holmium* attacks on Jibril Rajoub, the head of the Palestinian FA and Palestinian IOC. A member of the central committee of the Fatah faction that controls the PA and a former Fatah head of security, Rajoub has served time in an Israeli prison, something Zionist supporters repeatedly seek to promote (Cornibe 2016).

Hamas, Fatah and "Fun Runs"

Not all the difficulties experienced by Palestinian soccer players and Olympians can be laid at the door of the Israeli authorities. This complexity is increased when discussing the different political structures in the West Bank and the Gaza Strip. Very different approaches exist between Hamas, who govern in the Gaza Strip, and the Palestinian Authority (PA) who govern in the West Bank. The PA has a direct lineage to the PLO and was for a long period seen as the legitimate authority of the Palestinian people. However, in recent times, the PA has come under increasing criticism for not effectively representing the Palestinian people and adopting an increasingly neoliberal approach to government (Abunimah 2014). Hamas is an Islamist movement which, since being elected in 2006, has governed in Gaza Strip. During this time, it has repeatedly challenged the Israeli military and fought against the blockade which has resulted in greater popularity and allowed them to challenge an increasingly weakened PA/Fatah government in the West Bank. It is not possible here to offer a full account of their different politics, interpretations, religious and secular, and the "divide and rule" tactics used by the Israelis, but one notes the long-standing blockade of the Gaza Strip, and the very limited power held by the PA in the West Bank and their lack of control over security, land, water, movement of people and goods, industry and trade (Hass, 2013).

The tensions between the PA and Hamas have significantly affected all aspects of sport, including the suspension by the PFA, of the soccer league, split between the West Bank and the Gaza Strip, between 2007 and 2010. Differences between Fatah and Hamas are also evident in their approach to "fun runs." As a conservative Islamists organization Hamas is far more restrictive on the sporting activities of Palestinian women in the Gaza Strip. In April 2013, the United Nations Relief and Works Agency cancelled its third annual Gaza marathon after Hamas refused to allow the 370 women who registered to take part (Donnison, 2013; Greenwood and Balousha 2013; Khoury 2016; Tait 2013).

This short section has highlighted some of the tensions within Palestinian society and their impact on the development of sporting structures, not only recreationally but also at an international level. Whilst some of the difficulties have been self-inflicted, much more significant concerns relate to the actions of the Israeli state.

Israeli Actions Preventing the Development of Palestinian Sport

This section discusses how every aspect of Palestinian sport is affected by the actions of the Israeli state. It begins by identifying the restrictions placed on the movement of individual athletes and sports teams between the Gaza Strip and West Bank, and the travel restrictions faced by those seeking to play in international tournaments, along with restrictions placed on officials and equipment. More significantly is the evidence that suggests there is an unwritten policy of targeting individual Palestinian athletes and sporting infrastructure. This section considers the evidence and suggests possible motives. By necessity many of the examples are drawn from news media organizations and human right groups located in Israel and the OPT.[13]

In 2014 the Palestinian Football Association (PFA) published a report with a Palestinian NGO which documented the systematic obstruction of the development of Palestinian soccer (Jennings, Kuttab and Shalabi-Molano 2014). The report detailed the extensive restrictions placed on the movement of players and officials, military violence against players, the prevention of stadium construction and pitch developments, and military actions which had prevented youth tournaments and training schemes from taking place. Further examples are detailed in the Palestine Football Association document "Sports Under Siege: Israeli Transgressions Against Palestinian sports" (PFA 2017) which details the damage caused to the sporting infrastructure and how athletes, officials, coaches, visiting players and the shipments of sports equipment have been affected by what are seemingly random acts by Israeli officials.

One of the most significant influences on the development of Palestinian sporting identity, and the emergence of a sporting hero, is the lack of free movement of players and teams between Gaza and West Bank. As was noted earlier, Palestinian international soccer players have faced restrictions from Israeli authorities who regularly refuse travel permits on the grounds of national security. Israel decides which foreign players and teams can enter the OPT for games or tournaments with numerous examples of Israel banning soccer players from moving between Gaza and the West Bank. In 2016, after representation had been made to soccer's world governing body, FIFA, Israel was forced to allow players from Gaza to enter the West Bank to play the final match of the Palestine soccer cup (Hawwash 2016). Palestinian athletes, like the majority of those living in the OPT, are routinely denied permits to travel. This is a specific problem for those involved in team sports when, if they want to leave to participate in a training camp or competition, it is rare that all the players are granted travel permits—this often results in the whole trip being cancelled (Tawfiq 2016).

Organized marathon/fun runs in the region are far from straightforward and present particular challenges when the route crosses dividing lines ("borders") in disputed territories (Coppieters 2012). In 2012, the Arab Council called for a boycott of Adidas as the only non–Israeli sponsor of the Jerusalem marathon (AFP 2012; Eslam 2012). In 2013 all 22 athletes from Gaza were prevented from participating in the first Bethlehem marathon (which is located in the West Bank), because Israel refused to issue travel permits to move between the two territories (Donnison, 2013; Tait 2013). Similar travel restrictions imposed by the Israelis limited the event in 2014 and 2015 with only a very limited number of permits issued. In 2016, over 100 athletes from Gaza (including Nader Masri who represented Palestine in the 2008 Beijing Olympics) were prevented from running in the fourth annual Palestine Marathon, again due to Israeli refusal to issue travel permits (Khoury 2016). In response to criticism, the Israeli state, blamed the Palestinians for not submitting their applications in sufficient time to process the necessary travel documentation. Another example of citing "security concerns" was when Israel detained the coach of a blind Palestinian karate team for "suspected involvement in terrorist activity."

> The coach, along with five of his students were stopped by Israeli forces at the Erez border crossing earlier this week while trying to re-enter Gaza. The five blind and vision-impaired students, all under 18 years old, were travelling with four sighted students from the same karate school on their way back from Dubai where they had been competing in an international tournament [Shuttleworth 2016].

It is not just the athletes who are affected with officials and team equipment often denied travel permits. In 2016 three Palestinian Olympic representatives from Gaza (including the head of the Palestinian delegation, Issam Qishta), were initially denied travel permits to join their team at the Rio Olympics (Al Jazeera 2016). The Palestinian National Olympic Committee stated the athletes had to travel to the Rio 2016 Games without any of their necessary equipment after the Israeli authorities had quarantined it along with the team's uniforms (Khalaf 2016; Hawwash 2016).

In 2008/09 Israeli military actions in Gaza caused significant damage to Gaza's sports infrastructure when the Rafah National Stadium and Palestinian FA (PFA) buildings were destroyed along with damage to 20 sports clubs and 10 fields caused by Israeli airstrikes (BBC, 2012; Tawfiq, 2016). In 2013 and in response to the Israeli bombing, FIFA announced they would invest US$4.5m into Palestinian soccer and build a headquarters for the PFA, a soccer academy, two artificial pitches and rebuild the national stadium. However, reconstruction was constrained due to Israeli restrictions on the importation of building materials into the Gaza Strip (U.N. 2016). Similarly, donations of sports equipment from international sports organizations face restriction on entry to the OPT while the Israelis check to see if they could be used for terrorist activity.

There has been the suggestion that the Israeli state has deliberately targeted individual Palestinian soccer players in order to prevent them from becoming successful. One of the most high-profile cases was that of Mahmoud Sarsak, a former member of the Palestinian national soccer team. In 2009 Gaza-based Sarsak, 22, was arrested whilst entering the West Bank to take part in a training session. He was accused of being a member of Islamic Jihad and of being involved in violent anti–Israeli actions. However, he was never charged, nor given a trial, with his family denied visitations during his entire detention. In 2012, after two years in prison without trial, Sarsak began a hunger strike to protest his detention. During his 92-day hunger strike representation was made to the IFA from UEFA and FIFPro (an organization representing professional soccer players), and from FIFA President Sepp Blatter who wrote to express his "grave concern" about the illegal detention of Palestinian soccer players. Sarsak ended his hunger strike in exchange for early release; after detention without charge for three years, his soccer career was over. It was claimed that Sarsak had been detained because "Israel was afraid that he would become a sporting hero for his people" (Zirin 2014). Sarsak is just one example of many young, aspiring soccer players who have been targeted by the IDF with numerous media reports available to indicate the extent to which this is happening (Gelblum 2014; Nieuwhof 2013; Wall 2014; Zirin 2014).

In an attempt to highlight the "double-standards" on the movement and restrictions on the development of Palestinian football, the Palestine Football Association (PFA) tabled a motion at FIFA's fifth congress in 2015, which asked for Israel's suspension from the organization. The case centered on the presence of six teams from Israeli settlements in the Occupied West Bank who played in the Israeli league (Baker 2016; Bloomfield 2017). The PFA and various human rights groups (including Human Rights Watch) argued the presence of these settlement teams violated various United Nations Security Council resolutions and FIFA's own statutes which prohibit a member association from holding games on the territory of another member association without permission (Dorsey 2016). In response, Israel claims the appellation "occupied territory" is disputed and should be resolved through wider "peace negotiations."

In response to claims they are deliberately targeting and disrupting Palestinian sport, the Israeli state claims all action is taken on the grounds of national security. Free movement of players and officials has become an increasingly significant source of tension between the Palestinian and Israeli FAs and, by association, between soccer's governing bodies and national governments. Whilst the Israeli Football Association (IFA) has claimed it has worked to support the movement of Palestinian soccer players to attend training and matches, the Israeli state has a default position that Palestinians are using sport as a cover for terrorist activities. The IFA have admitted that the security concerns of the Israeli state override all other concerns and arguments. Arrest and detention (with or without charge), expulsions, torture, collective punishments (including house demolitions), shooting, and border closure are all justified on the basis of ensuring state security. In the struggle for public opinion various Israeli advocacy groups (nominally independent but pro–Israel and often funded by Zionist supporters) claim that the Palestinians are using and abusing the basic values of international sportsmanship and the spirit upon which sport is founded. A solitary example involving Samah Fares Muhamed Marava, a Palestinian soccer player, was presented by a prominent Zionist group:

> Marava, of Qalqilya, left Israel with his team on a soccer tour in April. While in Qatar, he met with Talal Ibrahim Abd al-Rahman Sarim, a member of Hamas's military wing, where he received money, a cellphone and written messages that he was to bring to Hamas terrorists in his hometown. The Shin Bet (Israel's internal Security Agency) said Marava "cynically exploited" his status as a soccer player to leave the country and make contacts with foreign Hamas agents [United with Israel 2016].

International Support for the Palestinians

After renouncing terrorism and moving to civil protests (intifadas), international support for the Palestinians has significantly increased and coalesced around the Boycott, Disinvestment and Sanctions (BDS) movement. The Israeli state and its supporters have responded with a public relations campaign ("hasbara"—see Dart, 2016), and moved from "warfare to lawfare" and accusing those who support the BDS movement as being anti-Semitic.

There are persistent, if problematic, comparisons of Israel with apartheid South Africa and on the use of a sporting boycott (Dart 2017; Di Stefano and Henaway 2014; MacLean 2014). Outside of sport, significant expressions of support for the Palestinians come from the International Solidarity Movement (Coy 2012; Higgins-Desbiolles 2009) and the "Gaza flotilla" activists (Archibald and Miller 2012; de Jong 2012). Another area that has seen significant activity is academia (Rose and Rose 2017) and the campus-based advocacy event known as "Israel Apartheid Week" (Barrows-Friedman 2014). The arts and cultural sectors have been active supporters of the Palestinians (including Ken Loach, Alice Walker, and Naomi Klein), with others opposed to any form of boycott (JK Rowling, Iain McEwan, Elton John, Lady Gaga, Rihanna, Madonna) who prefer either a non-political approach or advocate "bridge-building" between the Israelis and Palestinians (The Guardian 2015). One of the highest profile supporters of the Palestinians is musician Roger Walters (Pink Floyd) who recently claimed that many individuals were reluctant to publicly criticize Israeli policy for fear of being labeled anti–Semitic (Gallagher 2016).

Sports organizations and individual athletes have, arguably, been less vocal in supporting the Palestinians, especially when compared to the sport boycott of apartheid South Africa. One high point in the support for the Palestinians was when Israel was excluded from various sporting competitions in the Middle East and South Asia in the 1970s before they eventually found a "home" in European sporting competitions. More recently there has been an upturn in support for the Palestinians such as that expressed by the Algerian soccer team who stated they would donate all its FIFA 2014 World Cup money to Gaza in response to the damage caused by Israel's "Operation Protective Edge"[14] (Chandler 2014). Support has also been expressed by English cricketer, Moeen Ali, who was reprimanded by his governing body for wearing wrist bands embossed with the phrases "Save Gaza" and "Free Palestine" during an international match (Burdsey 2015) and the Egyptian Judo athlete, Islam El Shehaby, who refused to shake hands with his Israeli opponent during competition at Rio 2016 (Elia 2016). Support has also been expressed by soccer players Eric Cantona, Cristiano Ronaldo, Eden Hazard and Joey Barton (Rice 2014; Palmer 2014). Soccer fans, most notably Scottish club Glasgow Celtic FC, have used the presence of Israeli soccer teams in European club competitions to bring attention to the Palestinian cause; their actions resulted in them being sanctioned by football's governing body (Coyle 2017). In 2017 eleven NFL players were invited on an all-expenses-paid trip to Israel with six refusing to attend (Sommer 2017). As part of an attempt to highlight the PR element to this promotion ("hasbara"—see Dart, 2016), a number of high-profile advocates, including John Carlos, Harry Belafonte, Danny Glover, Angela Davis, and Alice Walker, signed an open letter asking the NFL players to consider withdrawing from the delegation (Hill 2017).

What Chance a Palestinian Sporting Hero?

This essay has discussed the significant challenges that face Palestinian athletes, and the potential for a Palestinian sporting champion to emerge and use sport as a platform to speak up for the Palestinian people. The main factors preventing the emergence of a Palestinian sports star include the lack of sporting infrastructure (facilities, organization, coaching), the lack of free movement and the wide range of impositions placed on all those living in the OPT. Sport features low on the list of priorities for those living under occupation, and who lack the basic human rights of security, healthcare, freedom of movement, education and work. Palestinians continue to experience systematic ethnic cleansing, house/village/community demolitions, collective punishments, travel restrictions, state torture, detention without trial, assassination, mass unemployment, subsistence wages, poor living conditions, inadequate health services, sub-standard transport, housing shortages and inferior education.

There is the suggestion that the Israelis are deliberately targeting Palestinian sport to prevent the emergence of an athletic spokesperson. There are no successful or high-profile Palestinian athletes able to represent Palestinians on an international sporting stage with the prospect for an equivalent "Black Power salute" moment not promising. There is no figurehead, equivalent to Nelson Mandela or Desmond Tutu (or within sport, Dennis Brutus or Harry Edwards) who is able to represent the Palestinian cause. The emergence of an athlete able to draw attention to the Palestinian cause (similar to that of John Carlos and Tommy Smith) is perhaps more likely to come from outside the Palestinian community. This is unsurprising given how, as Chomsky (1999) has shown, the Israeli state has deliberately and consistently "removed" leaders from within the Palestinian community. There is always the potential for a "hero" to emerge from an unlikely source; one notes the "unlikely heroes" that have emerged to speak up against injustice, including the Civil Rights activist, Rosa Parks, and against the Pakistani Taliban, Malala Yousafzai. There is potential for a foreign-born athlete, of Palestinian heritage, to advocate the cause, but from the evidence of those representing Palestine at Rio 2016, this remains unlikely; like most athletes they seem to prefer to "keep politics out of sport." One potential avenue of support is via a Muslim athlete, such as English cricketer, Moeen Ali, who identifies with fellow Muslims (but, as noted earlier, they form one part of the Palestinian population). There is the suggestion of establishing a "common cause" (intersection) with the Black Lives Matter movement and athletes in the USA (Dabashi 2016;

Sidahmed 2016) and one waits to see if a "hero" will emerge to speak for the Palestinians. One also waits to see if the Palestinian cause will generate popular and widespread support such as that which emerged to challenge apartheid South Africa.

As noted at the start of this essay the notion of "90-minute patriots" and Hobsbawm's "11 shirts" view of national identity is perhaps more relevant when one looks at the disparity between what Palestine has in terms of sport and what it has in terms of a nation state. When the Palestinian men's national soccer team qualified for the 2015 Asian Cup and traveled to Australia to participate in their first international tournament, the team gave those in the Palestinian diaspora and Australian soccer fans an opportunity, albeit briefly, to see "Palestine" as a nation (Rego 2015; Moore 2015); however, just one week earlier the Australian government had voted at the UN not to convey nationhood upon Palestine (Carr 2015). This reveals the disconnect between "Palestine" as a sporting entity and an actual nation of Palestine.

In this essay I have tried to be objective and focus on key details and have argued that the Israeli state has, and continues to, hamper the development of Palestinian sport—be this of individual athletes, clubs, leagues, buildings and infrastructure, at the elite and grass-roots level. The Israeli state continues to control and restrict Palestinian movement in and out of the OPTs which some have seen as part of a deliberate policy in suppressing the use of sport as a platform for expressions of Palestinian national identity. For Young (2017) "targeting Palestinian sports is no accident. It is an insidious tactic in the overall strategy of crushing the resolve of the Palestinian people to remain steadfast on their land." As Tawfiq (2016) has concluded "the psychological effects of (often inconstant and seemingly random actions) by the Israeli state towards the issue of travel permits, and movement of players, equipment and logistics has a significant impact on all concerned."

The presence of the Palestinian national team at the Rio 2016 opening ceremony was a highly visible representation of the challenges faced by Palestinians who manage to compete in international sport. The athletes began to represent the diversity of the Palestinian people with the team contain individuals from the West Bank, the Gaza Strip, Israel and the Palestinian diaspora. The restriction on movement, the arbitrary detainments and detentions, and the closure of crossing points into and out of the OPT are compounded by a lack of sporting infrastructure. This essay has shown that Israel has consistently sought to, deliberately or otherwise, destroy (physically and symbolically) the aspirations of Palestinian athletes. Targeting sport has a ripple effect on wider Palestinian society and reduces the avenues available for expressions of national identity. Despite all this, soccer is leading the way, with the success of the Palestinian men's national team, perhaps being the best opportunity to represent Palestine on an international sporting stage. Athletes are important symbols of Palestine in national and international sport competitions, and whether they are successful or not, sport remains an important site to bring together Palestinian people, and their supporters, to create a physical sense of unity. This is especially important in their struggle for social justice, human rights and a homeland.

Notes

1. Jews who lived in the region before the creation of the state of Israel were known as Palestinian Jews. The Yishuv (Hebrew for settlement) is the term applied to Jews living in the region prior to the creation of the State of Israel.
2. The Israeli state continue to use laws from the Ottoman and British Mandate periods to justify their occupation of territory in the West Bank.
3. The West Bank was annexed by Jordanian Kingdom in 1950; this claim was relinquished in 1988.
4. As Bregman (2014) notes, the terms one uses to describe "the land" is often indicative of one's political leaning: "Palestine" used by those who are pro–Palestinian, the "Occupied Territories" by those on the broad left, the "Liberated Territories" and/or "Judea and Samaria" by right-wing Jewish supporters, and the "Administrative Territories" and /or Territories beyond the Green Line' by those sitting on the fence.
5. Compared with other human rights issues, the "Palestinian Question" is premised on a territorial dispute, rather than a racial/ethnic issue. There are increasing attempts by the Israeli state and Zionists to make "ethnicity" the crux of the debate because it "allows" them to accuse those who support the rights of the Palestinians and question the actions of the Israeli state of being antisemitic.
6. There are an estimated two million Palestinians in Jordan. Syria, Chile, Lebanon and Saudi Arabia each have an estimated Palestinian population of around 500,000.
7. Arab-Israelis (such as those from Circassian or Druze communities) can serve in the IDF which is essential for employment in Israeli society with Arab-Israelis members permitted to be elected to the Knesset (Israeli parliament).
8. Although Palestine played in qualification matches for the 1934 FIFA World Cup the team contained no Palestine Arabs.
9. A Palestinian league was re-established shortly after the Oslo Accords in the mid–1990s. The resurrected Palestinian league was set up as semi-professional and consisted of two regions: the West Bank and the Gaza Strip. The intention was for the champion of the West Bank to play against the champion of the Gaza Strip, with the winner declared as the national champion.
10. Many of the clubs in Gaza represent nothing more than small, claustrophobic neighborhoods with the Gaza league, unlike the West Bank league, not allowing foreign players (Ali Khaled 2015).
11. This was ten years before the United Nations recognized Palestine.
12. By comparison, the Israel sent 39 athletes in 2000; 36 in 2004; 43 in 2008; 37 in 2012, and 47 in 2016.
13. An extensive list of Israeli actions against individual athletes and sporting structured can be found at http://xssportpal.blogspot.co.uk/. While the content of the site cannot be independently verified it is very comprehensive and detailed. Additional information on Israeli activity is detailed in *Israeli Occupation Transgressions Against Palestinian Sports, 2016, 2017*, which identifies numerous, often unexplained, arrests and detentions of individual athletes and officials working for Palestinian sports organizations.
14. Israel's *"Operation Protective Edge"* was a 50-day assault on the Gaza Strip which resulted in more than 2,000 Palestinians deaths and significant damage to the infrastructure and living conditions.

References

Abunimah, Ali. 2014. *The Battle for Justice in Palestine*. Haymarket.
Abou Jalal, R 2017. "Meet the Men Behind Gaza's First Female Sports Club." *Al Monitor*. www.al-monitor.com/pulse/originals/2017/03/palestine-gaza-women-sports-academy.html
AFP. 2012. "Arab Sports Council Boycotts Adidas Over Jerusalem Marathon." *Al Arabiya News*. https://www.alarabiya.net/articles/2012/04/05/205608.html
Al Jazeera. 2016. "Israel Blocks Olympics-Bound Palestinian from Travel," News, *Al Jazeera*. http://www.aljazeera.com/news/2016/08/israel-blocks-olympics-bound-palestinian-travel-160802202751580.html.
Ali Khaled. 2015. "Football in Times of Crisis: Palestine's Game Endures in the Face of Tragedy." *The National*. http://www.thenational.ae/sport/football/football-in-times-of-crisis-palestines-game-endures-in-the-face-of-tragedy.
Allen, Dean. 2013. "'National Heroes': Sport and the Creation of Icons." *Sport in History* 33 (4): 584–94. doi:10.1080/17460263.2013.850782.
Anderson, Benedict R. 2006. *Imagined Communities: Reflections on the Origin and Spread of Nationalism*. Verso.
Arabiya News, Al. 2014. "Football Proving Popular for Palestinian Women—Al Arabiya English." https://english.alarabiya.net/en/sports/2014/03/21/Football-proving-popular-for-Palestinian-women-.html.
Archibald, David, and Mitchell Miller. 2012. "Full-Spectacle Dominance? an Analysis of the Israeli State's Attempts to Control Media Images of the 2010 Gaza Flotilla." *Journal of War & Culture Studies* 5 (2): 189–201. doi:10.1386/jwcs.5.2.189_1.
Associated Press. 2017. "Palestinian Women Try to Bring Baseball to Gaza." *VOA*. http://www.voanews.com/a/palestinian-women-baseball-gaza-strip/3773931.html.
Bairner, Alan. 2015. "Assessing the Sociology of Sport: On National Identity and Nationalism." *International Review for the Sociology of Sport* 50 (4–5): 375–79. doi:10.1177/1012690214538863.
Bakan, Abigail, and Abu-Laban, Yasmeen. 2009. "Palestinian Resistance and International Solidarity: The BDS Campaign." *Race & Class* 51: 29–54.
Baker, Peter. 2016. "Home Teams Are Israeli, but Turf Is in West Bank—*New York Times*." *New York Times*. https://www.nytimes.com/2016/09/25/world/middleeast/israeli-palestinian-soccer-west-bank.html?_r=3.
Barghouti, Omar. 2011. *Boycott, Divestment, Sanctions. The Struggle for Palestinian Civil Rights*. Haymarket.
Barr, James. 2012. *A Line in the Sand: Britain, France and the Struggle That Shaped the Middle East*. Simon & Schuster.
Barrows-Friedman, Nora. 2014. *In Our Power: U.S. Students Organize for Justice in Palestine*. Just World Books.
BBC. 2012. "Q&A: Israel-Gaza Violence." *BBC News*. http://www.bbc.co.uk/news/world-middle-east-20388298
Ben-Porat, Amir. 2008. "Death to the Arabs: The Right-wing Fan's Fear." *Soccer & Society* 9 (1): 1–13. doi:10.1080/14660970701616662.
———. 2016. "The Usual Suspect: A History of Football Violence in the State of Israel." *Sport in History* 36 (1): 98–116. doi:10.1080/17460263.2015.1016549.
Bernish, Claire. 2016. "Israel's Apartheid Policies Create Hurdles for Team Palestine on the Road to Rio." *Mint Press News*. https://www.mintpressnews.com/israels-apartheid-policies-create-hurdles-team-palestine-road-rio/219254/.
Bloomfield, Aubrey. 2017. "FIFA Must Take Action on Israeli Settlement Clubs." *Al Jazeera*. http://www.aljazeera.com/indepth/opinion/2017/01/fifa-action-israeli-settlement-clubs-170106135455991.html.
Bregman, Ahron. 2014. *Cursed Victory: A History of Israel and the Occupied Territories*. Allen Lane.
Brentin, Dario. 2013. "'A Lofty Battle for the Nation': The Social Roles of Sport in Tudjman's Croatia." *Sport in Society* 16 (8): 993–1008. doi:10.1080/17430437.2013.801217.
Burdsey, Daniel. 2015. "Un/making the British Asian Male Athlete: Race, Legibility and the

State." *Sociological Research Online* 20 (3). http://www.socresonline.org.uk/20/3/17.html.
Carpenter Les. 2015. "The NBA's First Palestinian? Sani Sakakini's Remarkable Basketball Odyssey." *The Guardian*. www.theguardian.com/sport/blog/2015/aug/03/the-nbas-first-palestinian-sani-sakakinis-remarkable-basketball-odyssey
Carr, Bob. 2015. "Australia's UN Vote on Palestine Does a Disservice to All Sides, Including Israelis." *The Guardian*. https://www.theguardian.com/commentisfree/2015/jan/14/australias-un-vote-on-palestine-does-a-disservice-to-all-sides-including-israelis.
Chandler, Rick. 2014. "Algeria to Donate World Cup Money to Palestine, Says Report." *Sports Grid*. http://www.sportsgrid.com/uncategorized/algerian-soccer-team-received-as-heroes-reportedly-will-donate-world-cup-money-to-palestine/.
Chomsky, Noam. 1999. *The Fateful Triangle: The United States, Israel and the Palestinians*. Pluto.
Coppieters, Bruno. 2012. "The Organisation of Marathons in Divided Cities: Brussels, Belfast, Beirut and Jerusalem." *The International Journal of the History of Sport* 29 (11): 1553–76. doi:10.1080/09523367.2012.702106.
Cornibe, Bruce. 2016. "Palestinian Olympics Chairman: Terrorists, Not Athletes, Are 'Heroes.'" *CounterJihad*. https://counterjihad.com/palestinian-terror-supporter-involved-olympics.
Coy, Patrick G. 2012. "Nonpartisanship, Interventionism and Legality in Accompaniment: Comparative Analyses of Peace Brigades International, Christian Peacemaker Teams, and the International Solidarity Movement." *The International Journal of Human Rights* 16 (7): 963–81. doi:10.1080/13642987.2011.642144.
Coyle, Matt. 2017. "Celtic Supporters Hand Over £176,000 to Palestinian Charities." *STV News*. https://stv.tv/news/west-central/1379386-celtic-supporters-hand-over-176-000-to-palestinian-charities/.
Dabashi, Hamid. 2016. "Black Lives Matter and Palestine: A Historic Alliance—Al Jazeera English." *AlJazeera*. http://www.aljazeera.com/indepth/opinion/2016/09/black-lives-matter-palestine-historic-alliance-160906074912307.html.
Dart, Jon. 2016. "'Brand Israel': Hasbara and Israeli Sport." *Sport in Society* 19 (10). doi:10.1080/17430437.2015.1133595.
_____. 2017. "Israel and a Sports Boycott: Antisemitic? Anti-Zionist?" *International Review for the Sociology of Sport* 52 (2): 164–88. doi:10.1177/1012690215583482.
De Jong, Anne 2012. "The Gaza Freedom Flotilla: Human Rights, Activism and Academic Neutrality." *Social Movement Studies* 11 (2): 193–209. doi:10.1080/14742837.2012.664901.
Di Stefano, Paul, and Mostafa Henaway. 2014. "Boycotting Apartheid from South Africa to Palestine." *Peace Review* 26 (1): 19–27. doi:10.1080/10402659.2014.876304.
Dorsey, James M. 2016. "Shifting Sands: Volatile Political Transitions in the Middle East and North Africa." *World Scientific*. doi:10.1142/9643.
Elia, Nada. 2016. "A New Milestone: BDS at the Olympics—Mondoweiss." *Mondoweiss*. http://mondoweiss.net/2016/08/milestone-the-olympics/.
Galily, Yair, and Ben-Porat, Amir. 2008. *Sport, Politics and Society in the Land of Israel: Past and Present*. Edited by Amir Galily, Yair, and Ben-Porat. Routledge.
Gallagher, Paul., 2016. "Roger Waters: Pink Floyd Star on Why His Fellow Musicians Are Terrified to Speak Out Against Israel." *The Independent*. http://www.independent.co.uk/news/people/roger-waters-pink-floyd-israel-boycott-ban-palestine-a6884971.html
Gelblum, Ben. 2014. "Soccer Is Under Fire in Palestine—VICE." *VICE*. https://www.vice.com/en_us/article/football-israel-palestine-discrimination-fifa.
Gilmore, Inigo. 2005. "Arab Players Hailed as Heroes in Israel's World Cup Campaign—Telegraph." *The Telegraph*. http://www.telegraph.co.uk/news/worldnews/middleeast/israel/1487028/Arab-players-hailed-as-heroes-in-Israels-World-Cup-campaign.html.
Greenwood, Phoebe, and Balousha, Hazem. 2013. "Gaza Marathon Cancelled by UN After Hamas Bans Women from Participating." *The Guardian*. https://www.theguardian.com/world/2013/mar/05/gaza-marathon-cancelled-hamas-bans-women.
The Guardian. 2015. "JK Rowling Explains Refusal to Join Cultural Boycott of Israel." *The*

Guardian. https://www.theguardian.com/books/2015/oct/27/jk-rowling-explains-refusal-to-join-cultural-boycott-of-israel.

Harif, Haggai, and Yair Galily. 2003. "Sport and Politics in Palestine, 1918–48: Football as a Mirror Reflecting the Relations Between Jews and Britons." *Soccer & Society* 4 (1): 41–56. doi:10.1080/14660970512331390723.

Hass, Amira. 2013. "Palestinian Mohammed Assaf Wins Arab Idol—Middle East—Haaretz." *Haaretz.* http://www.haaretz.com/middle-east-news/.premium-1.531385.

Hassan, David. 2013. "Introduction: What Makes a Sporting Icon?" *Sport in History* 33 (4): 417–26. doi:10.1080/17460263.2013.850263.

Hawwash, Kemel. 2016. "Hey Israel, Give Palestinians a Sporting Chance." *Middle East Eye.* http://www.middleeasteye.net/columns/give-palestine-sporting-chance-israel-967625887.

Henry, Ian P., Mahfoud Amara, and Mansour Al-Tauqi. 2003. "Sport, Arab Nationalism and the Pan-Arab Games." *International Review for the Sociology of Sport* 38 (3): 295–310. doi:10.1177/10126902030383003.

Higgins-Desbiolles, Freya. 2009. "International Solidarity Movement: A Case Study in Volunteer Tourism for Justice." *Annals of Leisure Research* 12 (3–4): 333–49. doi:10.1080/11745398.2009.9686828.

Hill, Marc Lamont. 2017. "Why I Applaud the NFL Players Who Spoke Out Against Israel." *The Huffington Post.* http://www.huffingtonpost.com/entry/applaud-nfl-players-spoke-against-israel_us_58a741e9e4b037d17d278dbc.

Hobsbawm, Eric. (1990) *Nations and Nationalism Since 1780: Programme, Myth, Reality.* Cambridge University Press.

———, and Terence Ranger (Eds.) (1983). *The Invention of Tradition.* Cambridge University Press.

Holt, Richard, and Dino Ruta. 2015. *Routledge Handbook of Sport and Legacy: Meeting the Challenge of Major Sports Events.* Routledge.

Hunter, John S. 2003. "Flying the Flag: Identities, the Nation, and Sport." *Identities Global Studies in Culture and Power.* 10: 409–25. doi:10.1080/10702890390253308.

IMEU. 2013. "Israel's History of Assassinating Palestinian Leaders." *Institute for Middle East Understanding.* https://imeu.org/article/israels-history-of-assassinating-palestinian-leaders.

Jennings, Mariabruna, Jonathan Kuttab, and Susan Shalabi Molano. 2014. *"Israel Hinders Football in Occupied Palestine: Detailed Report and Executive Summary)."* http://xssportpal.blogspot.co.uk/2014/08/israel-hinders-football-in-occupied.html.

Kaufman, Haim, and Yair Galily. 2007. "Reading Sports in Palestine: The Early Days of Sport Reports in the Hebrew Mandatory Press." *Israel Affairs* 13 (3): 586–604. doi:10.1080/13537120701531676.

———, and ———. 2009. "Sport, Zionist Ideology and the State of Israel." *Sport in Society* 12 (8): 1013–27. doi:10.1080/17430430903076316.

Khalaf, Rayana. 2016. "Will Israel Allow Palestine's Olympic Gear to Reach Brazil? Confiscates Athletes Equipment and Uniforms." *Centre for Research on Globalization.* http://www.globalresearch.ca/will-israel-allow-palestines-olympic-gear-to-reach-brazil-confiscates-athletes-equipment-and-uniforms/5539426.

Khalidi, Issam. 2012. "Coverage of Sports News in Filastin, 1911–1948." *Soccer & Society* 13 (5–6): 764–76. doi:10.1080/14660970.2012.730777.

———, and Raab, Alon K. 2017. "Palestine and the Olympics—A History." *International Journal of the History of Sport,* 34 (13): 1403–1418. doi.org/10.1080/09523367.2018.1461622

Khalidi, Rashid. 2010. *Palestinian Identity : The Construction of Modern National Consciousness.* Columbia University Press.

Khalili, Laleh. 2009. *Heroes and Martyrs of Palestine : The Politics of National Commemoration.* Cambridge University Press.

Khoury, Jack. 2016. "More Than 100 Gaza Athletes Barred from Running in Palestinian Marathon—Israel News—Haaretz.com." *Haaretz.* http://www.haaretz.com/israel-news/.premium-1.712119.

Lieber, Dov. 2017. "Palestinians Send 6 Athletes to Rio—Half of Them Germans." *The Times of Israel*. 2016. Accessed February 10. http://www.timesofisrael.com/six-palestinian-athletes-head-to-rio-half-of-them-germans/.
Lim, Andrea. 2012. (ed) *The Case for Sanctions Against Israel*. Verso.
Ma'an News Agency. 2010. "Palestinian Paralympics Gets Boost from EU." http://www.maannews.com/Content.aspx?id=291861.
MacLean, Malcolm. 2014. "Revisiting (and Revising?) Sports Boycotts: From Rugby Against South Africa to Soccer in Israel." *The International Journal of the History of Sport* 31 (15): 1832–51. doi:10.1080/09523367.2014.934680.
Mallon, Bill, and Heijmans, Jerome, 2015. *Historical Dictionary of the Olympic Movement*. Rowman and Littlefield.
Menary, Steve. 2007. "When Is a National Team Not a National Team?" *Sport in Society* 10 (2): 195–204. doi:10.1080/17430430601147039.
Mendel, Yoni. 2017. "The Palestinian Soccer League: A Microcosm of a National Struggle." *+972*. https://972mag.com/palestinian-soccer-league-gears-up-for-nailbiter-final/106184/.
Monier, Hawa. 2016. "PC Olympics Special: Two Teams Making History—Team Palestine and Team Refugees." *Palestine Chronicle*. http://www.palestinechronicle.com/pc-olympics-special-two-teams-making-history-team-palestine-refugee-team/.
Montague, James. 2009. "Women Flock to See First Female Football Game in West Bank." *CNN*. http://edition.cnn.com/2009/SPORT/football/11/06/palestinian.womens.football.westbank/
_____ 2015. "'Soldiers Without Weapons': Palestine Football's Painful Journey." *CNN*. http://edition.cnn.com/2015/01/11/football/palestine-asian-cup-japan-football/
Moore, Glenn. 2015. "Asian Cup 2015: Palestinians Flying the Flag for a Nation of Two Halves." *The Independent*. http://www.independent.co.uk/sport/football/international/asian-cup-2015-palestinians-flying-the-flag-for-a-nation-of-two-halves-9978829.html.
Morris, Benny. 1999. *Righteous Victims: A History of the Zionist-Arab Conflict, 1881–1999*. Knopf.
_____. 2008. *1948: A History of the First Arab-Israeli War*. Yale University Press.
Mutch, Thembi. 2016. "Surfing in Palestine: Everyday Life in the Occupied Territories." *The Guardian*. https://www.theguardian.com/artanddesign/2016/may/22/surfing-in-palestine-the-occupied-territories-as-youve-never-seen-them-before-tanya-habjouqa.
Nieuwhof, Adri. 2013. "How Israel Derails the Promising Careers of Palestinian Football Stars." *The Electronic Intifada*. https://electronicintifada.net/blogs/adri-nieuwhof/how-israel-derails-promising-careers-palestinian-football-stars.
Omar, Eslam. 2012. "Egypt Forced to Wear 'Pro-Israel' Adidas Kit Despite Arab Boycott." *Ahramonline*. http://english.ahram.org.eg/NewsAFCON/2017/39055.aspx
Palmer, Ewan. 2014. "Cristiano Ronaldo Versus Israel: Eric Cantona, Eden Hazard and the Football Stars Backing Palestine." *International Business Times*. http://www.ibtimes.co.uk/christian-ronaldo-pro-palestine-footballers-israel-450487.
Pappe, Ilan. 1999. *The Israel/Palestine Question: A Reader*. Routledge.
_____. 2007. *The Ethnic Cleansing of Palestine*. Oneworld Publications.
_____. 2011. *The Forgotten Palestinians: A History of the Palestinians in Israel*. Yale University Press.
_____. 2014. *The Idea of Israel: A History of Power and Knowledge*. Verso.
PFA. 2017. "*Sports Under Siege Israeli Transgressions Against Palestinian Sports Israeli Transgressions Against Palestinian Sports*." Accessed March 8. http://cartonrougeapartheidisrael.weebly.com/uploads/1/2/6/0/12608354/rapport_anglais.pdf.
Rego, Nishadh. 2015. "Celebrating Palestinian Nationhood Through Sport: A Photo Essay." *Muftah*. http://muftah.org/celebrating-palestinian-nationhood-sport-photo-essay/#.WN4s_jvyvIU.
Rice, Simon. 2014. "Joey Barton and Yossi Benayoun Become Involved in Twitter Row Over Israel-Gaza Conflict." *The Independent*. http://www.independent.co.uk/sport/football/news-and-comment/joey-barton-and-yossi-benayoun-become-involved-in-twitter-row-over-israel-gaza-conflict-9628185.html.

Richardson, Louise. 2006. *What Terrorists Want: Understanding the Enemy, Containing the Threat.* Random House.
Rogan, Eugen., 2016. *The Fall of the Ottomans: The Great War in the Middle East, 1914–1920.* Penguin.
Rose, Hilary, and Steven Rose. 2017. "Israel, Europe and the Academic Boycott." *Race Relations* 50 (1): 1–20. Accessed April 7. doi:10.1177/0306396808093298.
Rose, John. 2004. *The Myths of Zionism.* Pluto Press.
Said, Edward. 2003. *A Question of Palestine.* Random House.
Sand, Shlomo. 2012. *The Invention of the Land of Israel: From Holy Land to Homeland.* London: Verso.
_____. 2014. *How I Stopped Being a Jew.* Verso.
Schneer, Jonathan. 2011. *The Balfour Declaration: The Origins of the Arab-Israeli Conflict.* Bloomsbury.
Segev, Tom. 2000. *The Seventh Million: The Israelis and the Holocaust* (trans. H. Watzman). Owl Books.
_____. 2001. *One Palestine, Complete: Jews and Arabs Under the British Mandate.* Abacus.
Sherwood, Harriet. 2012. "Maher Abu Rmeileh Makes Palestinian Sporting History at London 2012." *The Guardian.* https://www.theguardian.com/world/2012/jul/24/maher-abu-rmeileh-palestinian-olympics.
Shor, Eran and Yonay, Yuval, 2010. "'Play and shut up': The Silencing of Palestinian Athletes in Israeli Media." *Ethnic and Racial Studies* 34(2): 229–247. doi.org/10.1080/01419870.2010.503811
Shuttleworth, Kate. 2016. "Israel Detains Coach of Blind Palestinian Karate Team for 'Suspected Terrorist Activity'" *The National.* http://www.thenational.ae/world/middle-east/blind-palestinian-karate-team-detained-at-israeli-border-after-return-from-dubai-tournament.
Sidahmed, Mazin. 2016. "Critics Denounce Black Lives Matter Platform Accusing Israel of 'Genocide.'" *The Guardian.* https://www.theguardian.com/us-news/2016/aug/11/black-lives-matters-movement-palestine-platform-israel-critics.
Sinai, Allon. 2016. "Sinai Says: Arab Representation in Israel's Olympic Delegation Lacking, but Future Bright." *The Jerusalem Post.* http://www.jpost.com/printarticle.aspx?id=459615.
Smith, Adrian, and Dilwyn Porter. 2004. *Sport and National Identity in the Post-War World.* Routledge.
Sommer, Allison Kaplan. 2017. "Only Five NFL Players Show Up for Israel Trip, After Others Refuse to Be 'Goodwill Ambassadors.'" *Haaretz.* http://www.haaretz.com/israel-news/.premium-1.772237.
Sorek, Tamir. 2000. "Palestinian Nationalism in the 1940s: The Sports Column as an Identity Agent." *Zmanim* 70: 15–25 (in Hebrew).
_____. 2005. "Between Football and Martyrdom: The Bi-Focal Localism of an Arab-Palestinian Town in Israel." *British Journal of Sociology* 56(4): 635–661.
_____. 2007. *Arab Soccer in a Jewish State: The Integrative Enclave.* Cambridge University Press.
_____. 2013. "Sport, Palestine, and Israel." In: D. Andrews and B. Carrington (eds.), *A Companion to Sport.* Blackwell, 257–269.
_____. 2016. "'I Don't Identify': Palestinian-Israeli Fans of Israel's National Football Team." *Alternative Information Center.* http://www.alternativenews.org/index.php/features-02/199-i-don-t-isanddentify-palestinian-israeli-fans-of-israel-s-national-football-team.
Stanislawski, Michael. 2016. *Zionism: A Very Short Introduction.* Oxford University Press.
Sterchele, Davide. 2013. "Fertile Land or Mined Field? Peace-Building and Ethnic Tensions in Post-War Bosnian Football." *Sport in Society* 16 (8): 973–92. doi:10.1080/17430437.2013.801223.
Sugden, John. 2008. "Anyone for Football for Peace? the Challenges of Using Sport in the Service of Co-existence in Israel 1." *Soccer & Society* 9 (3): 405–15. doi:10.1080/14660970802009023.
_____. 2010. "Critical Left-Realism and Sport Interventions in Divided Societies." *International Review for the Sociology of Sport* 45 (3): 258–72. doi:10.1177/1012690210374525.

Suleiman, Amna. 2016. "100 Women 2016: The Woman Defying Gaza's Biking 'Ban.'" *BBC News*. http://www.bbc.co.uk/news/world-middle-east-38094578.

Tait, Robert. 2013. "Gaza Athletes Banned from Bethlehem Marathon." *Daily Telegraph*. http://www.telegraph.co.uk/news/worldnews/middleeast/palestinianauthority/10000805/Gaza-athletes-banned-from-Bethlehem-marathon.html.

Tawfiq, Mousa. 2016. "Palestinian Athletes Face Israeli Hurdles*The Electronic Intifada*. https://electronicintifada.net/content/palestinian-athletes-face-israeli-hurdles/18466.

Thomas, Ryan J., and Mary Grace Antony. 2015. "Competing Constructions of British National Identity: British Newspaper Comment on the 2012 Olympics Opening Ceremony." *Media, Culture & Society* 37 (3): 493–503. doi:10.1177/0163443715574671.

Thorpe, Holly, and Nida Ahmad. 2015. "Youth, Action Sports and Political Agency in the Middle East: Lessons from a Grassroots Parkour Group in Gaza." *International Review for the Sociology of Sport* 50 (6): 678–704. doi:10.1177/1012690213490521.

Times of Israel. 2015. "Palestinians Name Soccer Teams After Terrorists." *The Times of Israel*. http://www.timesofisrael.com/palestinian-soccer-teams-named-after-terrorists/.

_____. 2016. "Police Arrest Palestinian Soccer Coach Whose Team Posed with Photo of Terrorist." *The Times of Israel*. http://www.timesofisrael.com/police-arrest-palestinian-soccer-coach-whose-team-posed-with-photo-of-terrorist/.

Tobin, Jonathan. 2016. "Explaining Palestinian 'Heroes.'" *Commentary*. https://www.commentarymagazine.com/foreign-policy/middle-east/israel/explaining-palestinian-heroes-terrorism-tel-aviv/.

Traganou, Jilly. 2017. "National Narratives in the Opening and Closing Ceremonies of the Athens 2004 Olympic Games." *Journal of Sport and Social Issues* 34 (2): 236–51. doi:10.1177/0193723509360217.

U.N. 2016. "*COMMON COUNTRY ANALYSIS 2016 Leave No One Behind: A Perspective on Vulnerability and Structural Disadvantage in Palestine*." http://www.unsco.org/Documents/Special/UNCT/CCA_Report_En.pdf.

United with Israel. 2016. "Palestinians Using Sports to Bash Israel." *United with Israel*. https://unitedwithisrael.org/palestinians-using-sports-to-bash-israel/.

Vincent, John, Edward Kian, and Paul M Pedersen. 2011. "Flying the Flag: Gender and National Identity in English Newspapers During the 2006 World Cup." *Soccer & Society* 12 (5): 613–32. doi:10.1080/14660970.2011.599582.

Wall, James. 2014. "Does the IDF Target Palestinian Soccer Players?" *Wallwritings*. https://wallwritings.me/2014/03/17/does-the-idf-target-palestinian-soccer-players/.

Ward, Tony. 2009. "Sport and National Identity." *Soccer & Society* 10 (5): 518–31. doi:10.1080/14660970902955455.

Wenner, Lawrence A., and Andrew C. Billings. 2017. *Sport, Media and Mega-Events*. Edited by Lawrence A. Wenner and Andrew C. Billings. Routledge.

Wheeler, Carolynne. 2008. "Palestinian Football Team Plays on Home Soil for First Time." *The Telegraph*. http://www.telegraph.co.uk/news/worldnews/middleeast/palestinianauthority/3264501/Palestinian-football-team-plays-on-home-soil-for-first-time.html

Wiles, Rich. 2013. (ed) *Generation Palestine: Voices from the Boycott, Divestment and Sanctions Movement*. Pluto.

Young, Jane. 2017. "Israel's Fear of Palestinian Sports People." *Pundit*. pundit.co.nz/content/israels-fear-of-palestinian-sports-people

Zec, Dejan, and Miloš Paunović. 2015. "Football's Positive Influence on Integration in Diverse Societies: The Case Study of Yugoslavia." *Soccer & Society* 16 (2–3): 232–44. doi:10.1080/14660970.2014.961387.

Zirin, Dave. 2014. "A Red Line for FIFA? Israel, Violence and What's Left of Palestinian Soccer." *The Nation*. https://www.thenation.com/article/red-line-fifa-israel-violence-and-whats-left-palestinian-soccer/.

PART FOUR

Media Re-Presentation of Nationhood and Sport

Team Orders
Mass Media Complicity with State Nationalisms Expressed Through Motorsport

ZACHARY T. ANDROUS

Abstract

This essay analyzes mass media presentations of riders competing in the International Motorcycling Federation Road Racing World Championship (currently trademarked as MotoGP by rights holder Dorna Sports), to show how they discursively enact and reify state claims to national legitimacy by representing the riders as paragons of their state nationalities. This is important because mass media is an essential component of modern and contemporary nationalisms, acknowledged by theorists since Anderson's insistence on the crucial role of print capitalism in imagining nations. English, Italian, and Spanish dominate the linguistic market for MotoGP media; in Spanish (and Catalan) language coverage, the positions of high profile athletes on Catalan independence are reported, as are their responses to flags, anthems, and other Spanish symbols, but none of this makes its way into the English or Italian coverage.

The essay covers: discursive affirmation of and challenge to exclusively state nationalities in both official and journalistic representations of rider identity; narrative expression of state-based ethno-nationalisms that de-historicize national state identities like Spanish and Italian, rendering them timelessly infinite; Italian sports media coverage of the alleged "nationalistic influence" behind the controversy surrounding an Italian rider's accusation of collusion on the part of two riders from Spain to deny him the Championship in 2015, including the historical role of Italian media in state nationalism during Fascism; an expansion of Anderson's original concern with print capitalism to account for the contemporary mediascape and its essential role in supporting state nationalisms; and cracks in the narrative, including riders whose nationalities defy easy definition and the appearance of non-state languages. The dramatic risks associated with motorcycle road racing lend the sport a symbolic potency that makes it a particularly effective vehicle for arousing emotional responses in the spectators, serving to amplify the natural connection between sport and nationalism.

In this essay I analyze mass media presentations of riders competing in the International Motorcycling Federation (FIM) Road Racing World Championship Grand Prix to show how they discursively enact and reify state claims to national legitimacy by representing the riders as paragons of state-based identities. I also locate and attempt to amplify some of the cracks in that narrative consistency. I position the contemporary mediascape's treatment of state-based identities in terms of rider and country as the developed expression of the historical role of print-capitalism described by Anderson (2006, 36–46). To illustrate these tendencies, I analyze the narratives presented by the official commentary on two Grand Prix races, before going on to consider the Italian language coverage of the controversy that erupted at the end of the 2015 season after one rider accused two others of colluding to deny him the championship. Presuming no familiarity with MotoGP on the part of the reader, I first offer a brief overview of the sport that cannot hope to convey the spectacular nature of its visual aspect, much less the total sensory assault of witnessing a live event. I encourage readers to at least view some of the wide range of free videos available online, if not any of the various documentary films on the sport, to gain a better sense of what these athletes accomplish and endure. I then address the "terminological chaos" (Connor 1994, 89) in which the words state, nation, nation-state, and nationalism are mired, before offering my analysis of some of the 2015 season's mass mediation. Apart from my academic interests, fo i'tifo pe i'pilota Marco Simoncelli [I am actually a fan, of the rider Marco Simoncelli], and this amplifies the potency of my participant-observation. All translations from the Italian, including any errors they may contain, are my own.

Introducing MotoGP

The FIM Road Racing World Championship Grand Prix is the oldest organized motorsport competition in the world, dating from 1949. Since 1992 the Spanish corporation Dorna Sports (acquired by the international Bridgepoint Investment Group in 2013), has held exclusive commercial and broadcast rights to the World Championship, trademarked since 2002 as MotoGP, an abbreviation of the colloquial Motorcycle Grand Prix. Its defining characteristic is the racing of prototype motorcycles, designed and manufactured exclusively for the purpose of Grand Prix racing. These are competition machines rather than commercial motorcycles. While some of their innovations eventually influence consumer models, they are wholly unlike production motorcycles manufactured for sale; as a result, MotoGP is widely acknowledged to be the world's most competitive division of motorcycle racing. The World Championship is contested across three divisions: The Moto3 class, which races motorcycles with a 250cc engine capacity reaching top speeds of approximately 145 mph; Moto2, which runs 600cc machines with top speeds of 175mph; and MotoGP, as the premier class is officially known, running 1,000cc bikes reaching speeds of 225mph. As with other sports, dedicated aficionados follow the development of younger riders in the lower divisions, but the real focus is on the top class. Unless otherwise indicated, my discussion herein is restricted to the MotoGP division, particularly in respect to statistics regarding race wins and number of Championship titles won.

Visually, the prototype machines are unmistakably motorcycles: two wheels, seat over the engine, handlebars, exposed rider bent low over the gas tank. Once in motion, however, they are unmistakably a class apart from other motorcycles: whipping past in a roaring blur, leaning impossibly far over in the corners, and occasionally flipping over to suddenly catapult the rider through the air and crashing back down to the pavement. Beyond the action on the track, a Grand Prix race is a dramatic spectacle: the riders and their motorcycles are festooned with a garish harlequin of sponsors, logos, and nicknames, the stands are full of color-coordinated fans bedecked in flags, hats, and banners, and in an antiquated display of objectification, young female models dressed in sexualized versions of the team colors hold umbrellas that shade or shelter the riders as they sit on their motorcycles before the race begins. (Certain riders eschew the so-called umbrella girl in favor of their own wife or girlfriend in ordinary dress.)

As the name reflects, races originally took place on ordinary streets and roads temporarily closed to traffic. While some smaller competitions are still organized that way, national and international road racing competitions are now held on closed tracks built specifically for motor racing. These tracks are designed to demand the maximum from both riders, in terms of their abilities, and motorcycles, in terms of their versatility, handling, and horsepower. The tracks require immediate transitions from high-speed straight-line sections, in which the riders reach speeds over 200 miles per hour, to combinations of tight and sweeping corners that require the bikes to be leaned over at angles approaching 60 degrees, to say nothing of the second-to-second changes in direction, velocity, and gear. In a matter of less than ten seconds a rider may go from sixth gear at 220 miles per hour, down to second gear to take a corner at 45, then immediately back up to fifth and, without pausing there, back down to first or second, gaining and losing twenty, fifty, or over a hundred miles per hour with each curve of the track. Any given trajectory through a curve is known as a racing line. The inside line through a corner is shorter and thus usually the stronger position for a rider. A chicane, in which alternating left and right turns occur in close succession, provides an ideal opportunity for passing, as the longer outside line is immediately replaced by the shorter inside line. The conventional wisdom among fans is that the rider makes a greater difference than the motorcycle: two riders on the same machinery frequently perform very differently, so it is not simply a matter of having the fastest or best handling motorcycle available.

Crashes are not uncommon, ranging from relatively low speed slides that send riders skidding across the ground to dramatic displays of applied physics that send motorcycle and rider somersaulting through the air with devastating results. The riders wear rigid back and chest protectors and their state-of-the-art leather suits include gyroscopically triggered airbags to protect them from impact in the case that they are launched through the air. Serious injuries are surprisingly rare given the number of crashes, but they do occur: broken bones are by far the most common, with shoulders, hands, and feet being the most difficult to protect from the impact of crashes and thus the most susceptible to damage. Eventually most riders undergo surgery for arm pump, a condition in which the muscles of the forearm swell to the extent that they constrict blood flow to the area. A sobering dimension that amplifies the intensity for everyone involved is the occasional loss of life on track: Daijiro Kato and Marco Simoncelli each perished from injuries suffered during a race, in 2003 and 2011 respectively, while Luis Salom lost his life in an accident during practice in 2016. On those sad occasions one hears continuous acknowledgment, from commentators and fans alike, of the fact that everyone involved, most of all the riders, knows the risks that the sport carries.

Despite those risks, or perhaps in part because of them, the Championship boasts a massive global following, with local broadcast partners worldwide. The season typically comprises eighteen races run between March and November, with about half in Europe and the rest occurring in Asia and the Americas. Twenty-eight riders competed in the 2015 season. Points are awarded based on the order in which the riders finish: twenty-five points for first, twenty for second, sixteen for third, and so on down through the order to fifteenth place, which scores a single point. Sixteenth and below score no points. The rider with most total points at the end of the season is that year's World Champion. Giacomo Agostini won the championship in the top division eight times between 1966 and 1972, a record that has only been approached by one rider: Valentino Rossi, who won his first in 2001 and his seventh in 2009. Over the course of the 2015 season it seemed he was on track to win his eighth title to match Agostini's record, but with three races left Rossi accused two other riders of colluding to deny him the title and a major controversy erupted, the coverage of which clearly illustrates the degree to which state identities are naturalized in mass media discourse on the MotoGP World Championship.

The treatment of this controversy demonstrates the extent to which individual competitors are represented as absolute paragons of state-nationality, especially so in the case of Valentino Rossi, the sport's greatest superstar and highest value commodity. Rossi is important not only for being the highest profile rider the sport has ever seen, but also because Italy is a state with a notoriously poor record of creating a sense of corresponding national identity. I will come back to this controversy and look more closely at its treatment by the Italian press, after a broader consideration of the ways in which commentary on the Championship discursively enacts state claims to national legitimacy.

The expression "team orders" refers to a situation that potentially arises as a result of the way the competition is organized: each team typically fields two riders who, while working for the same employer, supported by the same sponsors, and riding the same motorcycles, nonetheless compete against one another on the track. Situations can arise in which one member of the team is already eliminated mathematically from Championship contention while the other is still has a possibility to take the title. From the perspective of management and its sponsors, the possibility of a Championship win is more important than the performance of a single rider, hence the so-called "team orders" to the rider already eliminated to not interfere with the effort of the other one still in contention. The enforced subsuming of the rider's individual competitive interest to the interests of the powerful few architects of the collective is, in its way, reminiscent to me of the ways in which individuals are compelled to subscribe to state identities that do not necessarily accord with their own. A further parallel could be drawn between team orders and the implicit understanding of the mass media that they are not to speak in any way that contradicts the unitary identification of the rider with his state citizenship.

But just as there is no real way for management to enforce team orders during a race, and no way to know with certainty what factors are affecting a rider's performance simply by observing them on track, thus introducing elements of doubt, certain indications of non-state nationalisms occasionally slip through and come across the channels of mass media that broadcast this sport around the world.

Terminology and Definitions

The terminological chaos long lamented by Walker Connor (1994, 89–117) has hardly improved in the intervening decades. In this essay I eschew the term nation-state in favor of distinguishing between a given nation and a given "territorial-political unit (a state)" (Connor 1994, 96). For the most part, states are unambiguous in respect to being bordered (although the specificity of the borders themselves can sometimes be ambiguous) and while some internal particulars are typically contested, the institutional apparatus responsible for the collective affairs of that territory is easily recognizable. On the other hand, I accept a degree of the ambiguity that Connor (1994, 92–95) associated with the concept of a nation and feel no need to make absolute claims as to the defining characteristics of nationhood or the root causes of nationalism. That said, I agree with Connor (1994, 95–99) that nations are characterized by the collective psychological phenomenon in which a sense of primordial heritage renders an experience of collective interest and identity with a population greater than one's own social world. For Anderson (2006), the imagined community of the nation is also political, if not territorial; but unlike the state, the nation is a community in the sense of "a deep, horizontal comradeship" (7), rooted in the perception of common origin described by Connor (1994, 92–94). Connor laments the sort of equivalent identification of nations with states implied by the idealistic and obfuscator hyphenation nation-state, and blames it for the common misperception that nationalism refers to loyalty to a state, rather than a nation. Given the persistent aspirations of modern states to force their citizenry to identify with them, I use the phrase state nationalism to identify the endeavor of a given state to replace the multiple nationalities existing within its borders with a single, state-based identification, as in the well-known cases of France, Spain, and Italy.

With this in mind, my use of terms like French, Spanish, or Italian, is limited to describing either the state itself (by which I mean the French Republic, Kingdom of Spain, and Italian Republic, respectively) or the citizenship of individuals in those states. When it comes to the identities of the individual riders, as opposed to their citizenship, a few clues are discernible from mass media as to the extent that a given rider may or may not identify with their state citizenship in terms of their own personal experience of identity. Some riders have been quoted in Spanish language publications reporting celebrity positions on the question of Catalan independence, but a given position on that issue is not necessarily a reliable predictor of a given person's own experience of identity. Language, on the other hand, remains a powerful symbol of identity and a means of both challenging and promoting identities on the part of both states and stateless nations. But even language choice is not an absolute predictor of an individual's identity or their position on an issue like national independence for a territory currently within the confines of a state. Just in my own experience I have met speakers of Corsican and Ligurian who oppose independence from France and identify primarily as Italian, respectively. However, the symbolic power of language transcends individual experiences so much so that the appearance of these languages presents a de facto challenge to the linguistic hegemony that is an essential component of both French and Italian state nationalism. So, while I do not make assumptions about riders' identities or political positions based on their use of non-state languages, I do note with interest the appearance of such languages and attempt to amplify their significance for the topics I address.

Theory and Scope

I distinguish between the mass mediation of the World Championship by Dorna Sports itself, as opposed to that presented by other national and international broadcasters. Dorna produces the only video feed available to its worldwide broadcast partners, so whether a fan watches the races through subscribing to Dorna's MotoGP.com website, on their own locally broadcast free television signal, or through a private commercial satellite or cable network, the stream of images, the changes from camera to camera, and the graphics displayed on the screen, are always and only what is generated by the Dorna crew of camera operators, producers, directors, and commentators. Local broadcast partners, even those broadcasting in English like BBC Sport or British Eurosport, typically provide their own commentators. Both Dorna and other broadcasters generate their own range of supporting features that profile riders, teams, sponsors, and locales through interviews, short videos, and the like.

My focus here is on the official commentators and, to a lesser extent, the graphic representations used in the official video production. I have never heard overtly political topics appear in the officially produced content: no references to current events, no signals from riders through signs or images and phrases added to their gear. Humanitarian and charitable causes appear from time to time, typically as organized events leading up to a given race, in which some riders will participate in some kind of ceremonial activity to demonstrate their support for the local charity. Apart from these sponsored events, individual riders rarely use their competition related appearances to promote causes, apart from an occasional piece of paper with a hashtag or website held up to a camera, and the positioning of a charity's logo amidst the riot of patches and logos of commercial sponsors that cover the riders' leather track suits. This silence on the part of riders in the official broadcasts makes an implicit statement, but also leaves open the space for explicit statements to speak beyond the direct content of their words.

For the analysis that follows I draw primarily on the discussion of language ideology offered by Kroskrity (2000), the techniques of Critical Discourse Analysis (CDA) presented by Fairclough (2001) and, more broadly Bourdieu's (1991) general critique of so-called legitimate language. While acknowledging the classically Sausserian concern with the linguistic code itself, Bourdieu (1991, 38) goes on to emphasize the importance of attending to "the social conditions of its production" to give "an adequate account of discourse." In other words, a given text will never be sufficient unto itself as an object of analysis, but will always require a consideration of the social context in which it was produced. Kroskrity (2000, 8) characterizes the ideological dimension of language as "the perception of language and discourse that is constructed in the interest of a specific social group," contending that this contradicts the "myth of the socio-politically disinterested language user or the possibility of unpositioned knowledge." This supports my own argument that the discursive content of MotoGP's mass mediation serves the interests of state claims to national identity, even if the states themselves are not directly responsible. Fairclough (2001, 27) defines ideological power as "the power to project one's practices as universal and 'common sense.'" I apply Fairclough's (2001, 27) principle that "institutional practices which people draw upon without thinking often embody assumptions which directly or indirectly legitimize existing power relations" to the spontaneous utterances generated by commentators during the race, as well as the commonsense language used to indicate riders' identities in mass mediated discourse generally. The presumed allegiances and rivalries salient to the 2015 controversy I discuss below provide some examples of the state nationalist ideology laid bare in the commonsense treatment of the issue. My analysis highlights certain images and discursive treatments that are in no way extraordinary or distinctive relative to the rest of the speech in which they are embedded, because "ideology is most effective when its workings are least visible" (Fairclough 2001, 71).

Reification of State-Based Identities

I argue that the mass mediated presentation of riders' and racetracks' origins and geo-political positions, respectively, constitute implicit expressions of state nationalism through the discursive reification of state-based identities. My argument draws on Anderson's (2006) historical analysis of nationalism's initial reliance on print capitalism, together with sociological and historical perspectives on the politicization of sport and the relationship between language, identity, and nationalism. "The convergence of capitalism and print technology ... created the possibility of a new form of imagined community, which in its basic morphology set the stage for the modern nation" (Anderson, 2006 46). Subsequently, states sought to harness nationalism's power to excite devotion in the masses by imagining nations that were essentially synonymous with the states themselves. The apocryphal proclamation by early statesman Massimo d'Azeglio in 1861, that "with Italy made we must now make the Italians," points up the historical reality that Italy came to be not because a nation of people sharing language, territory, and sense of common descent sought to organize themselves into a state, but rather because a territorially expansive state sought legitimacy by inventing a corresponding nation. The contemporary Italian state is as authoritatively established as any highly developed state in the world in terms of the political control of its territory. But in respect to the identity of its citizenry, it continues to struggle against the greater weight of pre–Italian languages and national and regional identifications. Fortunately for the Italian state, the secession movements that are serious about independence in Sicily, Sardinia, and Venice are relatively small. The larger right-wing Northern League for the Independence of Padania party used secession from Italy as part of its early rhetoric, but in recent years has downplayed the idea in favor of a more conventional far right platform. Spain, on the other hand, faces organized secession movements that are real forces within Spanish politics: Basque interests used violence to focus attention on their cause, while the much larger population of Catalonia has attempted to find political pathways to independence. The official position of the Spanish state in respect to both cases is that the state itself is indivisible.

In the first decades of the 21st century, Italy and Spain are each still struggling in their own ways to consolidate a national identity that corresponds to that of the state. The official MotoGP broadcast strictly adheres to the idealized vision in which an individual's identity is not only best represented by reference to their citizenship, but that their citizenship intrinsically entails a shared sense of common interest with other citizens. Riders' names are accompanied by a small flag and three letters abbreviating the state of which they are citizens every time they appear in a table showing starting or finishing position, Championship standings, or other quantitative comparisons. More stylized representations of the state flags typically appear in the graphics highlighting individual riders in a more artistic fashion, usually as part of the buildup during the pre-race broadcast. The circuits themselves are similarly represented in the table graphics with their small flags and three letter abbreviations, as well as materially in the decorative stylings of the facilities themselves. Finally, during the podium ceremonies, the anthem of the winning rider's state citizenship is played in abbreviated form, and the flags of the podium finishers (in first, second, and third places), are displayed behind them during the presentation of the trophies. For riders, their state citizenship is the only thing that ever appears in these representations, which in and of itself would be a notable expression of state nationalism. But the treatment of the racetracks differs in ways that serve to further reinforce the vision of a citizenry sharing a national identity synonymous of that with the state.

Among the eighteen races on the 2015 calendar appeared the Grands Prix of Spain (ESP), Italy (ITA), Catalunya (CAT), San Marino (RSM), Aragon (ARA), and Valencia (VAL). Catalunya, Aragon, and Valencia each use their regional or territorial flag, rather than the flag of the Spanish state, which is used for the Spanish Grand Prix, held in Andalusia. The Italian Grand Prix, held in Tuscany, shows the Italian flag, while the San Marino Grand Prix, shows the flag of the Republic for which it is named. The enclave state itself does not contain the racetrack, which lies in nearby Misano Adriatico, Italy, as reflected in the formal designation of the race as the Grand Prix of the Republic of San Marino and the Rimini Riviera, but it is always the flag of the Republic of San Marino, and never that of Italy, which appears in association with the race. The practice by which riders are accompanied only by the flag of their national state is particularly notable in the case of those riders who are Spanish citizens, because of the way in which the territorial and regional flags are used for the tracks, but not the riders. I read this as an expression of what I described above as state nationalism: a claim, in this case implicit, to the unified identity of the people despite the existence of degrees of regional and territorial autonomy. In other words, it expresses the notion that while there may be such a place as Catalunya or Valencia, people from those places are and can only be Spanish. This is further reinforced by the ways in which the commentators incorporate references to the riders' state identities, but at the same time, the commentary reveals some of the contradictions that result from treating state-based identities in a common-sense way.

Rider Identity

Identities that correspond with state citizenship are typically used to formally designate riders by the commentators, although in fairness, labels like Spaniard, Italian, or British are used interchangeably with other adjectival expressions that are the stock in trade of sports commentators: one may hear Valentino Rossi referred to as the Italian, the Yamaha rider, the former world champion, or as veteran announcer Nick Harris likes to say sometimes, a wily old campaigner. But it is precisely this subtle normalization of the state-based identities that renders them powerfully instructive, especially when they are adhered to strictly in the face of obvious contradictions. In this section I analyze the commentary and, to a lesser extent, the visual content, of two official MotoGP broadcasts from the 2015 season: The Grand Prix of the Republic of San Marino and the Rimini Riviera; and one of the four Grands Prix held in the Kingdom of Spain, the Grand Prix of Catalunya. In each case, the titular location of the race presents a series of ideological challenges to the premise of a nationally unified identity for the state's population, but the obvious contradictions are countered with the discursive naturalization (Fairclough 2001, 27–28) of the state's own ideology of national unity. To be clear, I am not necessarily attributing this to conscious choices about how to represent identity on the part of commentators or producers, because I have not had the opportunity to take this up with the individuals in question. Irrespective of their own opinions or the extent of the deliberateness of their choices, the broadcast stands on its own as a discursive object, and it is the commonsense language therein, broadcast to the world, with which I am concerned here.

The San Marino Grand Prix

The Republic of San Marino is an enclave state whose borders are contained entirely within the territory of the Italian Republic. The eponymous Grand Prix is held outside of the Republic proper (whose territory is too small to feature a suitable site for a racetrack) in the nearby Italian town of Misano Adriatico, adjacent to the popular beach resort area of Rimini. That said, everything about the race indicates that it is connected to San Marino: its abbreviation in the calendar is RSM, the hashtag displayed continuously throughout the video feed is #SanMarinoGP, the flags of the Republic are on display at the track and in stylized form in the on-screen graphics, and the first place trophy was presented to the winner by the Republic's Minister of Tourism and Sport.

Citizenship in San Marino is not easy to come by: it transfers only to those who are born to a Sammarinese parent, or by naturalization after thirty years' legal residence within the Republic. In the 2015 season Alex DeAngelis was the only rider across all three classes to boast San Marino citizenship and, just as with every other rider's state citizenship, DeAngelis' name is always accompanied by the flag of the Republic in the race graphics. DeAngelis is not a particularly competitive rider, so the commentators rarely have occasion to say his name apart from when they rattle off the starting positions just before the race begins. During the Argentine Grand Prix DeAngelis started from the last position, prompting commentator Nick Harris to proclaim, "and completing the grid, the man from San Marino" in a typical color commentary style. At the San Marino Grand Prix, where DeAngelis again started from last on the grid, Harris called him "the local boy, Alex DeAngelis." But in the same review of the starting grid, the other commentator, Matt Birt, described Valentino Rossi, who is decidedly not from San Marino, as "the home hero Rossi." The only other mention of DeAngelis came when he crashed out early in the race in an incident with another rider. The two commentators mentioned both riders' names repeatedly as they confirmed who was involved and remarked on it being a relatively high-speed crash, but in the rapid response style of addressing an accident, there was no adjectival embellishment of either rider. Prior to this, DeAngelis had worked his way up to as high as fifteenth, considerably better than his starting position in twenty-sixth, but not close enough to the front to warrant any time on camera prior to the crash, nor any mention by the commentators.

Valentino Rossi, on the other hand, was as usual a major target for both the camera and the commentary. Rossi's hometown of Tavullia is only 14 kilometers by road from the racetrack in Misano Adriatico. About rider Andrea Dovizioso, Harris said "it's very much his home race here, lives just up the coast at Forli," while a graphic showed Dovi's number over a stylized Italian flag, directly above the hashtag for the SanMarinoGP. It goes on through the buildup prior to the start, where the commentators arguably have more time to fill with colorful characterizations: in the run-up to a break Harris exclaims "here on the Adriatic coast of Italy!" and on the return he speaks of "Valentino Rossi in front of his home crowd." In respect to the staggered positions on the first row of the starting grid, Harris explains that "number forty-six [Rossi] the local hero, he's got the inside line [advantageous, in third position], but it's Jorge Lorenzo in pole [more advantageous, in first position]." Finally, as the red lights are lit to indicate the race will start in a few seconds at the moment they are extinguished, Harris pronounced "let battle commence here in Italy!" His utterance is technically correct, being that the track is located in Italy, and the Grand Prix's location is officially shared between two different states. But as states, San Marino and Italy are not interchangeable. In respect to the track, the commentators automatically refer to it as Misano, a natural abbreviation of its full name: Misano World Circuit Marco Simoncelli, which is the graphic displayed in the upper corner of the screen for the duration of the broadcast. For example, as Rossi began improving his position, Harris pronounced "everybody at Misano is going absolutely crazy, they're urging on, the local boy's in third place, but in these conditions he's closing all the time." But the presumed affinity between the riders of Italian citizenship and the place in which they are racing ends up overshadowing the legitimacy of San Marino as a thing apart from Italy. Within a minute of the comment quoted immediately above, Harris had said "Lorenzo leads from Marquez, but everybody in Italy is now on their feet: Rossi is on the charge in third place!" Again, this is lexically accurate in terms of the specific location of the venue, but the association of Rossi's localness with the entirety of Italy leaves little conceptual space for San Marino as a separate entity. A more radical slippage between these categories takes place later in the race, when Jorge Lorenzo crashes out, dealing a major blow to his Championship hopes with the loss of all possible points from that race. Birt, rather than Harris, called this one: "Drama in the MotoGP World Championship ... he's crashed out of the Misano GP, huge, huge moment in the 2015 World Championship, Lorenzo out of the race!" Misano is the track, but San Marino is the titular host of the race. All of this serves to discursively erase the legitimacy of San Marino, and underscores the state nationalist premise that everything within the boundaries of the state identifies exclusively and entirely with that state.

The Catalunya Grand Prix

The treatment of the four Grands Prix held in Spain further reinforce the tendency to treat state claims to absolute nationality as paradigmatic, especially in respect to the identification of individual riders: one of these four, held in Jerez, Andalucía, is nominated as the Grand Prix of Spain. The other three are designated as the Grands Prix of Catalunya, Aragon, and Valencia. The Spanish Grand Prix is represented in on-screen graphics by the flag of Spain, while the others are represented by the flags of their autonomous territories (as every administrative region in Spain is called; this is simply the language of the Constitution, which is clear on the indivisibility of the Spanish state and its conflation with a claimed Spanish nation, and does not imply any extraordinary autonomy). The slippages of rider identity in the case of Spain indexes a different set of factors than San Marino and Italy. The Republic of San Marino is a sovereign state separate and distinct from Italy; its position as an enclave microstate presents certain conceptual challenges to the paradigm of a state's territorial unity. In the case of the Grands Prix held in Spain, however, they index a decidedly more active challenge to the paradigm of territorial unity insofar as one of the cities hosting a Grand Prix is the capital of an autonomous territory agitating for independence.

In the first decades of the 21st century, the independence movement in Catalonia is an internationally visible element of Spanish and European politics. In the era of Brexit and immigration crises, nationalist and secessionist political movements garner increased attention, be they nations seeking secession from states or states seeking secession from interstate federations like the European Union, the Eurozone, and NATO. While political issues on the whole are absent from the narratives of MotoGP commentators, it is impossible to dissociate the issues from their primary symbols, such as flags, landscapes, territories, and languages. Similar sorts of slippages and evident contradictions that I identified in respect to the San Marino Grand Prix are also evident here, albeit in starker contrast given the context of Catalonia.

In the same way that the Grand Prix of San Marino is represented graphically by the flag of the Republic, the Grands Prix of Catalonia, Aragon, and Valencia are each represented by the local flag of that region, while the Grand Prix of Spain, held in Andalucía, is represented by the Spanish flag. Riders from any region of Spain, however, are only ever represented with the Spanish flag, in on-screen graphics and should they ascend the podium, and the Spanish national anthem, should they win the race. One of the most obvious cases from the 2015 race was the case of Aleix Espargaro, whose first name is distinctively Catalan. Espargaro was starting from pole position for just the second time in his career, and in the routine review of positions on the starting grid Nick Harris pointed out that Espargaro "was born and bred just round the corner." A few minutes later, as the race was about to start, Harris said "what a day for Aleix Espargaro, local boy, really local, two miles away, born and bred next to the circuit." Clearly Espargaro is Catalan. But when he is shown on the starting grid, the stylized graphic of his name and number appear against a billowing Spanish flag above the hashtag #CatalanGP in the onscreen graphic. Yet the flag used to represent the racetrack itself in the graphics is the flag of Catalonia. The fact that these apparent contradictions require no explanation demonstrates the extent to which ideology operates as commonsense: the contradiction is simply ignored, and any apparent differences or inconsistencies between the two identities are treated discursively as if they do not exist.

I interpret this as follows: while Spain may include regions with distinctive identity features, like names, flags, and locations, the people themselves can only be Spanish. So at a race in Catalonia, with Catalan flags, a rider with a Catalan name, known to be "really local" by the commentators, is called "the Spaniard" and "the Spanish rider" in the other references to him before he crashed out with only five laps remaining, which prompted Matt Birt to say "aw, Aleix Espargaro has crashed out of his home race … what a nightmare for the pole position man." Other riders from Catalonia, including Dani Pedrosa and Marc Marquez, as well as Jorge Lorenzo from the Balearic Islands, are all called either Spaniards or Spanish and, in this broadcast at least, never any other kind of toponymical reference. (I recall hearing Lorenzo referred to as Mallorcan at least once, but not in any of the six 2015 races whose commentary I analyzed for references to rider and racetrack identities.) Each of these riders is in some way referred to as being at their home race, home track, or in front of their home fans. I am not arguing that this is a way of rendering Catalonia and Spain synonymous or even interchangeable; instead, I interpret this as a commonsense expression of the ideological claim that every individual who is a citizen of the Spanish state should necessarily, automatically, and exclusively identify as Spanish. Territories and administrative divisions, like Catalonia, can have their own names and flags and local boys in the race, but the boys themselves are Spanish. The ideological nature of this discursively rendered unitary state nationality is thrown into sharp relief by the context of the Catalan independence movement, which is predicated on the notion that no relationship between the people of Catalonia and the Spanish state is necessary whatsoever. The examples I have outlined thus far are characteristic insofar as they come from relatively routine examples of World Championship commentary. But with just two races left in the 2015 season, the sport's highest profile rider, veteran Valentino Rossi, accused Honda rider Marc Marquez, who had already been mathematically eliminated from the Championship, of interfering with him to aid his Yamaha teammate Jorge Lorenzo. The commonsense ideology of state nationalist identity provided a ready framework for scripting the controversy, as I will show in the following sections.

The 2015 Controversy

It is difficult to convey the degree of Valentino Rossi's significance. He is second only to Giacomo Agostini for the number of World Championships he has won, and Agostini and Rossi are the only two riders ever to win more than five titles in the premier class. Agostini competed well before the era of the celebrity athlete emerged, and while Rossi may not have surpassed Agostini's record, he is by far the highest profile sports professional in Italy. He routinely appears in Forbes' list of the top ten earning athletes worldwide, making him the highest paid Italian athlete. Italians who don't know the names of any other racers, who profess no interest in sport whatsoever, recognize Valentino Rossi. Beyond Italy, his following is worldwide, as is his commercial empire of merchandise and sponsorship. His affable, easygoing nature and affinity for the limelight only helps the fact that Rossi is a natural talent who spent his prime years completely dominating the sport: he took the world championship title every year between 2001 and 2005, lost it in 2006 by crashing out of the very last race of the season in an unforced error, before taking it again 2008 and 2009. But he has not won a championship since: in 2010 Rossi suffered a major injury, and 2011 and 2012 were spent riding for Ducati, whose motorcycle had taken only a single championship since entering the competition in 2003, a dream pairing for many Italian fans that ultimately proved fruitless. In 2013 he returned to Yamaha, the machine with which he won four of his world championship titles, but he has yet to claim another, leaving him one short of matching Agostini's record and two short of surpassing it. In the heady years of Rossi's five consecutive

Championship titles it seemed all but certain that he would conquer Agostini's record and cement his place in history as the undisputed king of Grand Prix motorcycle racing. But as the pace of his winning slows and more years pass without another Championship, his ultimate ascension to the winningest of all time appears increasingly unlikely. In 2015 Rossi was thirty-six years old, making him the second oldest rider to win a race in the modern era of the sport. Had he won the Championship that year, to tie Agostini's record, he would have been the oldest Championship winner ever. But the tide of the sport had turned by then to the next record-shattering superstar, a rider setting records for being the youngest rather than the oldest. In 2013, his debut season in the premier class, 20-year-old Marc Marquez set records for being the youngest rider ever to start from pole position, the youngest rider ever to set a fastest race lap, to ever win a race, and the youngest to win two, then three, then four races in succession. He finished the season as the first rookie to win the title since 1978, and the youngest to do so since 1983. Marquez won the Championship by just four points, which is the difference between finishing one place apart in any given race, a very narrow margin. Rossi finished that year fourth in Championship, with 237 points, whereas the top three riders had all broken 300. Marquez took the title again in 2014, electrifying the sport with his charming combination of cheerful youthfulness and seemingly effortless domination.

Marquez got off to a slow start in 2015, coming in fifth in the first race to Rossi's first. Marquez crashed out of the third race after he and Rossi made contact in what was immediately ruled a racing incident, which is to say something that normally happens in the course of a race and not resulting from irresponsible or unsportsmanlike riding. Marquez crashed again on his own three races later, and again in the next race after that, all but eliminating him mathematically from Championship contention before they were even halfway through the season. Rossi led the Championship in points for almost the entire season, with 28-year-old Jorge Lorenzo, who had won the Championship in 2010 and 2012, trailing him closely; with two races left in the season Rossi was eleven points ahead of Lorenzo and was positioned to take the Championship. In the pre-race press conference, Rossi accused Marquez of having deliberately interfered with him in the previous race to help Lorenzo, going on to say in a subsequent interview that he believed it was because Marquez had a longer term goal of surpassing Rossi's total number of Championship titles, and so it was in his interest to ensure Rossi did not gain another. These kinds of accusations are relatively rare, and the media played up the rivalry in predictable ways. So much rancor had developed that the traditional pre-race press conference, which had earlier been exploited by Rossi as a platform to make his original accusation, was cancelled before the final race. Lorenzo won the final race and with it the Championship, but Rossi's accusations had cast a shadow of doubt over its legitimacy.

Some examples of the coverage of this controversy in the Italian language sporting press will further illustrate ways in which mass media discourse presents commonsense versions of ideological claims about state nationality. This is instructive because Italy is widely considered to be one of Europe's weakest states in respect to the population's identification with the state and has one of the world's oldest and best established traditions of sports journalism. *La Gazzeta dello Sport* is a daily newspaper covering all sport that began publishing in 1896, with a daily circulation of over 200,000 and a readership that must be much higher, since many of those copies are delivered to cafes where they are read and discussed by several people throughout the day. *Moto Sprint* is a weekly magazine dedicated to motorcycle competitions that began publication in 1976, the year after Agostini won his final premier class World Championship. Many informal interviews have started with someone's comment when I am purchasing Moto Sprint at a news stand, and I typically inquire as to the role of digital media versus print; many of these anonymous informants have explained to me that the real commentary, the real depth of analysis and opinion, is still found in the pages of the publications, while updates, scores, and the like are what they look for online. I have no quantitative or systematic data to back this up; it is simply one of the myriad general impressions that has emerged out of a decade of ongoing, every day, ethnographic observation of the foreign society in which I live.

Like any MotoGP fan in Italy, I followed the last weeks of the 2015 season very closely, and not only with scholarly interest. In writing this essay I have made every effort to base my analysis on the data I find in the textual objects, rather than allowing my opinions and emotions as a fan to influence my reasoning. But in the interest of fully disclosing my positionality, I feel it appropriate to explain my opinion of the controversy that dominated the last weeks of that historic season. Of the innumerable conversations I had with friends and strangers alike during those tense weeks, I must acknowledge in particular the discussions I had with my girlfriend Jennifer, who had never followed any kind of motorsport before she became drawn into the 2015 season by virtue of my interest. Throughout the controversy we watched the races, press conferences, and other media appearances together, and neither read anything about it in the Italian or Anglophone press without promptly discussing it with the other, so I formed my opinions in tandem with her. Rossi's accusation had to do with the Australian Grand Prix, and I provide the following summary of the action as I saw it to help frame the context of his later accusation.

Before Rossi made his comments, neither of us had noticed anything unusual about the race. Lorenzo had started from the front row of the starting grid, while Rossi started from the third row because of a poor qualifying performance; Lorenzo got into the lead during the first lap, while Rossi, who had settled into seventh during the first lap, took several laps to work his way up to the battle for second. A familiar scenario unfolded in which Rossi's Yamaha was outpaced on the long straight portion of the track by the more powerful Honda and Ducati of Marquez and Andrea Iannone respectively, only to take back the positions in the tight corners where the less aggressive Yamaha engine gives it better handling. Meanwhile Lorenzo, on his Yamaha, was far enough ahead in first place to not get caught up in the three-way battle for second until about two-thirds of the way through the race, by which time the trio of Marquez, Iannone and Rossi had caught up to Lorenzo. Marquez and Lorenzo began taking and re-taking first place from one another, while Rossi and Iannone did the same with third. With five laps to go, Rossi had passed Iannone and was faced with passing Marquez, who defended his position as any rider would: adjusting his racing line to "close the door," or occupy the space through which the other rider would have to pass. Doing so necessarily slows both riders, but allows the rider in the lead to maintain their advantage. This is a standard tactic and there is nothing extraordinary about it in terms of racing comportment. Andrea Iannone continued to fight and at one point made a very aggressive move to pass both Rossi and Marquez at the same time, dropping Rossi and Marquez back to fourth and third. These were the positions at the start of the last lap: Rossi in fourth behind Marquez, Iannone, and Lorenzo in the lead. Marquez and Iannone traded positions three times before Marquez was able to hold his advantage in second. As Marquez managed to pass Lorenzo into first, Rossi was fighting all out with Iannone for third place: Rossi forced his way past with a very aggressive move, and Iannone immediately did the same back, actually bumping Rossi's bike with his own. Ultimately, Iannone managed to hold onto third place, just as Marquez managed to hold onto first. Lorenzo and Rossi, the only two in contention for the Championship, finished second and fourth, respectively.

Marquez and Iannone were both out of Championship contention at this point in the season, but both appeared to us to be racing to win nevertheless. Fans and riders universally recognize that riding to win in every race, irrespective of the Championship standings, is a core principle of the sport. Essentially, Rossi accused Marquez of violating this sacrosanct principle of the competition, which is one of the worst insults that can be made against a rider's integrity. Neither of us really believed Rossi's accusation, especially because it looked to us like Iannone had done more to hold him up than Marquez when it really mattered. The sporting press in any language had nothing to say about it after the race because Rossi waited until the press conference that opened the following race to say anything, and nothing seemed untoward on the basis of how the race looked to watchers, professional and amateur alike. I recall thinking at the time that Rossi was trying to plant seeds of doubt to save face in the case that he ended up losing the closely contested Championship fight with Lorenzo. It seemed disingenuous to talk about Marquez in the prior race but not Iannone. It was not hard to anticipate Rossi's accusation becoming a self-fulfilling prophecy and, in fact, in the next race Marquez appeared to be racing against Rossi rather than for the win. The commentators talked it up, calling it epic, personal, a dogfight, the battle of the season, and so on. Just a few laps into the race, Rossi had caught up to Marquez and the back and forth began, with Marquez clearly doing everything he could to keep Rossi from staying ahead of him. With 15 laps to go, Rossi was ahead of Marquez and raised his arm in a gesture typically used when a rider has a problem to let other riders know that they can safely pass; in this case, Rossi was clearly making the request to Marquez to stop challenging Rossi's passes and let him proceed with his race. If anything, Marquez responded by becoming even more aggressive, and attempting on the next lap to pass Rossi on the outside line of a curve (which is typically impossible, as the outside trajectory is appreciably longer than the inside line). Commentator Nick Harris called the action: "Rossi gets up the inside, Rossi's back into third place, what can Marquez do, side by side they come," and Matt Birt began, "ooh, Marquez thought about riding around the outside of Rossi at turn twelve, brave in the extreme that would have been, [shouting] he rides around the outside of turn thirteen instead, he absolutely mugs Rossi on the outside, Rossi looks really..." and at that very moment Marquez crashed, after making contact with Rossi, who clearly pushed Marquez with his leg, although it was never clear if that was the initial contact or a response to contact initiated by Marquez. After some excited talking over each other, the first legible comment came from Birt, who said while a replay was being shown "well, you've got to say, Valentino Rossi looks over his left shoulder, he slowed right down in turn number fourteen, there was contact between Marquez, a shake of the head from Marc Marquez, and you feel with some justification." Harris followed immediately with "there's going to be repercussions from that incident, I can promise you."

And there were: Race Direction ruled that Rossi had deliberately forced Marquez off his racing line, and Rossi was penalized according to the established system, which resulted in his being forced to start the next, final race of the season from last place on the grid, all but guaranteeing Lorenzo's victory in the race and the Championship. On October 27, 2015, MotoSprint ran the sardonic headline "SHAME: The Championship ends in disgust. Marquez plays dirty, and makes Rossi lose his nerve, who then takes a kick at the title. In Valencia he will start from last. Feel sorry for Lorenzo." So the question appears settled: even though Rossi's actions were in clear violation of written rules, Marquez's violation of unwritten rules provoked it and thus Marquez is responsible for wrongdoing. Inside the magazine, the cover story opens on page eleven with a two-page spread of Marquez and Rossi on track, with the same text as the cover, and an additional piece of text alongside an insert shot of Lorenzo: "Spain Connection: Marquez gave Lorenzo a big hand in the contest against Rossi." Elsewhere the magazine reports various iterations of Rossi's claim that Marquez has a long term goal of limiting Rossi's Championship titles so that it will be easier to surpass him in the contest to be the winningest of all time, but in the spread that opens the story, they propose another explanation based on the common citizenship between Marquez and Lorenzo. A quote from Graziano Rossi, Valentino's father and retired Grand Prix racer, takes the premise of a Spanish connection further: "The organizers of the World Championship [Dorna Sports] are Spanish and they have allowed Marquez to pursue his only objective: to prevent Valentino from winning." Including the quote from Rossi's father was a particularly significant editorial choice for the following reasons.

The sixteen thumbnail quotes in the "Rossi vs Marquez for and Against" feature on page twenty-one included two celebrities; eight former riders who have each won multiple World Champion titles (including Loris Capirossi, who was serving as MotoGP Safety Advisor in 2015), but none of whom were currently competing in the Championship; six team managers who were currently competing, including Marquez's; and Graziano, credited as "father of Valentino," and who had never won a World Championship during his racing career. With no disrespect intended to the elder Rossi's racing career, he is not in the same league as those who have won multiple Championships, he is not involved in the World Championship in any way beyond being a spectator, and he is not a celebrity on the order of the pop star and television personality also quoted. Rossi's father taking his son's side in the debate is predictable and expected. A Spanish conspiracy, on the other hand, is not only exciting and intriguing, it was not suggested by anyone else quoted in that feature: the comments from the racing professionals and the celebrities each in their way address the central sportsmanship question of whether Marquez not riding to win justified Rossi's reaction against him. Only Rossi's father invokes forces larger than the riders, with the ideologically commonsense claim that the Spanish management wants Spanish World Champions.

In the final race of the season at Valencia, Rossi's penalty required that he start from last position, twenty-eighth on the starting grid. He mounted a valiant effort, aided by some riders who allowed him past, battled by others who were sooner or later out fought, and eventually finished in fourth, losing the Championship to Lorenzo by just five points. In the headline of the November 10, 2015, issue Moto Sprint pulled no punches: "The Big Swindle: Marquez escorts Lorenzo and keeps back Pedrosa. Rossi's catching up is useless. The title is the Spaniards.'" Appearing in smaller font above the main headline: "Rossi: 'They really fixed this race'" [lit. "they did a big cookie," a slang expression from horse racing indicating a method of administering performance enhancing drugs to a horse, and now used commonly in football to refer to match fixing]. The historic *Gazzeta dello Sport* ran the following headline above the fold on November 9, the day after the race: "What a Fix!" [lit. What a Big Cookie!], followed by "Catching up not enough, Rossi attacks Marquez: 'he protected Lorenzo.... I deserved the title, I led [the Championship] from the first race. What a disgrace the last laps.' Jorge admits: They [Marquez and Pedrosa, who finished behind Lorenzo and ahead of Rossi] helped me, like this the title remains in Spain.'" In the same headline box is a preview of the Commentary by Umberto Zapelloni: "Our Champion is Vale. In the record books is Lorenzo's name. In the record of our hearts is Valentino's." Inside of that issue, the Italian sportswear manufacturer Dainese ran a full page ad showing Valentino on a victory lap, smiling through his visor, hand held high, with the phrase "Proud of Our Champion." Rossi is one of over twenty riders in various international competitions sponsored by Dainese (Marquez and Lorenzo are sponsored by AlpineStars, the other major manufacturer of protective gear for the Championship).

Conclusion: Interpeting the Controversy

In terms of the controversy between Rossi's technical violation of the rules versus Marquez's violation of their spirit, there are two things to address: the possessive pronouns on the one hand and the insistence that the Championship would have gone to Rossi on the other. The second of these could be more easily dismissed as typical fan style brag talk, were it not so closely bound up with the former. In fact, as a discursive claim, they are virtually inseparable: the acknowledgment that Rossi is the rightful Champion is only meaningful if he is "ours" and his status as such is simultaneously the basis for recognition of his status as the rightful Champion. The ideologically commonsense presumption here is that if you are reading these articles, or seeing these advertisements, in Italian, that you necessarily identify with the collective identity implied by the linguistic competence sufficient to be reading an Italian newspaper in the first place. This fundamentally state nationalist logic was bluntly proclaimed by Lin Jarvis, the Yamaha team boss ultimately responsible for managing both Rossi and Lorenzo, when he was asked in a press conference about the challenges of managing both of the two feuding riders: "I think one thing that helps is that I'm not either Italian or Spanish; that's said as a joke, but it's also not a joke. If you are able to be neutral, remain neutral, it's very important because there's a lot of nationalistic influence can come: if you're Spanish, you should support the Spanish, if you're Italian, you should support the Italian perhaps." Embedded in his statement are a series of ideological claims that underlie self-evident, commonsense understandings of what identity, citizenship, and nationality mean. Jarvis is connecting his ability to remain neutral to the fact that he does not share citizenship with either rider, which is an indirect way of saying that if he were either Spanish or Italian, he would not be able to remain neutral because of "nationalistic influence." From a certain perspective, this could be taken as an indication that Jarvis believes the Spanish riders collaborated to deny Rossi the Championship because the influence of state nationalism is so strong that it cannot be avoided among and between citizens, hence Jarvis' claim that his neutrality is based on his being neither Spanish nor Italian. By extension, Jarvis' comment could be interpreted as lending support to the claim made by Rossi's father, that the Dorna corporation was itself responsible for creating the conditions that favored the Spanish riders over the Italian. (It may be worth pointing out doing so would have probably worked against Dorna's own economic interests, since Rossi is by far the most widely celebrated and followed MotoGP rider worldwide, and had he managed to tie Agostini's all-time record in 2015, which would have kept alive the hope that he would go on to surpass it, interest in the Championship would have surely spiked.)

Whether statements made through broadcast media by individual commentators or participants, or headlines and photo captions in print media, the direct association between a rider, their citizenship, and their presumed values and allegiances, serve to discursively construct these individual athletes as paragons of their respective state identities. Even in the face of obvious contradictions and inconsistencies, as in the difference between being Catalan and being Spanish, or being in San Marino and being in Italy, the overarching logic of state nationalism is enforced through its naturalization as commonsense. Apparent and even evident contradictions, as when Aleix Espargaro sends Twitter messages in Catalan language, or when Marco Simoncelli's pit board displayed a congratulatory message in his local dialect of the Romagnolo language rather than Italian when he won a World Championship are visible to any and every spectator who tunes in to the broadcasts. These examples are salient for contemporary political issues, as well as for the more fundamental attempt to forge a national identity for the state. Today's multimedia, multiplatform content generation may be the evolved form of Anderson's print capitalism, but the use of language as a vehicle of ideology continues to be a central mechanism of state aspirations to national legitimacy.

REFERENCES

Anderson, Benedict. 2006. *Imagined Communities: Reflections on the Origins and Spread of Nationalism*. Rev. ed. London: Verso.

Bourdieu, Pierre. 1991. *Language and Symbolic Power*. Translated by Gino Raymond and Matthew Adamson. Cambridge: Polity.
Connor, Walker. 1994. *Ethnonationalism: The Quest for Understanding*. Princeton: Princeton University Press.
Crash.net. 2015. "MotoGP Valencia: Jarvis: Enough of the Polemics, Let's Move On." http://www.crash.net/motogp/news/225035/1/jarvis-enough-of-the-polemics-lets-move-on.html.
Fairclough, Norman. 2001. *Language and Power*. 2d ed. Harlow: Pearson.
Kroskrity, Paul V. 2000. "Regimenting Languages: Language Ideological Perspectives." In *Regimes of Language: Ideologies, Politics, and Identities*, edited by Paul V. Kroskrity, 1–34. Santa Fe: School of American Research.

Taking Our Ball and Staying Home

Nationalistic Exceptionalism and Cultural Imperialism in U.S. Sports Coverage and Leagues

JARED BAHIR BROWSH

Abstract

When the United States failed to qualify for the 2018 World Cup, Fox, who acquired the rights to the event in 2011, reduced its on-the-ground coverage in Russia and struggled to market the event without an American presence. Since the 19th century, sports have been one of the main sources of national identity for those living in the United States and has been used as a tool for cultural imperialism and proof of American exceptionalism for over a century. This essay examines media coverage and professional league marketing to show the evolution of this nationalistic attitude toward sports in the United States, from the dearth of media attention toward sports that lack American involvement and dominance to the constant attempts to expand the footprint of domestic professional sports league in the United States around the world through expansion and player recruitment.

On October 10, 2017, the United States Men's National Soccer Team (USMNT) took the field in Couva, Trinidad, with control over their fate in the Confederation of North, Central American and Caribbean Association Football (CONCACAF) tournament that determines what teams from the Confederation qualify for the Fédération Internationale de Football Association (FIFA) World Cup that was taking place the next summer in Russia. Widely considered one of the top three teams in the CONCACAF, USMNT was seen as one of the favorites going into the fifth round of the tournament, known a the Hexagonal or "Hex" where the final six teams left in the tournament play a home and home series, with each squad playing ten games total and the top three teams automatically advancing to the World Cup.[1]

The USMNT had not performed as expected throughout the tournament, struggling to find consistency in their play. After automatically advancing to the fourth round they were in danger of not making it to the Hex after an opening win in their group a tie and a loss put them in danger of not making the top two of four teams in Group C. The would recover to win their group and move to the fifth round, but a loss to Guatemala, a team barely in the top 100 in the world, concerned many fans of the team.[2] Qualification was no smoother in the fifth round as two losses and a draw in the first four games put the United States toward the bottom of the rankings. The team again recovered, putting them in position to qualify for the tournament with just a draw against the 99th-ranked Trinidad and Tobago National Team. The last time they played in Trinidad in the fourth round of the CONCACAF the two teams drew, but like in the previous round the draw would be just enough to secure qualification.[3]

An upset to the two-island nation would not necessarily eliminate the USMNT since the teams they were competing against for the third qualifying spot, Panama and Honduras, were playing two teams widely considered superior the same day, Mexico and Costa Rica respectively. Combined with a U.S. loss, both of those teams would have to win their games to completely eliminate the United States, since the fourth spot in the fifth round still offered hope since that team would play the fifth-place team from the Asian Football Confederation qualifying tournament. First half goals by Trinidad and Tobago surprised many, but both Honduras and Panama trailed by a goal and each of their games still putting the United States 45 minutes away from the World Cup. Young star Christian Pulisic brought the USMNT within one early in the second half, but that hope turned to panic as Honduras took a 3–2 lead on Mexico and Panama tied Costa Rica a few minutes in the second half. Hope remained until Panama scored in the waning minutes of their match officially eliminating the United States from the world's largest soccer tournament.[4]

The unlikely elimination not only disappointed millions of United States' soccer fans, but executives at Fox Sports. Professional soccer has never experienced any where near the popularity of the "four major sports leagues" in the United States, but did see significant growth since the last time the USMNT missed the World Cup spurred by the improvement over the previous three decades, success of the Women's National Team, growth of Major League Soccer, and increased accessibility to international leagues like the Premier League in Britain and the United European Football Association (UEFA) Champions Leagues. However, even with this growing interest in professional soccer outside the United States where the MLS lags behind many European leagues in terms of talent, Fox had banked on the inclusion of the USMNT to draw in audiences, especially during the group stage where there is a lower concentration of star players and top teams. The lack of a U.S. squad combined with games airing in the early morning hours in the United States due to the time difference with host Russia brought up significant red flags for Fox executives and producers as they looked ahead to the tournament, which commenced in mid–June of the next year.[5]

Fox and Telemundo outbid other networks for the 2018 and 2022 Men's World Cups, along with the 2015 and 2019 Women's World Cups, in 2011 with a $1.1 billion joint offer to FIFA. ESPN and Univision had aired the World Cup in the United States since 1994, but Fox and the Comcast-owned Telemundo were awarded the tournaments after offering almost double the other two networks had given FIFA in their previous deal.[6] While the Spanish-language Telemundo felt good about their investment, which made up about 60 percent of the total bid with the qualification of Mexico and the overall more intense soccer fandom of their audience, Fox needed to adjust how they would promote and cover the event.

The approach to the latter was to try to advertise the upcoming tournament as a global event featuring the world's biggest stars facing off in the most popular single sport event. Unfortunately the campaign launched during the National Football Conference championship game in January 2018, and a significant portion of American football fans might not have recognized current players like Lionel Messi and Ronaldo. This possibility was not lost on marketers working with Fox as David Beckham, probably the most popular soccer player in the United States in spite of his retirement and lack of inclusion in the World Cup, and Deadpool, a Marvel superhero licensed to Fox who would be featured in a eponymous sequel later that year, also appeared in promotions for the tournament.[7] Later promotions featured intense graphics and short appearances by the world's top players as Fox promoted a "fist fight" for the Cup hoping the violent imagery typically reserved for their American football coverage would draw in fans that were planning to skip the tournament without the involvement of the United States.[8]

Fox's U.S.-centric approach had been evident for years. Most of their soccer announcers for not only MLS and USMNT but also international matches and tournaments were American.[9] The previous American television World Cup right holder, ESPN, employed a number of British announcers who were more familiar with soccer in Europe and globally. Their style was not only more similar to how soccer is announced around the world, but they often had more knowledge of players and teams outside CONCACAF, many of which represented the favorites to win the World Cup. Most of the broadcast teams primarily announce MLS games, which feature a lower concentration of World Cup participants than the Premier League and other European soccer organizations that the ESPN announcers had more experience covering. They did both employ primarily American commentators, but with the higher concentration of American announcers points to the assumption that Fox hoped that the familiar accents could draw more casual American viewers, especially for USMNT matches, while assuming diehard soccer fans would watch in spite of lack of international announcers, many of which have more experience covering a large portion of top World Cup participants.[10]

More evidence of the financial value the inclusion of the USMNT to Fox Sports along with the programming division's America-first approach came in 2015 when a closed bid for the 2026 World Cup was triggered by scheduling issues connected with granting Qatar the 2022 World Cup. The tournament was originally scheduled for the summer of 2022, but concern over high summer temperatures in the Middle Eastern nation led FIFA officials to push the World Cup back to November and December of that year when it would be cooler. They did consider February, but that would have created a conflict with the Winter Olympics and a March/April tournament would have conflicted with Ramadan in the first Muslim-majority nation to host the soccer tournament. Typically the World Cup competes only with baseball on the American summer sports schedule, but a move to fall has the World Cup up against early season basketball, hockey, and the most popular sport in the United States, football. Fox pays the NFL about $1.6 billion a year through 2022 to air football on their flagship network Thursdays and Sundays, four times what they agreed to pay FIFA for each of four World Cups they paid to air.[11] As a way to possibly make up for the schedule change, FIFA held a closed bidding process for Fox and Telemundo with the two networks agreeing to pay FIFA $300 and $350 million respectively for the rights to the 2026 World Cup.[12] Many felt was significantly less than what they could have solicited in an open bidding process.[13] Understanding the value of a North American hosted World Cup, the deal included a bonus of $180 million from Fox if the United States was one of the hosts of the tournament. This bonus was not only because the games would take place during prime watching hours for American audiences, but hosts typically get an automatic bid into the World Cup, an inclusion more valuable to the English-speaking United States audience that Fox hoped to attract with Telemundo's lower $115 million bonus for the same outcome representing some evidence of this value to Fox. With the 2026 World Cup bid representing the first shared by three nations there are questions whether FIFA would still allow the hosts to automatically qualify, however with a qualifying field increasing by 50 percent to 488 and the value it has to FIFA to include the host in the tournament it is likely that all three will avoid needing to qualify through the CONCACAF tournament that eliminated both the United States and Canada in 2018. This same reasoning is used in the Olympics as the host nation automatically qualifies for every event it desires to compete.[14]

As the world's biggest single sport event approached, Fox needed to decide how to cover the actual event. They assigned twelve announcers and commentators to broadcast the World Cup, but in the months leading up to the event they revealed that only four of those broadcasters would actual travel to Russia to call the games. The other eight would announce the matches from Fox studios in Los Angeles over 6,000 miles from Moscow. Their online coverage tried to appeal to casual fans with general discussions about what announcers looked forward to while visiting Russia and what will be the fan tradition popularized by the event, referencing vuvuzelas that were featured in the 2010 World Cup in South Africa. Further evidence of Fox's disconnect with soccer outside the United States was seen in their feature celebrating rising phenoms in the sport which included an American player and Senegalese professional who did not even make his national team's World Cup roster.[15]

Fox's commitment to sports outside the major four United States professional leagues and two top college sports has been inconsistent since the network launched in 1986. Many argue that Fox did not become a true competitor to the Big Three broadcast networks, NBC, CBS, and ABC, until 1994 when they won the bid for the rights to National Football League games which they still hold over two decades later. Two years later they acquired the rights to "America's Pastime" broadcasting games for Major League Baseball, uniting the two sports often connected to culture in the United States.[16] The next year Fox launched Fox Sports World, a network dedicated to international sports, particularly rugby, Australian Rules Football, and soccer. The digital tier cable network relied on low cost international fare, some of which coming from its sibling company Sky Sports through 21st Century Fox. Fox Sports acquired the U.S. rights to the English Premier League a year later outbidding ESPN. Fox Sports World showed a combination of live and tape delayed matches, continuing as the network transitioned to Fox Soccer Channel in 2006, dropping coverage of most of the other sports exhibited on the previous iteration of the network. To offset some of the costs Fox subcontracted coverage of games to ESPN, particularly after 2010 when a three-year, $80-million-dollar right deal began between Fox and the EPL. The same year Fox Soccer Plus was launched to complement the original network and its programming after they acquired the media rights to several leagues and channels on several cable systems from the Irish based Setanta Sports.[17] As the value of live sports continued to rise, NBC eventually outbid Fox for the Premier League and the network lost the rights to a number of other leagues to the growing beIn Sports.[18] With decreasing content and the impending launch of Fox Sports 2 in August 2013, it was announced that the soccer network would be replaced by the entertainment focused FXX in September of the same year.[19] They did agree to air FIFA tournaments, including the World Cups, in 2011, but when the contract kicked in for the 2015 Women's World Cup, Fox did not air games from the world soccer tournament on their niche soccer network. Like its sister station Fox Sports 1, the new network, which was rebranded from Fuel TV, focused on mainstream American sports with focus on combat and action sports, although it has expanded to include some Australian Rules Football and rugby, whose similarity to American football may explain its slow growth in the United States.[20]

Nationalistic Sports Coverage for a Nationalistic Audience

There is no doubt that audiences in the United States greatly prefer watching professional and college sports originated from their own country than anywhere else. In fact, many sports that are popular internationally that the United States does not excel at on the world stage, like soccer, are derided as being unworthy of American attention because they are boring or even unmasculine particularly compared to popular contact sports like American football.[21] Although Fox has shown some ambivalence toward international teams and leagues, they are not alone in their U.S.-centric approach. NBC's Olympic coverage has been criticized for too frequently prioritizing American athletes while ignoring the successes of other countries, pasteurizing the coverage for an audience they see as representing a Middle America that is white and often ignorant of sports or athletic success outside of their country's borders.[22] NBC has found some success with its Premier League coverage, but the coverage by NBC is sure to prioritize the American experience of watching the game.[23] Even ESPN, with its international presence, has struggled at times to balance this lack of familiarity of Americans with competition outside of the United States with meaningful in depth coverage of the sport.[24] It is clear American broadcasters are not willing to risk losing casual fans who may be turned off if U.S. storylines and figures are not centralized, especially when it is a sport without deep U.S., or at least North American, connections like baseball, football, or even basketball.[25]

Money and Coverage

Capitalism and money cannot be ignored when considering Fox, NBC, and other networks' approach to acquiring the rights and actually broadcasting the games. Intuitively the former should lead to the latter, but as Fox proved with subcontracting their English Premier League coverage to ESPN before being outbid by NBC at the end of the contract, that is not always the case. The problem is no longer whether sports outside the "big four" North American leagues and college athletics can draw an audience, as NBC's coverage of the English Premier League and the general growth of other sports through streaming has shown, but how much profit can it bring compared to other available content options.[26] Even as each of these media companies manage a number of networks and streaming services, they still have a finite amount of time on the schedule to maximize how much money they make.[27]

Another issue that arises when media companies are considering acquiring rights fees from international sports properties is how it fits, or conflicts with sports media rights they already own. Using the English Premier League as an example, whose season runs from August to May each year, many of the games happen on weekend mornings and afternoons, much like leagues in the United States. Fox is paying the NFL more than a billion dollars a year for the right to play football games every Sunday along with the hundreds of millions of dollars the media corporation pays college conferences like the Big Ten for the rights to football games every Saturday.[28] The Premier League directly conflicts with the entire American football season and much of the baseball season with Fox paying Major League Baseball over $600 million a year to broadcast the league's regular season and playoff games, including the World Series. Compare that to NBC's contract with the Premier League costing the media outlet under $200 million a year, the larger investment makes those rights and games a higher priority.[29] Fox is not going to pay to either broadcast content that directly conflicts with their properties they spent over $2 billion on, nor are they going to play any content that brings in a smaller audience, so there is very little financial reason for Fox to prioritize that programming. Even if you argue the audiences for soccer and American football/baseball may not crossover they still would be forced to disseminate conflicting promotional materials or marketing efforts for sports and events airing at the same time. The motivation for Fox to grow a Premier League audience if they were to reacquire the rights would be automatically limited, since it could take away from the audience for their other programming. It would also affect the way they could sell to advertisers and their overall revenue since businesses would question how they would balance both sets of rights. Considering sports are one of the few places where traditional commercial advertising still holds value, since live content, particularly competitions, lose value immediately after the original airing and results are released, outlets want to avoid anything that might negatively impact that revenue stream. NBC, a network whose weekly football game occurs on Sunday evenings, does not own any baseball rights, and their college football rights are limited to Notre Dame home games, and it does not have to be concerned with the same conflicts as Fox when it comes to airing Premier League matches.[30]

The conflict above does not even consider ancillary shows and content, which is a huge part of any sports network or programming unit at a large media conglomerate, particularly as it relates to each of their cable networks, streaming services, and digital properties which rely heavily on shows, articles, and other media about the games, leagues, and players. This content populates their website and fills the hours when games are typically not played and the outlets still want to draw an audience. When looking at a show like SportsCenter, ESPN's flagship news and highlights show, it is no accident that the NFL and NBA dominate coverage on the show, dedicating over half the program time to just these two leagues. ESPN and their parent company, Disney pays the NFL $1.9 billion a year to play one game a week on Monday nights and the NBA $1.4 billion to air games on the cable network and Disney's broadcast network, ABC.[31] To ensure they maximize this investment they not only set aside significant amount of news coverage and analysis to these two leagues, but schedule a number of shows, like NFL Primetime and the NBA focused The Jump to covering these American sports leagues every day.[32] They also employ more reporters, analysts, and commentators increasing the investment in the coverage. They hope to make the most of their money by featuring these personalities in as many ways as possible on television and all their outlets, including their website and ESPN+, their growing streaming service. This allows them to air more content from these entities while also offering an outlet for smaller leagues, like mid-major basketball conferences, that can draw strong regional audiences and help them recoup some of their larger rights investments by attracting subscribers to the service that costs sports fans an extra $5 a month beyond what they are already paying their service provider to see live sports. To maintain some credibility they do include limited coverage of leagues they do not own the rights, like the National Hockey League, and sports outside North America where most of the audience for the original ESPN, which broadcasts from Bristol, Connecticut, reside.

ESPN does have international outlets and subsidiaries in Latin America, Australia, Japan, and other regions and countries throughout the world that focus more on the sports popular in the countries their audiences originate, but the investment in leagues like the NFL still leads the parent network to include a sport with a limited fan base outside of the United States on these networks as the potential international growth of the sports not just benefits the league, but the outlets who can point advertisers toward international exposure for their products when selling sponsorship. This is why an international event like the Olympics can demand over $200 million for high level sponsorship, even though it only occurs every four years.[33] Reaching a captive audience that can be in the billions presents a unique opportunity for businesses, since most advertising tends to be limited by localities and borders, and there are fewer reliable ways to advertise as the audience becomes more fragmented and more options for entertainment are introduced.[34] Some research has also found that the association with sports can have an overall positive influence on stock prices and consumer opinions related to the business and product.[35] This association is only increased when the exposure is not just the hundreds of millions of potential consumers in United States, but also the billions around the world.

American Sports Exceptionalism and Cultural Imperialism Post–World War II

There were a number of attempts to spread American culture through sport before World War II, particularly after the Allied victory in World War I. Military personnel and missionaries tried to promote American ideals and display the country's athletic strength around the world, hoping this would be a way to spread American exceptionalism, ideology and nationhood through sports, much like Britain had done in the past. The Olympics and other international competitions offered potential opportunities to consolidate global sports competitions and help spread American culture throughout the world. This was mostly led by private organizations and individuals, but motivating this push was the increased success of the United States in these international competitions. The 1920 Summer Olympics was the first where the host nation did not win the total medal count, with the United States beating Sweden by 31 total medals.[36] They did have the most gold medals in the 1912 Olympics, but Sweden, who hosted these games in Stockholm, had two more total medals. Travel had long been a barrier for participating countries, with nations outside of the host country or continent sending smaller teams of athletes. During the St. Louis games in 1904 the United States won 239 of 280 total medals since most countries only sent a few athletes to America for the games.[37] These international events like the 1920 Olympics and the 1919 Inter-Allied Games not only presented opportunities for the United States to show their athletic prowess, but also spread American influence on other nations. The United States was becoming an international power, but many countries balked at the opportunity to Americanize their sporting culture during the interwar period, placing their own nationhood above American approaches to various sports.[38]

World War II not only helped accelerate the United State journey to becoming a superpower, but created an environment where American sports and their connected culture and ideas could spread more easily, especially with the focus on cultural imperialism as American leaders moved away from physically influencing nations on the ground through the military and other colonialist means. This was most evident during the Cold War, where the struggle between capitalism and communism was often fought through the United States and USSR's attempts to spread their culture and ideologies throughout the world.[39] Patriotism and sport had become inseparable during the war as a number of athletes joined the military and by the end of the war the national anthem was played before football games, a tradition that quickly spread to other sports and events.[40] Using the Olympics to spread ideas and communicate American dominance and exceptionalism helped the event grow as the idea of a nation as a team grew and became profitable, leading to increased corporatization of the competition, which continues today.[41]

The events pitting the United States and the USSR were especially popular, with victory being linked to advancement of the ideologies each nation represented. The clearest example of this was during the 1980 Winter Olympics when the United States beat the USSR team in the semifinals of the hockey competition in what has become known as the "Miracle on Ice." This was significant not only because the United States was seen having significantly less talent, but also due to the rumors that the United States may boycott the Summer Olympics in Moscow, which would ultimately lead to the two superpowers not competing in the Summer Olympics, where the Americans have more success, again until 1988, with the Soviets boycotting the 1984 Summer Olympics in Los Angeles. Lost in that moment was the fact that Soviet teams, and their satellite territories like East Germany dominated the games throughout the 1970s and 1980s by using professional level players who kept their amateur status by being paid by the state.[42] The United States tried to keep the moral high ground, but eventually losing in this manner led them to push for professionals to be allowed to compete for their nation in certain sports, particularly basketball, leading to the Dream Team in the 1992 Barcelona Summer Olympics after a bronze medal finish for the U.S. in 1988. The Unified Team, which consisted of 12 of the 15 former Soviet nations, still beat the United States in the medal count in the 1992 Summer Olympics, but the collapse of the Soviet Union helped fuel American sport exceptionalism in the Olympics over the last two decades as the sport became more reliant on American corporations like McDonald's and Coca-Cola, which also helped fuel the United States' cultural imperialism throughout the world.

Even though the United States did not dominate the Olympics until the 1990s, they could still point to the success in certain sports and the spread of American sports in other countries as proof of American influence along with the movement of the International Olympic Committee toward a more capitalist approach, which was fully cemented by the 1984 Summer Olympics in Los Angeles. The United States was the only country to bid to become a host for the 1984 games partially because of the losses accrued by Montreal and Canada during the 1976 Olympics. Much of the 1984 games were funded by corporate sponsorship and television rights, leading to a new era of profitability for the Olympics spurred on by this American corporate approach, which continues today through traditional sponsorships and other connections formed by the presence of these corporations like McDonald's, which started their relationship with the Olympics in the 1970s and increased through their "You Win, They Win" promotion in 1984, a connection that continued through 2018's winter games.[43]

American Sports League Exceptionalism Goes Global

Americans are always ready to flex their strength in international multi-sport competitions like the Olympics, however, American nationalism and exceptionalism is most evident in sports leagues headquartered or centered in the United States. Baseball plays the "World Series" every year and declares a world champion even though no other country is involved or competes against Major League Baseball teams outside of exhibitions. At least the Little League World Series, which includes players under 13 years of age, includes international teams even though a team from the United States is guaranteed a spot in the championship game and hosts the event every year in Williamsport, Pennsylvania.[44] Both basketball and football also declare the champions of the NBA and NFL respectively as world champions in spite of the fact neither plays meaningful games against international teams, although the NFL would be hard pressed to do so, and may be the world champions in a sport played almost exclusively in the United States.[45] Fans of the leagues may argue that these are considered the top leagues in their respective sport, but the English Premier League, which is considered by many the top soccer league in the world, does not declare their team the world champions since it would be seen as ridiculous in the soccer world. Even the winner of the UEFA Champions League which pits the top club teams in Europe does not have the arrogance to declare their winner the champion of the entire world. The fact that the United States is physically isolated from other countries and their professional leagues have been around longer than most leagues in the same sport in other countries may help make fans and the leagues themselves feel more comfortable with declaring uncontested world dominance and avoid more significant pushback for these claims.[46]

Strengthening these claims is the increased presence of players outside the United States in these leagues. By the 2016–2017 season, over a quarter of the NBA were born outside of the United States with larger salaries attracting top players from 42 other countries.[47] The increasing salaries are linked to the massive media rights deals, including the NBA which brings in about $2.6 billion a year from ESPN and Turner Sports.[48] This media rights market has grown in other countries as well, which may explain a small dip in the international presence on American professional basketball courts, however the prevalence of foreign born players in leagues like the NBA or MLB, with about 27 percent of players born outside the United States, only encourages the world champion idea among these leagues and professional clubs.[49]

Salary is not the only explanation for the increase. In basketball, for example, the success of the Dream Team in the 1992 Summer Olympics helped to increase the NBA presence outside of the United States, as many fans had their first consistent exposure to the league's top players like Michael Jordan. For example, one of the players considered the best foreign born of all time, Dirk Nowitzki, whose mother played for the German national team, wanted to come to a U.S. university after seeing the Dream Team play in 1992 to increase his chances of making the NBA. Although required military service derailed that path he would still play against some Dream Team players in 1997 famously scoring 52 in a game against NBA professionals before being drafted by the Dallas Mavericks in 1998.[50] By 2001, the NBA launched Basketball Without Borders, running clinics for young international players around the world, not only to provide players with resources and support to improve, but also recruit players to American universities and the NBA. League All-Stars like Joel Embiid and Marc Gasol help make up the over three dozen players from Basketball Without Borders to be drafted in the NBA, with a number more playing at American universities. The staff is made up of college and NBA coaches and players who use the program to both coach and scout players. The program does provide exposure and other opportunities to young basketball players outside of the United States, however, there is a feeling of imperialism connected to the process as these NBA figures go around the world collecting talent on behalf of their American employer.[51]

Major League Baseball has been engaging in similar types of international recruitment and scouting since the 1950s. All of the franchises in MLB have facilities in the Dominican Republic and all but two teams have the same in Venezuela. Just under 20 percent of MLB rosters are made up of players from just these two nations, with 31 percent of professional baseball players and 50 percent of minor leaguers identifying as Latino, although some of them are born in the United States.[52] The Latino players who are born outside the United States face a long journey from the fields of their home country to multi-million dollar contracts as franchises take advantage of the financial struggles many of them face as they fight for their dream to make it to the Major League. Whereas top talent from the United States can receive large signing bonus or have the option to play baseball in college to improve their skill while, ideally, getting an education, players from the Caribbean and Latin America are often signed for the minor league minimum, $1,100 a month, even though they train throughout the year and play close to 200 games each season along with practice and other work required of a professional baseball player.[53] For the franchise this is a low risk proposition which can lead to finding the next Juan Marichal or David Ortiz for a fraction of what they would pay an American-born player with similar skill and potential. The presence of these teams not only leads to direct exploitation, but ancillary companies like Nike help increase the influence of American culture in these nations, similar to how other political and economic interests originating in America exploit labor and resources in Latin America and many other lower socio-economic countries throughout the world.[54] This exploitation is only increased when considering many of these players do not speak English and are here on work visas, giving them very few ways to advocate for themselves, especially since any complaints could end their career as teams could just move on to the next low-wage player who does not create conflict within the organization.[55] As the national sport in both the Dominican Republic and Venezuela, participation is high among citizens, leading to a large pool of players that can be taken advantage of by enterprising teams in Major League Baseball.[56]

Another country where baseball serves as the national sports is Cuba. Until 2018, Players from the island nation have been historically cut off from Major League Baseball due to the United States' embargo against Cuba, but that has not stopped franchises in the leagues from working with recruiters and human traffickers to smuggle talented players out of Cuba so they can defect and play in the league, ignoring federal law while risking the life of the player.[57] This gives the teams supporting this activity an advantage in signing the player, since players from outside of the U.S. and Canada are not subject to the draft. Teams make efforts to then sign the player before they are able to talk to an agent, who could secure more money for their client, since Cuban players often are already talented professionals who could command more money on the open free agent market. The circumvention of these regulations proves how far teams are willing to go to secure proven, affordable talent, so it is no surprise they are also willing to sign teenagers from across Latin America for below minimum wage as low risk investments.[58]

As noted above, this imperialism, until recently, had been fairly subtle and kept behind the scenes as recruiters and coaches would scout the player and determine whether it was worth the relatively small investment to bring them to the United States to play in the minor leagues or at American universities.[59] If they pan out it would be celebrated, especially if marketing departments can connect their story to the American "rags to riches" or Horatio Alger myths that continue to this day despite evidence that social and economic mobility described by Alger is not available to most people, particularly the poor and people of color who do not receive the same opportunities due to the wealth gap and systemic discrimination.[60] As media and commerce continues to become more globalized, professional football, baseball, and basketball leagues in America continue to work to increase the visibility of their global brand, players in these leagues are making more trips to other countries, not only for vacation or to participate in programs like Basketball Without Borders, but to compete in exhibitions against teams in that country and within their own league, and more recently, regular season games.

Out of Bounds: U.S. Professional Leagues Crossing Borders

The NFL has been playing exhibition games in Canada since the 1950s, with their first game outside of North America occurring in Tokyo in 1976 as the league tried to spread participation and, more importantly, fandom outside of the United States and Canada. Many of these early games in the 1940s through early 1960s pitted teams from the NFL and Canadian Football League, but by the 1980s, two NFL teams were regularly traveling throughout the world to play exhibition games unsurprisingly dubbed the American Bowl in 1986, with three different exhibition match-ups taking place in London, Sweden, and Montreal in 1988. The game in Sweden, which included Minnesota highlighting their Scandinavian origins of their Vikings mascot, was played in Gothenburg and was sponsored by Volvo, which was founded in the city.

In 1989, the league voted to establish the World League of American Football (WLAF, later NFL Europe League and then NFL Europa) as a spring developmental league, which opened play in 1991. The league attempted to form the Intercontinental Football League in Europe in 1975, but the idea was abandoned partly because the independent World Football League was established the same year. The WFL never actually expanded beyond the United States, with its furthest team located in Hawaii. Although developing young talent was the stated purpose, the NFL hoped the fringe NFL prospects who were playing in Europe to improve and display their ability to play in the larger league could help familiarize and draw European audiences to American football and the NFL. The first two seasons of the WLAF included teams based in America, and aside from the New York/New Jersey Knights the teams in the United States were located in markets that did not have an NFL team at the time like Birmingham, Alabama, and Sacramento California. Because of travel and budget issues the league suspended the 1993 and 1994 seasons before reemerging with teams exclusively in Europe. Eventually the desire of franchises and coaches to develop players personally led to a drop in talent and attention and the league was eliminated in 2007.[61]

The same year NFL Europa folded the league introduced the International Series, which was originally named Futbol Americano for the first game in Mexico City before the NFL rebranded to appeal to English-speaking fans particularly in the United Kingdom, featured two teams playing a regular season game either in Mexico or London, two of the three countries the NFL is considering for international expansion.[62] The third, Canada, hosted several Buffalo Bills games between 2008 and 2012, first as an exhibition and then as a regular season game as a part of the Buffalo-Toronto Series (BTS) as the league and franchise tried to grow its fan base in the city across the border about 90 minutes away from the American city. The BTS series was a hard sell since Canadians have their own football league including two teams within forty miles of Toronto. The same year the league tried to establish the China Bowl, an exhibition that would have featured the Seattle Seahawks and the New England Patriots as a part of the lead up to the 2008 Summer Olympics. The Patriots actually had offices in China at time, but the recession led them to leave China and the game was cancelled as a result.[63]

The international appeal of baseball, basketball, and hockey removes the obstacle of familiarizing citizens with the games that American football faces, although NBA rules do differ some from the rules of the International Basketball Federation (FIBA) followed by most other teams around the world. This familiarity is partly due to the fact that there are other professional leagues around the world in those sports, some of which have talent comparable to their American counterparts. This has not stopped the NBA, MLB, and NHL from trying to expand the visibility of their teams and players on foreign soil. Like the NFL, which used to play games against the CFL, both leagues have featured both interleague and intraleague exhibitions while also playing regular season international games. These leagues also maintain heavy influence on international competitions since many of the most popular players in those tournaments compete in those leagues, leading to the same influence of American sports culture experienced at the Olympics.[64]

The NBA has, by far, played in the most international locations, featuring a number of games between NBA and Eurasian club teams, the first official exhibitions taking place in 1978 with the Washington Bullets playing in Israel,

China, and the Philippines. Displaying the NBA's influence on these international matches the rules of the league, versus the internationally recognized FIBA rules, were typically followed. The 1980s saw several more series with NBA and European teams facing off, expanding these competitions to West Germany and Switzerland. In 1987, the McDonald's Championships were launched, with NBA teams winning the tournament, which was held in Europe every year aside from the first, which took place in Milwaukee. The Atlanta Hawks also played in the Soviet Union against the national team in 1988, the first NBA team to take on the Cold War adversary.[65]

In 1984, the first game between two NBA teams on foreign soil took place in Italy and by 1991 the NBA was playing several exhibitions internationally each year, including a number of games in China the first of which featuring the Houston Rockets in 2004, whose center at the time, Yao Ming, helped popularize the NBA in the Asian nation leading to the China Games. The NBA has greatly decreased exhibitions played in Europe between NBA teams, possibly due to the increased popularity of leagues in Europe, several of which have NBA level players with a number of players making their way to the American league competing against other top players both in terms of talent and salary. Teams in the NBA still play several games a year against European clubs with NBA teams winning the vast majority of games.[66]

The NBA rebranded these international exhibitions the Global Games continuing to play exhibitions in China along with a couple preseason games in Brazil. Consistent international regular season games started in 1990 in Japan with NBA teams playing two games series five times through 2003. After an eight year gap, the league has played yearly regular season games in either London or Mexico City since 2011, two countries without leagues featuring talent comparable to the NBA or even the NCAA, which oversees colleges on all levels that will schedule teams against international clubs and national teams.[67] There is no doubt these games, and the legacy of the 1992 Dream Team, has helped the NBA grow its fan base throughout the world, but its efforts have been especially lucrative in China with the league and associated business, like Nike, bringing in billions in revenue with the NBA arguably China's most popular international sports league.[68]

Major League Baseball also hopes to make inroads in China, although no games have been played there, the league has sent teams to play exhibitions in other nations around the world. The MLB Japan All-Star series has been played in Japan every other year between 1986 and 2006 putting all stars from MLB and Nippon Professional Baseball on the same field. The series was renewed in 2014 and 2018 with the MLB all-stars taking on the Japanese national team. International regular season games were first played in Mexico in 1996, a three-game series between the San Diego Padres and the New York Mets.[69] The league continued to play a regular season series every four years in Japan, Australia, or Mexico. They plan on increasing regular season international games in 2019 including their first games in London between the New York Yankees and Boston Red Sox.[70] Although not technically international, the Montreal Expos played 43 games in 2003 and 2004 in San Juan, Puerto Rico as the league considered moving the team to the Caribbean Commonwealth.[71]

The NHL's attempts at international exposure has been less one-sided than the other three major sports leagues, with foreign teams frequently coming to play on North American soil. These exhibitions and games still aimed to show American superiority in the sport and increase the visibility of the NHL, although the games between NHL and teams in other countries have been more evenly split than similar competitions in MLB and NBA.[72] The league had its first international exhibition series in 1938 between the Detroit Red Wings and Montreal Canadiens throughout Europe. A second tour of Europe and a Japanese series followed in 1958 and 1976 respectively with two NHL teams playing several games through the continent and Asian country.[73] The Super Series had Soviet teams traveling to the United States to take on NHL team. The Super Series was played regularly between 1976 and 1991 with Soviet teams winning 55 games to NHL teams 33 games with the two sides tying ten times. The NHL all-stars team also split a two game series against the Soviet national team in 1987.[74] The league increased the tournaments against European teams through the 1980s and 1990s along with having more exhibitions between NHL teams in foreign countries like Japan and England. Five seasons between 2007 and 2011 opened with NHL Premiere with several NHL teams traveling to Europe to play exhibitions against club teams before playing regular season games against each other. Much like MLB and NBA, the NHL is also looking to expand to China playing exhibitions there starting in 2017.[75] The same year the NHL Global Series renewed the scheduling of yearly regular season games in Europe.[76]

It is important to note that the NHL has long been last of the four major sports leagues in North America in popularity, struggling to receive the same viewership and attention in the United States as its three counterparts. Some reasons for this may be low participation due to the high cost of entry including equipment and access to facilities, which limits participation.[77] Some also say the sport does not translate well to television because of the fast pace and difficulty seeing the puck.[78] While these issues contribute to a smaller hockey fanbase in the United States, the NHL also suffers many of the problems that soccer faces in the country. Many of the stars of the sport are not American, and like in soccer, the United States does not dominate, seen as a second-tier entrant in most international competitions. Just over a quarter of the league originate from the United States, although this disconnect between American fans and hockey is reduced some by the presence of teams in major American cities for decades, with the Original Six's American teams being founded in the 1920s, an advantage over Major League Soccer in the United States, which was founded in 1993.[79]

Executives in the NHL have recognized this gap as they look to expand their visibility in China and Europe, even scheduling games earlier in the day on weekends to attract a larger European audience who want to see their countries' star players. Two of the league's most popular players, Russian Alexander Ovechkin and Canadian Sidney Crosby, although popular, do not have the same recognizability as players of similar talent in other leagues, like LeBron James or Tom Brady, with NHL stars being absent from lists ranking popular athletes in the United States and around the world.[80] The long history of dominance in hockey by countries other than the United States, particularly by the Soviets during the Cold War and Canada, whose connection with their official national winter sport is well known and displayed in the NHL with nearly half the league originating from the United States' northern neighbor, limits the national pride Americans may feel watching the sport as it competes for fans against the other three leagues, particularly the NBA whose season runs almost concurrent with the NHL's season.[81]

Conclusion

American nationalism, and the related exceptionalism and imperialism, have been connected to sports culture in the United States for over a century. Americans, physically and psychologically separated from the rest of the world except when it is economically or culturally advantageous, ignore or disparage sports and athletes in other countries expecting the rest of the world to fawn over American sports and athletes. Since World War I, but especially after World War II, attempts to spread American sports culture on the ground in foreign nations and in the media continue to grow as streaming makes it easier than ever to access these competitions and the growing business presence in countries like China and England ensure there is direct contact with the citizens of these countries where leagues and teams see future growth. There are consistent rumors the NFL and NBA are considering franchises in London as they look to take their leagues intercontinental, something the NFL tested through Spring leagues before global broadcasts were as ubiquitous as they are today as a result of advancements in broadcasting.

Capitalism and money are always going to be a main motivator in these attempts at expansion and cultural imperialism, but there also seems to be a level of pride ensuring American sports organizations and teams dominate around the world both in following and in competition, with American corporations following closely as they look to enter other markets not just through advertising but connecting themselves with the leagues and players working to expand their influence in other markets. Each year we celebrate international viewership numbers of North American "World Championships" assuming the whole world will tune into our sports, in spite of the fact it may not even be played in the countries expected to watch. There is no doubt some international organizations, like the English Premier League, are also working to profit from this sports globalization, but as Fox's reaction to the United States not qualifying for the 2018 World Cup shows, American nationalism is still a driving force in sports fandom and connected sports coverage. It is fitting that New England's NFL franchise has been so successful, since patriotism and sports are inextricably connected in the United States.[82]

NOTES

1. Martin Rogers, "The United States' World Cup Failure Is Looking Worse Every Day," *USA Today* June 19, 2018, https://www.usatoday.com/story/sports/columnist/martin-rogers/2018/06/19/united-states-world-cup-usmnt/713096002/.
2. Steven Goff, "U.S. National Soccer Team Concedes Two Early Goals in World Cup Qualifier Against Guatemala," *Washington Post*, March 25, 2016, https://www.washingtonpost.com/news/soccer-insider/wp/2016/03/25/u-s-national-soccer-team-concedes-2-early-goals-in-world-cup-qualifier-against-guatemala/?utm_term=.d5354237bcdd.
3. Conor Dowley, "USMNT Misses 2018 World Cup After Embarrassing Loss to Trinidad and Tobago," *SB Nation*, October 10, 2017, https://www.sbnation.com/soccer/2017/10/10/16456564/usa-vs-trinidad-and-tobago-final-score-2018-world-cup-qualifying-results.
4. Roger Gonzalez, "USA Eliminated from 2018 World Cup After Shocking Loss to Trinidad and Tobago," *CBS Sports*, October 11, 2017, https://www.cbssports.com/soccer/news/usa-eliminated-from-2018-world-cup-in-following-shocking-loss-to-trinidad-and-tobago/.
5. Associated Press, "Mostly American World Cup Announcers for Fox Despite No U.S.," *USA Today* https://www.usatoday.com/story/sports/soccer/2018/04/25/apnewsbreak-mostly-american-world-cup-announcers-for-fox/34231679/.
6. Jere Longman, "Fox, Telemundo Win World Cup Bid," *New York Times* October 21, 2011, https://www.nytimes.com/2011/10/22/sports/soccer/fox-and-telemundo-win-us-rights-to-2018-and-2022-world-cups.html.
7. Jason Lynch, "How Fox Sports Is Marketing the World Cup to U.S. Viewers with No Home Team to Root For," *AdWeek*, June 12, 2018, https://www.adweek.com/tv-video/how-fox-sports-is-marketing-the-world-cup-to-u-s-viewers-with-no-home-team-to-root-for/.
8. Aaron Timms, "Fox Replaces ESPN's Cult of British Accents with Maximum Volume at World Cup," *The Guardian*, June 11, 2018, https://www.theguardian.com/football/2018/jun/11/fox-sports-world-cup-coverage.
9. AP, "Mostly American World Cup Announcers."
10. Timms, "Fox Replaces ESPN's."
11. Kurt Badenhausen, "The NFL Signs TV Deals Worth $27 Billion," *Forbes*, December 14, 2011, https://www.forbes.com/sites/kurtbadenhausen/2011/12/14/the-nfl-signs-tv-deals-worth-26-billion/#67d3af6a22b4.
12. Associated Press, "ESPN, Univision Mad at No-Bid Sale of World Cup Rights," *USA Today*, February 13, 2015, https://www.usatoday.com/story/sports/soccer/2015/02/13/espn-univision-angry-at-fifa-no-bid-sale-of-us-wcup-rights/23387205.
13. Richard Sandomir, "Why FIFA Made Deal with Fox for 2026 Cup," *New York Times*, February 27, 2015, https://www.nytimes.com/2015/02/27/sports/soccer/why-fifa-made-deal-with-fox-for-2026-cup.html.

14. Stephen Pettigrew and Danyel Reiche, "Is There Home-Field Advantage at the Olympics?," *FiveThirtyEight*, August 9, 2016, https://fivethirtyeight.com/features/is-there-home-field-advantage-at-the-olympics/.

15. "Phenoms of the 2018 World Cup," *Fox Sports*, May 29, 2018, https://www.foxsports.com/soccer/fifa-world-cup/phenoms?pn=2&abTest=jw-player-stats.

16. Nate Freeman, "Is Football Now America's Pastime?," *Samford University Center for Sports Analytics*, January 3, 2018, https://www.samford.edu/sports-analytics/fans/2018/Is-Football-Now-Americas-Pastime.

17. Ciaran Hancock, "Fox Sports to Buy U.S. Operation of Setanta," *Irish Times*, January 11, 2011, https://www.irishtimes.com/business/fox-sports-to-buy-us-operation-of-setanta-1.1267081.

18. Associated Press, "NBC Wins $250m Rights to Broadcast English Premier League in U.S.," *The Guardian*, October 29, 2012, https://www.theguardian.com/sport/2012/oct/29/nbc-250m-english-premier-league-epl-broadcast-us?newsfeed=true.

19. Ken Fang, "Say Goodbye to Fox Soccer," *Awful Announcing*, March 29, 2013, https://awfulannouncing.com/2013/say-goodbye-to-fox-soccer.html.

20. John Ourand, "With 1 Not Done, Fox Goes for 2," *Sports Business Daily*, January 21, 2013, http://www.sportsbusinessdaily.com/Journal/Issues/2013/01/21/Media/Fox-Sports-2.aspx?hl=Fox%20Sports%202&sc=1.

21. Ben Fountain, "American Exceptionalism: The Great Game and the Noble Way," *The Guardian*, April 9, 2016, https://www.theguardian.com/us-news/2016/apr/09/american-exceptionalism-us-election-2016-baseball-lincoln-walt-whitman.

22. Todd VanDerWerff, "NBC's Coverage of the Olympics Is Atrocious. There's a Simple Reason Why," *Vox*, August 11, 2016, https://www.vox.com/2016/8/11/12433144/nbc-olympics-bad.

23. Richard Sandomir, "NBC Retains Rights to Premier League in Six-Year Deal," *New York Times*, August 11, 2015, https://www.nytimes.com/2015/08/11/sports/soccer/nbc-retains-rights-to-premier-league-in-six-year-deal.html.

24. Stefan Fatsis, "Soccer Fans: ESPN World Cup Coverage Earns Penalty," *The Wall Street Journal*, July 4, 2006, https://www.post-gazette.com/sports/other-sports/2006/07/05/Soccer-fans-ESPN-World-Cup-coverage-earns-penalty/stories/200607050250.

25. Michael Mandelbaum, "The New Republic: Soccer and U.S. Exceptionalism," *NPR*, June 25, 2010, https://www.npr.org/templates/story/story.php?storyId=128103553.

26. Matt Yoder, "NBC Claims a Record Number of Total Viewers for a Premier League Season in 2017–2018," *Awful Announcing*, May 18, 2018, https://awfulannouncing.com/soccer/nbc-claims-a-record-number-of-total-viewers-for-a-premier-league-season-in-2017–2018.html.

27. Juan Pablo Manterola, "Online Streaming Is the Future of Sports Broadcasting: It's Not 'If' You'll Cut Cable, but 'When,'" *Forbes*, April 14, 2017 Https://www.forbes.com/sites/forbesagencycouncil/2017/04/14/online-streaming-is-the-future-of-sports-broadcasting-its-not-if-youll-cut-cable-but-when/.

28. Teddy Greenstein, "Big Ten Announces Six-Year Deal with ESPN, Fox Sports Worth $2.64 Billion," *The Chicago Tribune*, July 24, 2017, https://www.chicagotribune.com/sports/college/ct-big-ten-espn-fox-sports-20170724-story.html.

29. Sandomir, "NBC Retains Rights to Premier League."

30. John Ourand, "The Escalation of Sports-Rights Fees Can Be Traced to a 2008 ESPN Deal," *Sports Business Journal*, May 3, 2018, https://www.bizjournals.com/newyork/news/2018/05/03/escalation-of-sports-rights-fees-traced-to-espn.html.

31. Jimmy Traina, "Here's What ESPN Pays for Most of Its Sports Rights," *Sports Illustrated*, June 26, 2017, https://www.si.com/extra-mustard/2017/06/26/espn-sports-rights-cost.

32. Patrick Burns, "What I Learned from a Year of Watching SportsCenter," *Deadspin*, July 26, 2013, https://deadspin.com/what-i-learned-from-a-year-of-watching-sportscenter-5979510.

33. Charles R. Taylor, "Sponsorship and Advertising Trends in the 2016 Rio Olympic Games: Three Things to Watch For," *Forbes* August 4, 2016, https://www.forbes.com/sites/onmarketing/2016/08/04/sponsorship-and-advertising-trends-in-the-2016-rio-olympic-games-three-things-to-watch-for/#5e0929cc18c7.

34. Scott Roxborough, "Rio Olympics Worldwide Audience to Top 3.5 Billion, IOC Estimates," *The Hollywood Reporter,* August 18, 2016, https://www.hollywoodreporter.com/news/rio-olympics-worldwide-audience-top-920526.

35. Rich Gentile, "The Impact of Corporate Sports Sponsorship," *Seton Hall Sports Poll,* November 13, 2015, https://blogs.shu.edu/sportspoll/2015/11/13/the-impact-of-corporate-sports-sponsorship/.

36. "Antwerp 1920," *International Olympic Committee* https://www.olympic.org/antwerp-1920.

37. "St Louis 1904," *International Olympic Committee* https://www.olympic.org/st-louis-1904.

38. Steven W. Pope, "Rethinking Sport, Empire, and American Exceptionalism," *Sports History Review,* 38 (2007): 96–100, https://core.ac.uk/download/pdf/56121.pdf.

39. Gerald R. Gems, *The Athletic Crusade: Sport and American Cultural Imperialism* (Lincoln: University of Nebraska Press, 2006) 39.

40. Becky Little, "Why the Star-Spangled Banner Is Played at Sporting Events," *History,* September 25, 2017, https://www.history.com/news/why-the-star-spangled-banner-is-played-at-sporting-events.

41. Gem, *The Athletic Crusade,* 31.

42. E.M. Swift, "A Reminder of What We Can Be: The 1980 U.S. Olympic Hockey Team," *Sports Illustrated,* October 28, 2014, https://www.si.com/olympic-ice-hockey/2014/10/28/reminder-what-we-can-be-1980-us-olympic-hockey-team-si-60.

43. Reuters, "McDonald's Ends Olympics Sponsorship Deal Early," *CNBC,* June 16, 2016, https://www.cnbc.com/2017/06/16/mcdonalds-ends-olympics-sponsorship-deal-early.html.

44. "World Series," *Little League* https://www.littleleague.org/world-series/.

45. Steven Wells, "Dear America: You Can't Be World Champions If No One Else Takes Part," *The Guardian,* November 18, 2008, https://www.theguardian.com/sport/blog/2008/nov/18/american-sports-nfl-nba-mlb.

46. *Ibid.*

47. Meredith Cash and Shayanne Ga, "NBA's Trend of Increasing Number of International Players Appears to Be Slowing Down," *Business Insider,* October 16, 2018, https://www.businessinsider.com/growing-number-of-foreign-born-players-in-nba-slows-2018-10.

48. John Lombardo and John Ourand, "ESPN, Turner Will Pay a Combined $24B in New Nine-Year NBA Media Rights Deal," *Sports Business Daily,* October 6, 2014, https://www.sportsbusinessdaily.com/Daily/Issues/2014/10/06/Media/NBA-media.aspx.

49. Stuart Anderson, "27% of Major League Baseball Players Are Foreign-Born," *Forbes,* April 27, 2017, https://www.forbes.com/sites/stuartanderson/2018/04/27/27-of-major-league-baseball-players-are-foreign-born/#167fd0ee7712.

50. Mike Tierney, "The '92 Dream Team Paved the Way for Global Players to Make Mark in NBA," *The National,* May 25, 2011, https://www.thenational.ae/the-92-dream-team-paved-the-way-for-global-players-to-make-mark-in-nba-1.375766.

51. "Basketball Without Borders," *NBA* http://global.nba.com/basketball-without-borders/.

52. Anderson, "27% of Major League Baseball Players."

53. Mike Elk and Karina Moreno, "Baseball, Latino America's Pastime, Faces New Challenges in Age of Trump," *The Guardian,* March 29, 2018, https://www.theguardian.com/sport/2018/mar/29/baseball-latino-trump-mlb.

54. Alan Klein, *Sugarball: The American Game, the Dominican Dream* (New Haven: Yale University Press, 1991), 6–8.

55. "Does Major League Baseball Exploit Latino Players?," *NBC News,* October 24, 2014, https://www.nbcnews.com/news/latino/does-major-league-baseball-exploit-latino-players-n228316.

56. Pope, "Rethinking Sport," 100–103.

57. David K. Li and Mary Murray, "Cuban Baseball Players Will No Longer Have to Defect to Join MLB," *NBC News,* December 19, 2018, https://www.nbcnews.com/news/sports/cuban-baseball-players-will-be-able-sign-mlb-contracts-without-n950106.

58. Jon Wertheim, "Exclusive: The Evidence That Persuaded U.S. Department of Justice

to Investigate MLB Recruitment of Foreign Players," *Sports Illustrated*, October 2, 2018, https://www.si.com/mlb/2018/10/02/fbi-investigation-mlb-atlanta-braves-los-angeles-dodgers.

59. "Does Major League Baseball Exploit Latino Players?"

60. Stefan Kanfer, "Horatio Alger: The Moral of the Story," *City Journal*, Autumn 2000, https://www.city-journal.org/html/horatio-alger-moral-story-11933.html.

61. Jon Gold, "10 Years After NFL Europe's Demise, Alumni Remember League Fondly," ESPN, June 23, 2017, http://www.espn.com/nfl/story/_/id/19638357/oral-history-10-years-nfl-europe-demise-alumni-such-kurt-warner-remember-developmental-league-fondly.

62. Thomas Barrabi, "NFL 'Nearer Than Ever' to Permanent London Team, Exec Says," *Fox Business*, October 13, 2018, https://www.foxbusiness.com/features/nfl-nearer-than-ever-to-permanent-london-team-exec-says.

63. Mike Reiss, "Patriots' Game in China Off," *Boston Globe*, April 2, 2007, http://archive.boston.com/sports/football/patriots/articles/2007/04/02/patriots_game_in_china_off/.

64. Matthew Rocco, "MLB: World Baseball Classic Key to Global Ambitions," *Fox Business*, March 3, 2017, https://www.foxbusiness.com/features/mlb-world-baseball-classic-key-to-global-ambitions.

65. Rob Peterson, "Open-ing the World to the NBA," *NBA*, October 8, 2004, http://www.nba.com/china2004/mcdonalds_open_041008.html.

66. "History of Games Played by NBA Teams in Europe," *NBA* http://www.nba.com/europelive/history.html.

67. "History of the NBA Global Games," *NBA Global* http://www.nba.com/global/games2013/all-time-international-game-list.html.

68. Mike Ozanian, "Mark Tatum Talks About the NBA's Enormous Success in China and Its Impact on Team Values," *Forbes* February 26, 2018, https://www.forbes.com/sites/mikeozanian/2018/02/26/mark-tatum-talks-about-the-nbas-enormous-success-in-china/#37732ac5518b.

69. "Major League Baseball Returns to Japan in 2018 and 2019," *MLB* https://www.mlb.com/news/major-league-baseball-returns-to-japan-in-2018-and-2019/c-274713114.

70. Associated Press, "MLB Says That Regular-season Games Will Be Played in Asia and in England in 2019 and 2020," *ESPN* July 28, 2017, http://www.espn.com/mlb/story/_/id/20186657/mlb-announces-games-played-overseas-2019-2020.

71. Michael Farber, "Montreal Expos the Team Without a Country Will Play in Canada and Puerto Rico. and Pray for Help," *Sports Illustrated*, March 31, 2003, https://www.si.com/vault/2003/03/31/340618/5-montreal-expos-the-team-without-a-country-will-play-in-canada-and-puerto-rico-and-pray-for-help.

72. Jeff Jacobs, "What Is So Super About This Soviet Super Exhibition Series?," *LA Times*, January 9, 1989, http://articles.latimes.com/1989-01-09/sports/sp-169_1_super-series.

73. Sheng Peng, "Learning from the NHL in Japan," *NHL*, September 22, 2017, https://www.nhl.com/kings/news/learning-from-the-nhl-in-japan/c-291246710.

74. Jacobs, "What Is So Super?"

75. "NHL Overseas History," *NHL*, November 2, 2018, https://www.nhl.com/news/history-of-international-nhl-games/c-559166.

76. Kevin Skiver, "NHL Plans to Head Back to Europe Next Season for Global Series, Including Opener in Prague," November 1, 2018, *CBS Sports*, https://www.cbssports.com/nhl/news/nhl-plans-to-head-back-to-europe-next-season-for-global-series-including-opener-in-prague/.

77. Benjamin Rains, "The Business of the NHL as Hockey's Popularity Slips in U.S.," *Nasdaq*, January 22, 2018, https://www.nasdaq.com/article/the-business-of-the-nhl-as-hockeys-popularity-slips-in-us-cm908815.

78. "Which Is the Sport of the Future?," *NBC Sports Boston*, December 13, 2017, https://www.nbcsports.com/boston/home-page/nba-nfl-nhl-nba-which-is-sport-of-the-future.

79. Sam McCaig, "Where in the World Do NHL Players Come From?," *The Hockey News*, October 14, 2018, https://thehockeynews.com/news/article/where-in-the-world-do-nhl-players-come-from.

80. "World Fame 100 2019," *ESPN*, March 12, 2019, http://www.espn.com/espn/feature/story/_/page/worldfame100/espn-world-fame-100-top-ranking-athletes#.
81. Sam Riches, "When Sport Defines a Nation," *Pacific Standard*, January 2, 2015, https://psmag.com/social-justice/when-sports-defines-nation-identity-hockey-canada-summit-series-98094.
82. Howard Bryant, "Sports and Patriotism," *ESPN*, July 4, 2013, http://www.espn.com/espn/story/_/id/9449554/sports-patriotism.

REFERENCES

Anderson, Stuart. "27% of Major League Baseball Players Are Foreign-Born." *Forbes*, April 27, 2017 https://www.forbes.com/sites/stuartanderson/2018/04/27/27-of-major-league-baseball-players-are-foreign-born/#167fd0ee7712.
"Antwerp 1920." *International Olympic Committee* https://www.olympic.org/antwerp-1920.
Associated Press. "ESPN, Univision Mad at No-Bid Sale of World Cup Rights." *USA Today*, February 13, 2015 https://www.usatoday.com/story/sports/soccer/2015/02/13/espn-univision-angry-at-fifa-no-bid-sale-of-us-wcup-rights/23387205.
Associated Press. "MLB Says That Regular-season Games Will Be Played in Asia and in England in 2019 and 2020." *ESPN* July 28, 2017 http://www.espn.com/mlb/story/_/id/20186657/mlb-announces-games-played-overseas-2019–2020.
Associated Press. "Mostly American World Cup Announcers for Fox Despite No US." *USA Today* https://www.usatoday.com/story/sports/soccer/2018/04/25/apnewsbreak-mostly-american-world-cup-announcers-for-fox/34231679/.
Associated Press. "NBC Wins $250m Rights to Broadcast English Premier League in US." *The Guardian*, October 29, 2012 https://www.theguardian.com/sport/2012/oct/29/nbc-250m-english-premier-league-epl-broadcast-us?newsfeed=true.
Badenhausen, Kurt. "The NFL Signs TV Deals Worth $27 Billion." *Forbes*, December 14, 2011 https://www.forbes.com/sites/kurtbadenhausen/2011/12/14/the-nfl-signs-tv-deals-worth-26-billion/#67d3af6a22b4.
Barrabi, Thomas. "NFL 'Nearer Than Ever' to Permanent London Team, Exec Says." *Fox Business*, October 13, 2018 https://www.foxbusiness.com/features/nfl-nearer-than-ever-to-permanent-london-team-exec-says.
"Basketball Without Borders." *NBA* http://global.nba.com/basketball-without-borders/.
Bryant, Howard. "Sports and Patriotism." *ESPN*, July 4, 2013 http://www.espn.com/espn/story/_/id/9449554/sports-patriotism.
Burns, Patrick. "What I Learned from a Year of Watching SportsCenter." *Deadspin*, July 26, 2013 https://deadspin.com/what-i-learned-from-a-year-of-watching-sportscenter-5979510.
Cash, Meredith, and Shayanne Ga. "NBA's Trend of Increasing Number of International Players Appears to Be Slowing Down." *Business Insider*, October 16, 2018 https://www.businessinsider.com/growing-number-of-foreign-born-players-in-nba-slows-2018–10.
"Does Major League Baseball Exploit Latino Players?" *NBC News*, October 24, 2014 https://www.nbcnews.com/news/latino/does-major-league-baseball-exploit-latino-players-n228316.
Dowley, Conor. "USMNT Misses 2018 World Cup After Embarrassing Loss to Trinidad and Tobago." *SB Nation*, October 10, 2017 https://www.sbnation.com/soccer/2017/10/10/16456564/usa-vs-trinidad-and-tobago-final-score-2018-world-cup-qualifying-results.
Elk, Mike, and Karina Moreno,. "Baseball, Latino America's Pastime, Faces New Challenges in Age of Trump." *The Guardian*, March 29, 2018 https://www.theguardian.com/sport/2018/mar/29/baseball-latino-trump-mlb.
Fang, Ken. "Say Goodbye to Fox Soccer." *Awful Announcing*, March 29, 2013 https://awfulannouncing.com/2013/say-goodbye-to-fox-soccer.html.
Farber, Michael. "Montreal Expos the Team Without a Country Will Play in Canada and Puerto Rico. and Pray for Help." *Sports Illustrated*, March 31, 2003 https://www.si.com/vault/2003/03/31/340618/5-montreal-expos-the-team-without-a-country-will-play-in-canada-and-puerto-rico-and-pray-for-help.

Fatsi, Stefan. "Soccer Fans: ESPN World Cup Coverage Earns Penalty." *The Wall Street Journal*, July 4, 2006 https://www.post-gazette.com/sports/other-sports/2006/07/05/Soccer-fans-ESPN-World-Cup-coverage-earns-penalty/stories/200607050250.
Fountain, Ben. "American Exceptionalism: The Great Game and the Noble Way." *The Guardian*, April 9, 2016 https://www.theguardian.com/us-news/2016/apr/09/american-exceptionalism-us-election-2016-baseball-lincoln-walt-whitman.
Freeman, Nate. "Is Football Now America's Pastime?" *Samford University Center for Sports Analytics*, January 3, 2018 https://www.samford.edu/sports-analytics/fans/2018/Is-Football-Now-Americas-Pastime.
Gems, Gerald R. *The Athletic Crusade: Sport and American Cultural Imperialism*, Lincoln: University of Nebraska Press, 2006.
Gentile, Rich. "The Impact of Corporate Sports Sponsorship." *Seton Hall Sports Poll*, November 13, 2015 https://blogs.shu.edu/sportspoll/2015/11/13/the-impact-of-corporate-sports-sponsorship/.
Goff, Steven. "US National Soccer Team Concedes Two Early Goals in World Cup Qualifier Against Guatemala." *Washington Post*, March 25, 2016 https://www.washingtonpost.com/news/soccer-insider/wp/2016/03/25/u-s-national-soccer-team-concedes-2-early-goals-in-world-cup-qualifier-against-guatemala/?utm_term=.d5354237bcdd.
Gold, Jon. "10 Years After NFL Europe's Demise, Alumni Remember League Fondly." *ESPN*, June 23, 2017 http://www.espn.com/nfl/story/_/id/19638357/oral-history-10-years-nfl-europe-demise-alumni-such-kurt-warner-remember-developmental-league-fondly.
Gonzalez, Roger. "USA Eliminated from 2018 World Cup After Shocking Loss to Trinidad and Tobago." *CBS Sports*, October 11, 2017 https://www.cbssports.com/soccer/news/usa-eliminated-from-2018-world-cup-in-following-shocking-loss-to-trinidad-and-tobago/.
Greenstein, Teddy. "Big Ten Announces Six-Year Deal with ESPN, Fox Sports Worth $2.64 Billion." *The Chicago Tribune*, July 24, 2017 https://www.chicagotribune.com/sports/college/ct-big-ten-espn-fox-sports-20170724-story.html.
Hancock, Ciaran. "Fox Sports to Buy US Operation of Setanta." *Irish Times*, January 11, 2011 https://www.irishtimes.com/business/fox-sports-to-buy-us-operation-of-setanta-1.1267081.
"History of Games Played by NBA Teams in Europe." *NBA* http://www.nba.com/europelive/history.html.
History of the NBA Global Games." *NBA Global* http://www.nba.com/global/games2013/all-time-international-game-list.html.
Jacobs, Jeff. "What Is So Super About This Soviet Super Exhibition Series?" *LA Times*, January 9, 1989 http://articles.latimes.com/1989-01-09/sports/sp-169_1_super-series.
Kanfer, Stefan. "Horatio Alger: The Moral of the Story." *City Journal*, Autumn 2000, https://www.city-journal.org/html/horatio-alger-moral-story-11933.html.
Klein, Alan. *Sugarball: The American Game, the Dominican Dream* New Haven: Yale University Press, 1991.
Li, David K., and Mary Murray. "Cuban Baseball Players Will No Longer Have to Defect to Join MLB." *NBC News*, December 19, 2018 https://www.nbcnews.com/news/sports/cuban-baseball-players-will-be-able-sign-mlb-contracts-without-n950106.
Little, Becky. "Why the Star-Spangled Banner Is Played at Sporting Events." *History*, September 25, 2017, https://www.history.com/news/why-the-star-spangled-banner-is-played-at-sporting-events.
Lombardo, John, and John Ourand. "ESPN, Turner Will Pay a Combined $24B in New Nine-Year NBA Media Rights Deal." *Sports Business Daily*, October 6, 2014 https://www.sportsbusinessdaily.com/Daily/Issues/2014/10/06/Media/NBA-media.aspx.
Longman, Jere. "Fox, Telemundo Win World Cup Bid." *New York Times* October 21, 2011 https://www.nytimes.com/2011/10/22/sports/soccer/fox-and-telemundo-win-us-rights-to-2018-and-2022-world-cups.html.
Lynch, Jason. "How Fox Sports Is Marketing the World Cup to U.S. Viewers with No Home Team to Root For." *AdWeek*, June 12, 2018 https://www.adweek.com/tv-video/how-fox-sports-is-marketing-the-world-cup-to-u-s-viewers-with-no-home-team-to-root-for/.

"Major League Baseball Returns to Japan in 2018 and 2019." *MLB* https://www.mlb.com/news/major-league-baseball-returns-to-japan-in-2018-and-2019/c-274713114.
Mandelbaum, Michael. "The New Republic: Soccer and US Exceptionalism." *NPR*, June 25, 2010 https://www.npr.org/templates/story/story.php?storyId=128153553.
Manterola, Juan Pablo. "Online Streaming Is the Future of Sports Broadcasting: It's Not 'If' You'll Cut Cable, but 'When.'" *Forbes*, April 14, 2017, https://www.forbes.com/sites/forbesagencycouncil/2017/04/14/online-streaming-is-the-future-of-sports-broadcasting-its-not-if-youll-cut-cable-but-when/.
McCaig, Sam. "Where in the World Do NHL Players Come From?" *The Hockey News*, October 14, 2018, https://thehockeynews.com/news/article/where-in-the-world-do-nhl-players-come-from.
"NFL History 1991–2000." *NFL* http://www.nfl.com/history/chronology/1991-2000.
"NHL Overseas History." *NHL*, November 2, 2018 https://www.nhl.com/news/history-of-international-nhl-games/c-559166.
Ourand, John. "The Escalation of Sports-Rights Fees Can Be Traced to a 2008 ESPN Deal." *Sports Business Journal*, May 3, 2018 https://www.bizjournals.com/newyork/news/2018/05/03/escalation-of-sports-rights-fees-traced-to-espn.html.
____. "With 1 Not Done, Fox Goes for 2." *Sports Business Daily*, January 21, 2013 http://www.sportsbusinessdaily.com/Journal/Issues/2013/01/21/Media/Fox-Sports-2.aspx?hl=Fox%20Sports%202&sc=1.
Ozanian, Mike. "Mark Tatum Talks About the NBA's Enormous Success in China and Its Impact on Team Values." *Forbes* February 26, 2018 https://www.forbes.com/sites/mikeozanian/2018/02/26/mark-tatum-talks-about-the-nbas-enormous-success-in-china/#37732ac5518b.
Peng, Sheng. "Learning from the NHL in Japan." *NHL*, September 22, 2017 https://www.nhl.com/kings/news/learning-from-the-nhl-in-japan/c-291246710.
Peterson, Rob. "Open-ing the World to the NBA." *NBA*, October 8, 2004 http://www.nba.com/china2004/mcdonalds_open_041008.html.
Pettigrew, Stephen and Danyel Reiche,. "Is There Home-Field Advantage at the Olympics?" *FiveThirtyEight*, August 9, 2016 https://fivethirtyeight.com/features/is-there-home-field-advantage-at-the-olympics/.
"Phenoms of the 2018 World Cup." *Fox Sports*, May 29, 2018 https://www.foxsports.com/soccer/fifa-world-cup/phenoms?pn=2&abTest=jw-player-stats.
Pope, Steven W. "Rethinking Sport, Empire,and American Exceptionalism." *Sports History Review*, 38, 2007, 92–120 https://core.ac.uk/download/pdf/56121.pdf.
Rains, Benjamin. "The Business of the NHL as Hockey's Popularity Slips in U.S." *Nasdaq*, January 22, 2018 https://www.nasdaq.com/article/the-business-of-the-nhl-as-hockeys-popularity-slips-in-us-cm908815.
Reiss, Mike. "Patriots' Game in China Off." *Boston Globe*, April 2, 2007 http://archive.boston.com/sports/football/patriots/articles/2007/04/02/patriots_game_in_china_off/.
Reuters. "McDonald's Ends Olympics Sponsorship Deal Early." *CNBC*, June 16, 2016 https://www.cnbc.com/2017/06/16/mcdonalds-ends-olympics-sponsorship-deal-early.html.
Riches, Sam. "When Sport Defines a Nation." *Pacific Standard*, January 2, 2015 https://psmag.com/social-justice/when-sports-defines-nation-identity-hockey-canada-summit-series-98094.
Rocco, Matthew. "MLB: World Baseball Classic Key to Global Ambitions." *Fox Business*, March 3, 2017 https://www.foxbusiness.com/features/mlb-world-baseball-classic-key-to-global-ambitions.
Rogers, Martin. "The United States' World Cup Failure Is Looking Worse Every Day." *USA Today*, June 19, 2018 https://www.usatoday.com/story/sports/columnist/martin-rogers/2018/06/19/united-states-world-cup-usmnt/713096002/.
Roxborough, Scott. "Rio Olympics Worldwide Audience to Top 3.5 Billion, IOC Estimates." *The Hollywood Reporter*, August 18, 2016 https://www.hollywoodreporter.com/news/rio-olympics-worldwide-audience-top-920526.
"St. Louis 1904." *International Olympic Committee* https://www.olympic.org/st-louis-1904.
Sandomir, Richard. "NBC Retains Rights to Premier League in Six-Year Deal." *New York*

Times, August 11, 2015 https://www.nytimes.com/2015/08/11/sports/soccer/nbc-retains-rights-to-premier-league-in-six-year-deal.html.

———. "Why FIFA Made Deal with Fox for 2026 Cup." *New York Times*, February 27, 2015 https://www.nytimes.com/2015/02/27/sports/soccer/why-fifa-made-deal-with-fox-for-2026-cup.html.

Skiver, Kevin. "NHL Plans to Head Back to Europe Next Season for Global Series, Including Opener in Prague." November 1, 2018, *CBS Sports*, https://www.cbssports.com/nhl/news/nhl-plans-to-head-back-to-europe-next-season-for-global-series-including-opener-in-prague/.

Swift, E.M. "A Reminder of What We Can Be: The 1980 U.S. Olympic Hockey Team." *Sports Illustrated*, October 28, 2014, https://www.si.com/olympic-ice-hockey/2014/10/28/reminder-what-we-can-be-1980-us-olympic-hockey-team-si-60.

Taylor, Charles R. "Sponsorship and Advertising Trends in the 2016 Rio Olympic Games: Three Things to Watch For." *Forbes* August 4, 2016 https://www.forbes.com/sites/onmarketing/2016/08/04/sponsorship-and-advertising-trends-in-the-2016-rio-olympic-games-three-things-to-watch-for/#5e0929cc18c7.

Tierney, Mike. "The '92 Dream Team Paved the Way for Global Players to Make Mark in NBA." *The National*, May 25, 2011 https://www.thenational.ae/the-92-dream-team-paved-the-way-for-global-players-to-make-mark-in-nba-1.375766.

Timms, Aaron. "Fox Replaces ESPN's Cult of British Accents with Maximum Volume at World Cup." *The Guardian*, June 11, 2018 https://www.theguardian.com/football/2018/jun/11/fox-sports-world-cup-coverage.

Traina, Jimmy. "Here's What ESPN Pays for Most of Its Sports Rights." *Sports Illustrated*, June 26, 2017 https://www.si.com/extra-mustard/2017/06/26/espn-sports-rights-cost.

Wells, Steven. "Dear America: You Can't Be World Champions If No One Else Takes Part." *The Guardian*, November 18, 2008 https://www.theguardian.com/sport/blog/2008/nov/18/american-sports-nfl-nba-mlb.

Wertheim, Jon. "Exclusive: The Evidence That Persuaded U.S. Department of Justice to Investigate MLB Recruitment of Foreign Players." *Sports Illustrated*, October 2, 2018 https://www.si.com/mlb/2018/10/02/fbi-investigation-mlb-atlanta-braves-los-angeles-dodgers.

"World Fame 100 2019." *ESPN*, March 12, 2019 http://www.espn.com/espn/feature/story/_/page/worldfame100/espn-world-fame-100-top-ranking-athletes#.

"Which Is the Sport of the Future?" *NBC Sports Boston*, December 13, 2017 https://www.nbcsports.com/boston/home-page/nba-nfl-nhl-nba-which-is-sport-of-the-future.

"World Series," *Little League* https://www.littleleague.org/world-series/.

VanDerWerff, Todd. "NBC's Coverage of the Olympics Is Atrocious. There's a Simple Reason Why." *Vox*, August 11, 2016 https://www.vox.com/2016/8/11/12433144/nbc-olympics-bad.

Yoder, Matt. "NBC Claims a Record Number of Total Viewers for a Premier League Season in 2017–2018." *Awful Announcing*, May 18, 2018 https://awfulannouncing.com/soccer/nbc-claims-a-record-number-of-total-viewers-for-a-premier-league-season-in-2017-2018.html.

About the Contributors

Zachary T. **Androus** is a U.S. anthropologist based in Florence, Italy, since 2006, where he operates the Florence Ethnographic Field School, and teaches the course Sport and Culture in Contemporary Italy for CEA Study Abroad. His research addresses the intersection of sport, nationalism, and identity in Europe; urban change in Italy; and the role of music in Corsican nationalism.

Ali **Bowes** is a lecturer on the sociology of sport at Nottingham Trent University. She completed her Ph.D. in the School of Sport, Health and Exercise Science at Loughborough University, where she studied the relationship between women's sport and English national identity. Her research interests center on feminist analyses of women's sport, focusing on women's professional golf.

Jomills H. **Braddock** II is a professor of sociology at the University of Miami, Coral Gables. His research examines school desegregation, the education of at-risk students, gender equity in sports, and the relations between athletic participation and academic and social development among adolescents. His interests are in informing public policy and practice, especially with issues of social justice and equity.

Jared Bahir **Browsh** is a mass communications scholar at the University of Colorado Boulder's College of Media, Communication, and Information. His research examines the political economics of media and culture, particularly the interaction between ownership, policy, and identity and how it influences representations of race, gender, ethnicity, and sexuality in popular culture.

Bruce S. **Burnside** is a doctoral candidate in anthropology and education at Teachers College, Columbia University. His work focuses on belonging and intercultural learning in Germany and Turkey and examines after-school centers for immigrant children, teacher narratives about the role of diversity in the classroom, and the debates surrounding the reconstruction of Berlin's royal City Palace.

Jon **Dart** is a senior lecturer in sociology and sport policy at Leeds Beckett University, where he teaches the sociocultural and political aspects of sport. With research interests in the political economy of sport, he has published on sport and the media, sport and protest, sport fandom, and sport politics in the Middle East. He coedited, with Stephen Wagg, *Sport, Protest and Globalization: Stopping Play*.

About the Contributors

Marvin P. **Dawkins** is a professor of sociology at the University of Miami, Coral Gables. His research focuses on issues of race and social equity in education, career aspirations and mobility, substance abuse and prevention, and sports. He also serves as the University of Miami's faculty athletics representative (FAR) to the ACC and NCAA.

Yannick **Kluch** is an assistant professor of sports communication and media at Rowan University, where he also serves as an affiliate faculty member for the university's Center for Sports Communication and Social Impact. His research focuses on cultural studies of sport, athlete activism, diversity and inclusion in intercollegiate athletics, and identity construction in sport.

Ashley B. **Mikulyuk** is a visiting assistant professor of sociology at Pacific University. She specializes in the sociology of education and examines issues related to educational inequality, diversity, and desegregation in U.S. society. She also conducts research on issues related to gender equity, including women's and girls' access to and success in sports participation.

Adrienne **Milner** is a lecturer in the Centre for Primary Care and Public Health at Queen Mary University of London. She studies health inequalities and the social determinants of health, as well as the effects of racial and sexual attitudes, policy preferences, and inequality on issues such as police brutality, discrimination of transgender individuals, and affirmative action.

Hendrik **Snyders** is a research associate in the Department of History at the University of Stellenbosch, South Africa, an accredited heritage practitioner, and the head of the Department of History at the National Museum in Bloemfontein. He has previously published in the fields of colonial, environmental and sport history as well as in heritage and memory studies.

Nicholas **Villanueva**, Jr., is an assistant professor of ethnic studies and the director of the critical sports studies program at the University of Colorado, Boulder. His first book, *Lynching of Mexicans in the Texas Borderlands*, won two national awards, including the National Association of Chicana & Chicano Studies Tejas Foco Nonfiction award for 2018. He is working on a project that examines the Latinx participants of the LGBTQ Rodeo.

Christina Sanchez **Volatier** is an assistant professor of sociology at Western New Mexico University. She specializes in social psychology, race and ethnic relations, and social theory. Her research explores socially constructed meanings and novelty grounded in everyday actions, as well as the democratic outcomes of sports participation by diverse identities.

Index

ABC (network) 63, 194, 197
Agostini, Giacomo 170, 181
Al-Atrash, Mary 147–148
Al-Sayad, Mayada 147–148
amateur 10, 28, 49, 51, 56, 59–60, 62–63, 133, 185, 199
American exceptionalism 18, 26, 190, 198–200, 207
Anderson, Benedict 1, 6, 12, 22, 74, 89, 91, 140, 167–168, 172, 174–175
Anderson, Carol 21
anti-Semitism 21, 141, 154–155
Apartheid 27, 47–48, 50, 52, 54, 56–59, 61–70
appropriate femininity 92, 98, 100–101, 106
Aryan superiority 26–28
athletes as warriors 102–103, 107
Atlantic Coast Conference 30

Big Ten Conference 196
behavior, unpatriotic 3, 9–10, 12, 17
boxing 29, 33–34, 36–39, 59
Brown v. Board of Education 26

Cape Gulf Club 49
CBS (network) 194
China 27, 61, 204–207
Coachman, Alice 28
college football 2, 20, 196–197
Communism 199
compulsory heterosexuality 92, 98, 100–101
Connor, Walker 172
Conservatism 21, 59, 64, 114, 140
critical discourse analysis 77, 85, 174
cyberbullying 15–17

Douglas, Gabby 14–17, 22
Dream Team 199, 201, 205

Els, Ernie 47
ESPN 192–197, 201

Facebook 16, 20, 131
femininity 91–93, 98, 100–102, 106–108, 110
Fox (network) 125, 190–197, 208

La Gazzeta dello Sport 183, 187
Gebrel, Ahmed 147
gender marking 92, 98, 101
Great Depression 50
great sports myth 1, 3, 6
Griffith-Joyner, Florence 28–29
gymnastics 3, 14, 17, 29, 33–38
heteronormativity 14, 92, 100

Hitler, Adolf 13, 26, 27
Holocaust 73
homogeneity 10, 12, 25, 30
homosexuality 92, 100

"imagined community" 4, 6, 9, 12–13, 22, 74, 88, 91, 141, 172, 175
infantilization 92, 98
International Motorcycling Federation 5, 167–169
Intifada 143–144, 146, 154
Israeli military 150–151, 153

Japan 205–206
Jim Crow 26
Joyner-Kersee, Jackie 28–29

Kaepernick, Colin 3, 9–13, 17–19, 22
Khoussa, Mohammed Abu 47
kneeling *see* national anthem and kneeling
Ku Klux Klan 15, 21

Latino athletes 29, 31, 32, 39, 201–202
lesbianism 100
LGBTQ 14
Locke, Bobby 47, 56
lynching 15–17

masculinity 2, 12, 91–93, 98, 101, 104–106, 195
media coverage 5, 27, 31, 73, 77–78, 82, 84, 92, 96–99, 101, 147–148, 167–168, 171, 183, 190, 192, 194, 196–197

NAACP 15
national anthem and kneeling 10, 19, 20

Index

national anthems 10–11, 14–16, 18, 19–22, 75, 90, 140, 149, 167, 180, 199
National Football League (NFL): and capitalism 11, 193, 196–197; Europa 203–204; fan base 9, 13; globally 203–204, 207–208; Hall of Fame 3; as an institution 3; and the military 18–19
National Hockey League 197, 204, 206–207
nationalism, feminist interpretations of 89
NBC 24, 31, 194–197
Nike 100, 202, 205
90-minute patriots 141, 157

Obama, Barack 26
"One-hundred-percent Americanism" 21–22
Owens, Jesse 13, 26, 28

patriotism 4, 6, 9, 11–13, 52, 73, 75–76, 80, 82, 84–85, 140, 199
Pickett, Tidey 28
Player, Gary 47, 56–57, 59, 61
Poage, George 28
Population Registration Act 52–53
Prohibition of Mix Marriages Act 52–53
protests 3, 9–13, 19–23, 56, 59, 62, 63, 65, 65, 143, 153–154

Quran 120–123, 130

racism 3–4, 9–10, 12–13, 15, 20–22, 24, 47–48, 55, 73, 149
rituals 75, 80, 103, 140
Roosevelt, Theodore 2, 18–19
Rossi, Valentino 171, 176, 178, 181, 185–187
Rudolph, Wilma 28
Russia 14, 17, 82, 190–192, 194

September 11th terrorist attacks 10, 127
Sewgolum, Papwa 47, 48, 57, 60, 65
Siegesfeier 71–73, 77–85
slavery 15, 17, 22, 28
social media 3, 9, 12, 14–15, 17–18, 106, 149
Soviet Union 27, 58, 199, 205–207
sport as battle 11, 103, 139
Stadler, Joe 28
Star Spangled Banner 18–19

Stokes, Louise 28
Strenuous Life 2, 18
Summer Olympic Games: 1896 (Athens, Greece) 28; 1904 (St. Louis, United States) 28, 198; 1908 (London, United Kingdom) 28; 1936 (Berlin, Germany) 13, 26–28; 1948 (London, United Kingdom) 26, 28–29; 1952 (Helsinki, Finland) 29, 146, 149; 1960 (Rome, Italy) 28, 30, 149; 1984 (Los Angeles, United States) 29, 199–200; 1988 (Seoul, South Korea) 28, 199; 1992 (Barcelona, Spain) 28, 199, 201, 205; 1996 (Atlanta, Georgia) 29, 146; 2008 (Beijing, China) 29, 152; 2012 (London, United Kingdom) 14, 17, 24, 26, 31, 34, 39–40, 146–147; 2016 (Rio de Janeiro, Brazil) 13–14, 17, 26, 138–139, 148–157

Taylor, John Baxter, Jr. 28
Telemundo (network) 192–193
Trump, Donald 21, 140
Tshabalala, Vincent 47, 48, 60, 63, 65
Twitter 16, 106, 131, 188

United States Men's National Soccer Team 190–193
U.S. military 3, 9, 11, 18–19, 199
University of Nebraska football team 20–21
University of Notre Dame 197

violence 15, 22, 56, 65, 151
Viroli, Maurizio 6, 12

white privilege 3, 9–10, 12–13, 15–16, 20, 22
White Rage 21
whiteness 12
Winter Olympic Games, 2014 (Sochi, Russia) 14

xenophobia 3, 13–14

Yacoub, Simon 147

Zimmerman, Christian 147–148
Zirin, Dave 11, 153

www.ingramcontent.com/pod-product-compliance
Lightning Source LLC
Chambersburg PA
CBHW032041300426
44117CB00009B/1146